Indian Village

INTERNATIONAL LIBRARY OF SOCIOLOGY AND SOCIAL RECONSTRUCTION

Founded by Karl Mannheim

Editor : W. J. H. Sprott

A catalogue of the books available in the INTERNATIONAL LIBRARY OF SOCIOLOGY AND SOCIAL RECONSTRUCTION, and new books in preparation for the Library, will be found at the end of this volume.

INDIAN VILLAGE

by

S. C. DUBE, M.A., PH.D.

Foreword by
MORRIS EDWARD OPLER

ROUTLEDGE & KEGAN PAUL LTD
Broadway House, 68-74 Carter Lane
London, E.C.4

*First published in 1955
by Routledge & Kegan Paul Ltd
Broadway House, 68-74 Carter Lane
London E.C.4
Printed in Great Britain
by Lowe & Brydone (Printers) Ltd
London N.W. 10*

*Second impression 1956
Third impression 1959*

Contents

Illustrations

Foreword

I N his informative and stimulating introduction to the present
volume, Dr. Dube has said, '. . . . what we need to-day is a
series of studies of village communities from different parts of
the country covering the many divergent patterns of organization
and ethos.' Dr. Dube has not only stated the need; he has shown
us what can be achieved in striving to meet it. His volume is a
solid study and one which will doubtless take its place among the
standard community studies made in various parts of the world
which he cites in his bibliography.

In a number of ways this volume is especially valuable and
challenging and is a tonic to present-day research into Indian
village life. In the first place, it is a total study, not in the sense
that it gives us all possible details concerning the village Shamirpet, but in the sense that it presents between two covers all important aspects of the culture of this community. Though the author
has been at pains to keep the account fairly general and un-
cluttered, the reader receives a convincing and reasonably adequate introduction to the historical, geographical, and political
setting and the social, economic, and ritual structure of the
village described. One puts the book down with a feeling that one
has really come to know Shamirpet, its background, people, and
problems quite well; even if everything about something is not
there, something about almost everything is given. This is almost
a departure in social science writing about Indian village life.
Such studies have tended to be topical, specialized, and often
too brief. Of attempts to give a sustained, many-sided picture of
an Indian community we have very few; there are Gertrude

vii

FOREWORD

Emerson's *Voiceless India* and William Wiser's *Behind Mud Walls*, both pioneer efforts, and a few others.

There are a good many reasons why more total studies of Indian villages have not been written to date, but one obvious reason should not be overlooked—the study of Indian village life yields material extremely complex and difficult to deal with in this manner. The village is a unity, yet half of its adult population, the women, come from outside communities with which the village is linked by complicated marriage relations. Each individual belongs to a caste which exercises a great deal of control over him, yet whose ruling group has jurisdiction far beyond the village confines. Each one of the many castes is a veritable subculture, with special traditions, prerogatives, rituals, food habits, and status, and this caste and its attributes is ordinarily a regional or national rather than a village phenomenon. Moreover, Indian culture and philosophy are old and rich. It is not easy to do justice to these background traditions which are the ultimate basis of much that goes on in present-day Indian village life and yet convey freshly and convincingly the localized, modern derivative of these historic impulses. And in this instance Dr. Dube's task was not made easier by the presence, in this village, of a sizeable group of Muslims. Consequently, at least on the religious side, he had two great traditions with which village activities had to be linked, and in terms of which they had to be interpreted. It was necessary to take into consideration all these outside influences and links, and still retain a focus on the village. Only those who have struggled with the intricacies of Indian village material and have before them the task of ordering it can fully appreciate Dr. Dube's accomplishment.

But this study has more to recommend it than that the author has given us ample coverage and has not been distracted from his central object. One of its attractions is that it rises above mere description; it provides analytical insights and provocative concepts. Students of Indian village culture and of folk culture in general will do well to examine Dr. Dube's definition and treatment of 'allied families' (as distinct from the lineage or general body of close relatives). Again, by analysing out six major factors which contribute toward status differentiation in Shamirpet, the author cuts through a bewildering maze of data and provides a key to the understanding of the relative status positions of the sub-

viii

FOREWORD

groups of the village and of individuals within these sub-groups. There is nothing remarkable or even particularly original in the factors he recognizes, but their application to the data in context is illuminating. It is the same with the identification of the new set of influences which, according to the author, are to-day playing upon the community. Whether the list is complete or not, it serves to explain much that has happened in the recent past and acts as a guide, or at least a hypothesis, to predict some future developments.

Dr. Dube's book has still another attribute which will intrigue many readers. He is not only interested in principles or factors which will illuminate specific aspects of the culture, but he is searching for abstractions of a higher level, integrating ideas which characterize and colour the entire culture. This quest is particularly marked in the concluding pages where 'the adjustment of the individual to the universe . . . peaceful adjustment and adaptation to the laws that control the universe,' and the tendency 'to view everything as hierarchically structured' are singled out as fundamental drives in the thought and activities of the group. The interest in discovering the kind and number of unifying and harmonizing principles which can be identified for any culture is strong to-day, and Dr. Dube's views of the binding forces in Indian culture and the effect of contemporary events upon them should receive close attention.

In the 'boiling down' of a large body of data to book size, it is often the sad fact that the vital essence is boiled off and a flavourless brew is left. Dr. Dube has off-set this necessity for general statement and summary by introducing source material and case material at strategic intervals. In this way, we are constantly reminded that even the statistics point to the joys and sorrows, triumphs and defeats of very real people and very vivid personalities.

The volume has one other characteristic which deserves attention. The data which have gone into it are the product of group research. It is, in fact, one of the first examples of what can be accomplished through a group, inter-disciplinary approach. More than eighteen staff members and students of Osmania University gathered the material under Dr. Dube's direction. Six faculties of the university were represented in the effort. Much of the material which the natural scientists collected is technical

FOREWORD

and specialized and will appear separately under appropriate auspices. But, because of this field method, Dr. Dube had excellent technical advice and solid material at his command in dealing with matters of agriculture, health, and nutrition—subjects which the social scientist may often have reason to touch upon with diffidence. Consequently, the book has a ring of authority which might be hard to achieve at points without this kind of collaboration. Group research is expensive, and it is not always easy to bring and keep together in amicable work relations specialists with different but highly-cherished vocabularies. There have been those who, not without reason, have questioned the whole business. Dr. Dube's book does much to dispel doubt and raise hope. He and his associates are to be congratulated.

Cornell University,
Ithaca, New York

MORRIS EDWARD OPLER

Acknowledgements

THIS study is an outcome of the Osmania University Social Service Extension Project which the author directed in 1951–52. Grateful acknowledgements are made to the University authorities for liberal allotment of funds and for enthusiastic support of the project. The author is particularly grateful to Nawab Ali Yavar Jung Bahadur, then Vice-Chancellor of the University, for his generous support of social research.

Messrs. Tuljaram Singh, R. Prakash Rao, P. R. Sirsalkar, P. L. Narsimha Rao, and T. Kanna Reddi worked on the research side in the Extension team, and assisted me in collecting and checking most of the data presented in this book. Dr. Hamid Ali Baig, Mr. Ghouse Mohiuddin, and Dr. Chandra Devi deserve special mention for their medical work, which won popularity for our team in the village, and for their reports on village health and nutrition. Dr. Ramchandra Rao, assisted by his unit, made investigations on cattle health in the village. Dr. Hashim Amir Ali, Dean, Faculty of Agriculture, took a special interest in our work; and through his agricultural unit we could get useful data on agriculture and economy in the village. Miss Sikander Siddiqi helped me with the study of the life-cycle and the religious festivals of the Muslims. My thanks are due to all these associates and collaborators.

Most of the chapters of this book were written in 1952–53 in London where I had an appointment as Visiting Lecturer in Indian Anthropology in the School of Oriental and African Studies, University of London. I had the benefit of discussing some of this material with Professor Christoph von Fürer-Haimendorf, Professor of Asian Anthropology in the University of London, and

ACKNOWLEDGEMENTS

with his wife, Mrs. Elizabeth von Fürer-Haimendorf. I acknowledge my gratitude to them for critical suggestions and for many kindnesses. I received much stimulation from Professor Raymond Firth and his seminar at the London School of Economics and Political Science. My friends Adrian C. Mayer and Burton Benedict discussed with me some of my field data. I recall with happiness the many delightful evenings I spent with them in London; and shall remember Mrs. Mayer and Mrs. Benedict for their hospitality. I have also to thank my friends Raymond and Bridget Allchin who read with great patience the first draft of this book and offered many valuable suggestions. Miss Catherine Brown typed the manuscript.

I am grateful to Professor S. Bhagavantam, Vice-Chancellor, Osmania University, for permission to publish this report and to Professor Morris E. Opler for his sympathy and encouragement. My wife has helped me in planning the research project, in analysng the field-material, and in preparing it for the press.

S. C. DUBE

Hyderabad, 1954

Introduction

I

INDIA is predominantly an agricultural and rural country. An overwhelming majority of her people live in the countryside. In undivided India it was estimated that there were over 700,000 villages within the country. Since partition this number has diminished, but the rural-urban ratio in the population still remains more or less the same. According to various estimates, 70% to 80% of India's population live in villages.

From time immemorial the village has been a basic and important unit in the organization of Indian social polity. It finds prominent mention in the classical texts of the land. For example, according to the *Rig-Veda* (generally dated in the latter half of the 2nd millennium B.C.) society developed in a series of ascending formations, starting from the family (*griha* or *kula*) and gradually extending to the village (*grama*), the clan (*vis*), the people (*jana*) and the country (*rashtra*). The term *grama*, still largely used in India for village, denoted an aggregate of several families sharing the same habitation. Besides mentioning that the village was headed by the *gramini*, chief of the village, the *Rig-Veda* does not give us any details regarding its internal structure or organization or its external affiliations. In post-vedic literature, particularly the epics, we have somewhat more detailed glimpses of the then existing settlements. The *Mahabharata* (*c.* 2nd century B.C.–2nd century A.D.) mentions several types of habitations and settlements, such as cattle farm (*ghosh* or *vraja*), small barbarian hamlets (*palli*), forts to protect surrounding settlements (*durga*), villages developing around the forts (*grama*), town (*kharvata* or *pattan*) and city (*nagara*). Through the *Mahabharata* we get an

I

INTRODUCTION

outline of the system of village and inter-village organization. According to the epic, the village was the fundamental unit of administration; and had as its head the *gramini*, who was its leader and chief spokesman; one of the major responsibilities of this headman was to protect the village and its boundaries in all directions within a radius of two miles. The administrative system was organized on the basis of grouping of villages, each group having its own recognized leader. Thus a group of ten villages was under a *das-gramini*, and this was the first unit of inter-village organization. Two such groups, that is twenty villages, used to be under a *vimsatipa*. A group of a hundred villages was headed by *satgramini* or *gram-satadhyaksha*. Finally, a group of a thousand villages was under an *adhipati*. Several later works touch upon this subject, but they do not add materially to our knowledge of the system of village and inter-village organization in ancient India. However, it will not be out of place to make a brief reference to the place of the village in the writings of Manu (*c.* 200 B.C.–2nd century A.D.), the Hindu law-giver, whose code still largely governs the structure of Hindu society. Manu distinguishes between three kinds of settlements: village (*grama*), town (*pura*) and city (*nagara*). According to him, the village was the fundamental unit of administration, with its own officers and organization. The *gramini* was the head of the village. Apart from the different spheres of socio-religious life in which the family, the clan, the caste and the village were all equally interested, the village as a unit had a number of responsibilities of its own. Thus the maintenance and management of several public utilities such as wells, tanks, ponds, reservoirs, embankments, cow-pens, groves, parks and pastures was under the village itself. Approximately a thousand villages constituted a country and were under a *sahasresa*; within this group were several divisions and subdivisions—a hundred villages under a *satesa*, twenty villages under a *vimsi*, ten villages under a *dasi* and finally the village itself under a *gramini*. Notwithstanding the passage of time, the village system in India still continues to have many of the characteristics described by Manu. Even to-day the village retains its semi-autonomous character. Invariably it has a recognized headman with a definite set of duties and functions. Groups of ten to twenty villages still join together to decide important cases and to discuss issues of common interest. A thousand villages or so constitute a culture-area, or at least a subculture-area, and the

2

rural community within this region invariably has a number of common cultural characteristics and social forms and values.

Yet we cannot regard the Indian village community as static, timeless and changeless. Time and the interplay of historical and sociological factors and forces have influenced the structure, organization and ethos of these communities in many significant ways.

II

To-day it is common to speak of the 'Indian village' or of 'the Indian peasant'. While it is true that many problems are common to the entire Indian countryside, this practice tends to give one an impression that the village as a social and cultural unit possesses a basically uniform organization and structure of values all over the Indian sub-continent. This would obviously be an over-simplified presentation of a rather complex situation. For a proper understanding of their social structure as well as of their problems, it is necessary to classify them into clearly distinguishable types. For such classification several criteria could be employed, including, among others, the following:

i. Size, population and land-area.
ii. Ethnic composition and caste-constitution.
iii. Pattern of land ownership.
iv. Structure of authority and power hierarchy.
v. Degree of isolation.
vi. Local traditions.

Each culture-area of India has its own nomenclature to classify the villages within its territory in respect of their size and population. In the Hindi-speaking parts of north and middle India it is usual to distinguish between *kheda* (a hamlet), *gaon* (a small village) and *kasba* (a large village). In Telangana, the Telugu-speaking part of the State of Hyderabad to which the village of Shamirpet described in this book belongs, a similar distinction is made between *gumpu, majra* and *grama*. The first of these denotes a tiny collection of huts, the second is a larger hamlet and the third is the village proper. The differences between these rural settlements are not confined only to their size and population. All three can be classified as belonging to the 'folk society', but they differ so greatly in their internal organization, economic self-sufficiency, patterns of adjustment with the outside world and the degree of influence and prestige in the wider rural community that any attempt to combine them would be tantamount to overlooking significant sociological facts. The residents of the large villages look upon themselves as the leaders of the rural community, regarding those from smaller villages as a little less civilized and those from small hamlets as rustics. The man from the smaller village is suspicious and critical about the ways of the people from bigger villages, but he has in his heart of hearts an admiration and respect for them. To him also the people living in still smaller settlements appear to be rather crude and rustic. As the division of labour in the community is governed to a very great extent by traditional caste occupations, and co-operative labour of a number of different castes is required not only for agricultural activities, but also for socio-religious life, the large village, having within its population all the occupational castes, has a comparatively more integrated and self-sufficient economic and socio-religious life than the smaller villages, which, in the absence of one or more occupational castes, may have to depend on some other settlement. Because of its multi-caste constitution, larger population and greater complexity of internal problems, the organization of the larger village is often remarkably different from that of smaller villages. In fact, some of the smaller villages and hamlets come to be regarded as appendages of the larger villages, and although they have considerable autonomy in domestic matters they are very greatly influenced by the views and preferences of their larger neighbour.

The ethnic and linguistic composition of a village, as well as its caste constitution, also determines its character. The structure, ethos and problems of a wholly tribal village will be very different from those of a village with a mixed or homogeneous population. A tribal village is often unitary in respect of its authority structure, the tribal authority itself being supreme in secular, ritual and cultural village matters. On the other hand, in the case of a village which has a mixed population of tribes on the one hand and Hindu castes on the other, or of two different groups of parallel Hindu castes separated from each other by the fact that they speak different languages and belong to different culture-areas, or of Hindus and Muslims, the nature of its internal organization and authority is bound to be different. If the diverse elements of its population have equal strength—numerical as well as economic—

4

it generally has a federal type of organization, in that each culture group within this settlement is semi-autonomous, and a common village authority drawn from all these groups has overriding powers for the community as a whole. In areas where there are intense or even pronounced inter-caste rivalries and tensions, the caste composition of the village will largely determine its patterns of inter-group adjustment.

It goes without saying that in a primarily agricultural country land must be greatly prized; and, with the great pressure of population and the conditions of private ownership, possession of land has not only an economic but a social and prestige value as well. Where all the land belongs to a landlord or is held by two or more landlords—as in the case of 'joint-villages'—the organization of the village is sure to be very different from that of a village inhabited by proprietary tenants. The general ratio of land distribution between two or more castes, between certain families or between one big landowner and the rest of the community may have a vital influence on the nature of village organization and problems.

No village in India is completely autonomous and independent, for it is always one unit in a wider social system and is a part of an organized political society. An individual is not the member of a village community alone; he also belongs to a caste, religious group or tribe which has a wider territorial spread and comprises several villages. These units have their own organization, authority and sanctions. Politically the villages are under the legislative, executive and judicial authority of the Indian Union and one of its constituent States. For administrative convenience these States are divided into districts, the latter being subdivided into *tehsils* or *taluquas*. In day-to-day administration the villages come into contact with the authorities and officials of this subdivision and of the district, although the laws of the State and the Union are binding on them. The village thus has independence and autonomy only in its domestic affairs. But who exercises the authority in this field? Is there a petty feudal landlord who has some administrative and judicial powers as well? Is there a government-recognized landlord who has arrogated to himself administrative powers? Or, has the village a *panchayat* (village council) constituted on the basis of local tradition? All the feudal states have been abolished in Republican India; but petty feudal estates still continue in some parts of the country, and effective steps have been taken in very few areas to abolish village landlordism. On the other hand, with a view to reviving village self-government, some State governments are establishing village councils with recognized legal powers, the members of which are appointed by the government. Locus of power in the community is another criterion in respect of which Indian villages often present very different pictures.

Nearness to or isolation from large administrative or industrial centres also has a bearing on the nature of the organization of a village and of its view of the world. Availability of or nearness to modern means of transport and communications also modifies the setting and fabric of a village, and in its classification it is necessary to take into account these vital factors.

Lastly, village settlements are governed by certain traditions—regional and local. The dress, speech and manners, as well as the lay-out of the village and construction of the houses, follow the prescribed patterns of the culture-area. Thus in the different areas we can naturally look forward to a certain degree of diversity in village organization. But apart from these regional variations villages have a corporate unity, and each one possesses an individuality of its own. Some villages are regarded as 'peaceful', others as 'difficult'. Some have a reputation for generosity and fair play, while others are notorious for their meanness. Some are known for being 'upright and strict'; others are criticized for their laxity. Love of litigation is a characteristic feature of some villages; ostentation and display of others; while still others may be very sensitive about their good name. Again, co-operativeness or its absence may characterize some villages. These attributes and qualities may have their roots in strong local traditions or in a combination of factors working at a particular time. But they do give a distinctive character to the village, and a study of the social ways, processes and motivations in such villages will not be without considerable sociological and psychological interest.

In view of the operation of factors delineated above, it is difficult to regard any one village as typical or representative of rural India as a whole. In fact, I would go a step further to say that such a village could hardly be regarded as representative even of its culture-area, except in a very general way. The problem before the social anthropologist and the sociologist is therefore a complex one, and what we need to-day is a series of studies of village communities from different parts of the country covering the many divergent patterns of organization and ethos. Until this is done our picture of social systems in rural India will remain vague and inadequate.

From the old ethnographic surveys and some preliminary studies published recently, an outline of the structure and organization of Indian villages is beginning to emerge clearly. Notwithstanding many significant differences, they have a number of structural similarities. In the north, middle and peninsular India, as well as in the eastern and western parts of the country, the following features characterize a very large number of villages.

1. As a territorial, as well as social, economic and ritual unit, the village is a separate and distinct entity. The residents of this settlement recognize their corporate identity, and it is recognized as such by others. It is not uncommon to find in them a sentiment of attachment towards their own settlement site. In several matters the village acts as a unit.

2. These settlements have a composite population comprising a number of groups belonging to different Hindu castes, and in some cases to tribes as well as to other religious groups. As far as the Hindu section of the population goes, these diverse groups are inter-dependent and integrated in the social, economic, ritual and administrative organization of the community. No caste alone is self-sufficient, for it requires the services of several other occupational castes which hold the monopoly of certain crafts and professions. This system of co-operative labour, based on a pattern of inter-caste relations approved by tradition, is not confined only to economic activities but also extends to ceremonial and ritual life. The hierarchical organization of castes within the community is so fixed in the structural patterns of rural India that the tribal as well as the non-Hindu (such as Muslim and Christian) segments of the population come to be regarded as other castes in the village.

In many parts of India, while maintaining their socio-religious identity, several of these non-Hindu groups have acquired some caste characteristics, particularly occupational specialization. For example, in some areas of rural India the Muslims function as an occupational caste variously, making fireworks, weaving, driving *tongas*, *ikkahs* and other hackney-carriages, selling vegetables or playing musical instruments.

3. The members of this local group are bound together by ties

7

of mutual and reciprocal obligations. Inter-personal and inter-group relations in several spheres of village affairs are governed by an established usage and social ethics. Breaches of the norms of the community and its established usage are dealt with either by the village elders or by a village council. The village council, speaking for the village, has the final authority of social ostracism through which it can effectively enforce its sanctions.

III

Modern community studies represent a very significant development in the field of social anthropology and sociology. The concepts and techniques formerly applied to the study and analysis of primitive and isolated tribal societies are now being adapted for the study of peasant communities, non-literate as well as literate, and also for the analysis of more complex and industrialized communities. This new direction in the focus of interest of an increasing number of social scientists and field-workers has inevitably led to important modifications in our conceptual framework and to a sharpening of our tools of research. The methodology of social sciences and techniques of field research have both gained very considerably from this new trend. The work of Robert Redfield, John Gillin, Sol Tax and Ralph Beals, among others, represents a substantial advance in this field, both in theory and in methodology. From Robert Redfield's *Tepotzlan: A Mexican Village* to Oscar Lewis's *Life in a Mexican Village: Tepotzlan Re-Studied* this branch of social anthropological enquiry has travelled far: the former inaugurated an epoch, which then appeared to be full of promise; the latter is a convincing proof of its maturity. On Middle America we now have a series of interesting and useful studies. In other parts of the world also important researches of this kind have been made. Studies of the great peasant societies of the East received encouragement and support from scholars both in Great Britain and in the United States. Malinowski's and Radcliffe-Brown's forewords to the works of Fei and Embree bear testimony to the interest evinced in community studies by the British social anthropologists. The work of Martin C. Yang and Francis L. K. Hsu received constructive support in the United States. A remarkable feature of some of these Far Eastern studies is that they were done not by Western scientists but by scholars

who were born and brought up more or less in the very social
setting that they were describing. Of course, the level of analysis
in these works differs considerably, ranging from somewhat
impressionistic accounts to fairly deep sociological and economic
analyses, but they constitute a departure of no mean significance
in anthropology as being symbols of an awakening of interest in
people for the anthropological and sociological study of their own
society. The range of such studies has indeed been wide enough
and has included several Western societies as well. Contributions
such as *The Polish Peasant in Europe and America* by W. I. Thomas
and Florian Znaniecki, *The Irish Countryman* by Conrad Arensberg,
Life in a Welsh Countryside by Alwyn D. Rees, although they are the
outcome of different research techniques and present different
levels of analyses, provide much useful material for comparative
studies. Mention must be made, in this connection, of the important and stimulating work of the Lynds and of the Warner school
in the analysis of more complex communities. *Middletown* and its
successor *Middletown in Transition* by R. S. and H. M. Lynd have
justly come to be regarded as classics in this field. *The Social Life
of a Modern Community* and *The Status System of a Modern Community*
by W. L. Warner and Paul S. Lunt, and *The Social Systems of
American Ethnic Groups* by W. L. Warner and Leo Srole, too, are
equally outstanding works in this class. Some of the works listed
above have provided the impetus for more community studies in
different parts of the world—in the so-called under-developed
areas as well as in technologically advanced, industrialized coun-
tries. At the present time very considerable field research either
has been done or is being done in many parts of the world—in
Middle America, in Puerto Rico (under the direction of Julian
Steward), in Great Britain (by the Edinburgh University, under
the direction of Kenneth L. Little) and in India (by the Cornell
group under the direction of Morris E. Opler, and by some Indian
universities).

Studies of modern communities as well as of non-literate or
technologically 'under-developed' societies whose traditions are
rooted in great civilizations of antiquity present a series of practical
and methodological problems. Modern communities are larger—
both in population and spatial distribution—compared with the
primitive societies hitherto studied by anthropologists. This
makes it difficult for the anthropologist and his associates to

have first-hand contact with more or less the entire community; and even at his best the scientist can have effective
acquaintance with only a small area of the territory. Necessarily,
therefore, he must work only in a few segments of the community,
whose selection, if it is to be sufficiently representative, raises
important methodological questions. Here we must have an adequate and effective sampling technique. The situation is further
complicated by the fact that within the general framework of a
modern community we have several subcultures. Besides certain
dominant values, there are divergent subsidiary values. The
community has its established norms, but the range of variation
in behaviour patterns is also very considerable. The sample to be
studied must take into account all these factors. Finally, the community must be studied in both its rural and urban settings, and
in this context due attention should be given to the vital interaction and inter-relations between its different components. The
actual research and the presentation of its results also raise a
number of complicated issues. Literary and historical evidence may
have developed some stereotypes about the community which may
be taken for granted by the research workers and may ultimately
colour the results of the whole research. It is easier to start with a
totally unbiased mind in a society about which nothing, or at any
rate very little, is known. In the case of historically well-known
societies, however, it is not easy to overcome an unconscious bias—
either for or against that society—for it may well have become a
habit of mind. Because of active political and economic interaction
between their communities, the prevailing complex of sentiments
and attitudes may determine the relations between those who are
studying and those who are being studied. These relations have to
be taken into account. Even in generally non-literate and under-
developed areas the people who are being studied are not totally
unaware of some of the wider implications of these studies. Sentiments of nationalism, caste or class-consciousness, local patriotism
and thoughts of the possible reactions and attitudes of the outside
world may govern their response to the enquiries being made by
the investigators. With regard to some phases of their life the
people may resist any investigation by 'outsiders' and may look
upon it as a most unwelcome intrusion. A field-worker born and
brought up within that very culture may, on the other hand, overlook certain trends and facts, and may even unconsciously seek to

rationalize and justify some elements in the life of his community. A proper scientific training can eliminate these dangers very considerably, but ideally the association of someone with a different cultural background with such a community research would perhaps provide the most satisfactory corrective. This would apply equally, but in the reverse, to the work being done in a community by 'outsiders' whose participation in the life and culture of this society may be so limited as to preclude the possibility of their having a firm grasp on the inner thought processes and subtle attitude patterns and value judgements of the members of the community. In this case utilization of properly trained collaborators from that very culture would be invaluable for the projected research. These points are quite important and cannot be dismissed lightly in planning serious community studies.

On the credit side, these community studies have several obvious advantages. They do not entail work in strange and difficult lands. They may be less romantic and not so very picturesque, but they certainly permit greater freedom of movement and also the use of practically all the amenities of modern civilization. The arduous conditions of research take only the more adventurous among the social scientists to remote islands and isolated tribal communities, but in the average community studies participation of a large number of investigators is possible because of the less difficult conditions of work. This permits team-work and also an inter-disciplinary approach. The investigator can gainfully use historical documents, literary evidence and government and administrative records. The language barrier in this case is not insurmountable, for even if the investigators are unacquainted with the language of the people they are studying, they can easily find bi-lingual people in the community itself who may have a working knowledge of the investigator's language. Finally, if the aims of research are properly explained to the people, and their confidence is gained by sympathy, tact and perseverance, the people themselves may come forward to offer intelligent co-operation.

Notwithstanding these advantages, there will still remain some of the problems and difficulties sketched above. But in the words of Gillin, from the methodological point of view 'there is nothing insuperably difficult about the solution of these problems'. He lists three requirements: '(1) Money in fair and substantial amounts; (2) large numbers of well-trained anthropologists; (3) the co-operation of specialists in other social and psychological sciences under an overall and integrated plan of investigation.'[1] If, however, it is intended to study only the social structure and organization, the specialists from other cognate sciences could be omitted; although their association would doubtless be of great value to the anthropologist. On the contrary, if depth-psychology has to be studied and problems having a bearing on personality have to be investigated, such inter-disciplinary co-operation is almost indispensable. Specialists in social statistics, agronomy and economics can help in the planning and conduct of such research in more ways than one.

In order that an adequate sample of all the subcultures is satisfactorily studied, and the norms of the society as well as the range of variation in behaviour patterns are sufficiently grasped, participation of a team of trained investigators is necessary. It has already been suggested that participation in such research of persons with differing cultural backgrounds, including some who actually belong to the community which is being studied, will be an invaluable aid towards proper subjective evaluation in the research itself and in its presentation also.

In India, where ways of life and thought are changing very fast, we require a large number of such community studies, both in rural and urban areas, in the different cultural regions of the country. We owe it to posterity that we leave careful records of contemporary life and cultures. As it is, for their historical and cultural interest alone such studies are worth undertaking. But their importance is greater at the present juncture because the country is undergoing significant technological changes, and it is necessary for us to assess and evaluate their human implications. Here we have the unique opportunity of making a 'pre-clinical' study of the communities as they are to-day, and then of studying them stage by stage under the impact of new technological factors. The social scientist can, in the first instance, make a really valuable contribution to social planning by publishing full and objective reports of his research; and as the volume of such data grows, ground will be prepared for the competent analysis of many problems of deeper theoretical interest. At the present time intensi-

[1] Cf. John Gillin, 'Methodological Problems in the Anthropological Study of Modern Cultures', *American Anthropologist*, Vol. 51, No. 3 (July–September 1949), pp. 392–399.

fication of community research is an urgent *desideratum*. As far as possible, in each culture-area it would be desirable to study one or more villages, a representative small town, two or three individual castes within the total network of inter-caste relations; and these studies could then be followed by more intensive investigations into specific problems, such as those of family and kinship, leadership and exercise of authority, social stratification, social change and personality. Preliminary studies can at best offer tentative hypotheses, but for theoretical developments of lasting significance we shall have to await more data gathered according to modern techniques of field research.

IV

This book is a descriptive study of the village of Shamirpet in the State of Hyderabad. It is an outcome of the Social Service Extension Project sponsored by the Osmania University and a plan of community study organized by the Department of Sociology and Anthropology. The Social Service Extension Project was organized in response to the call of educationists and national leaders to bring university students and teachers in contact with the realities of everyday life in the rural areas of the country. Shamirpet was selected because it was not far away from the city of Hyderabad and yet not near enough to be simply a suburban extension; was neither too large nor too small in respect of its area and population among the villages of this part of the country, and was fairly representative of the Telangana area of Hyderabad in its caste composition. Six faculties of the University—Arts, Agriculture, Veterinary Science and Animal Husbandry, Medicine, Engineering and Education—were each represented by one member of the staff and two or more post-graduate or senior students. Each unit was to do social work within its own special area of interest and technical competence. Funds were available for approved schemes, such as medical relief, introduction of modern methods of agriculture and animal care, adult education and cultural programmes, improvement of village sanitation and construction of better ventilated houses, etc. The Arts faculty was represented by post-graduate students of anthropology and trained research assistants, and was primarily responsible for the social and economic study of the village community. The other units had to study the problems arising in their respective fields, and were to help in doing specific investigations which were assigned to them from time to time. I had the privilege of directing both the research and the social service programme, and while the units were left free to a considerable extent in their respective welfare work, I was associated with the planning, direction and conduct of the research itself at every stage. The inter-faculty teams worked in the village for two summer vacations—extending to twenty weeks—and the anthropological unit remained in touch with the village for a whole year. At various stages the larger team included three women members —a doctor, a sociologist belonging to the Muslim community for work among the *purdah*-observing Muslim women, and an American lady, with training in psychology and anthropology, who was a 'guest' member of the team. The anthropology unit consisted of five members, each with post-graduate training in anthropology, four of whom spoke the regional language of the village and had spent many years in the countryside of the Telangana area of Hyderabad. Three of these members had previous training in practical field-work. As they were all Hindus by birth, we had further to seek the help of a woman lecturer trained in sociology for work among the Muslim women.

To begin with, the response of the village people was rather cold. For a short while we were regarded as missionaries; then as government agents brought into the village for organizing anti-communist propaganda. Some high-caste Hindus thought that we were there to instigate the low-caste untouchables to revolt against them. But our resources, especially our tents, crockery and cooks and buses, impressed them. The co-operation of highly placed officials rehabilitated us in the eyes of the village folk, and many of them who went to the city and made enquiries about us from educated relations returned to the village satisfied about our credentials. But more than all this, the excellent work of the Medical unit established rapport with the community, and the sympathetic welfare activities of the Agriculture, Veterinary and Education units further helped us to establish more intimate contacts with the people. They were benefiting by our presence: in the first two months 390 cases were treated by the Medical unit; several useful demonstrations were given by the Agriculture and Veterinary units, who also distributed vegetable seeds, plants of fruit-bearing trees and modern chemical fertilizers. The adult

14

education centre attracted many people from the village; both the library and cultural programmes became popular. The Engineering unit dug soakpits in the village, improved the village well and constructed several model smokeless ovens. This changed the attitude of the people considerably. To begin with the investigators making anthropological enquiry were regarded as a nuisance; now they were tolerated as inquisitive but friendly outsiders. In a few days there was a change for the better. We had never talked politics or religion, there was no propaganda or attempt at reform and no superiority of city-ways and sneering at the rustic ways of the village people in our attitude. Indifference turned into warmth and friendship, and at this point we intensified our anthropological investigations. At first a general sociological census of the community was taken, and later investigations of specific problems were started. A sample of 120 families representing different castes and levels of income, education and urban contacts was selected for intensive investigations. Episodic and topical life-histories were recorded from 80 people, besides 11 full biographies. This was done in a series of free-association interviews, which were controlled only in the final stages. Besides this the established method of participant observation and the usual techniques of anthropological enquiry were also used. The life-histories provide most of the material on inter-personal relations and attitudes, much of which has been translated in this book from the actual words of the informants. All the available village records were carefully studied, and as far as possible all the material collected was carefully checked. The research reports by other units on topics assigned to them—such as the medical examination of 1,200 people, a diet and nutritional survey, a survey of village agriculture and its problems, a survey of animal care and health— were carefully studied at the time of the preparation of this report and used at appropriate places; but most of them will be published, it is hoped, independently in professional journals.

My aim in this book has been to give a clear and intimate picture of some aspects of life in one Indian village. As the book is likely to be used by social anthropologists and sociologists as well as by others, I have endeavoured to keep my presentation fairly general. As our project had received considerable publicity in the Indian press we could not hide the identity of the village in a pseudonym. This in its turn has created several problems in the mode of presentation. The people of the village are proud and sensitive, and some of them would not like to be identified through the remembered incidents even though fictitious names and initials are used. Many concrete cases which I would have liked to cite have therefore been omitted. Anxiety to avoid unwanted legal complications has forced me to present one or two subjects in a somewhat roundabout manner. But some concrete cases had to be presented, and this I have done in a spirit of friendship and in the hope that I will not be misunderstood by the village people. Although this work is not based on a statistical enquiry, sufficient statistical checks were used during the investigations. In several parts of the book, however, I have just indicated the dominant norms and main lines of variation without attempting a statistical and tabular presentation. It is my belief that fruitful theoretical discussions must be based on research of a more extensive scale than that attempted in the field-work summarized in this book, and as such I have reserved a part of my field-material, which has possibilities of theoretical exposition, for subsequent studies both of an extensive and comparative nature. Problems of caste, kinship and lineage organization, social stratification, leadership and the exercise of authority will be dealt with more fully on the basis of further field-work which we soon hope to extend to other rural communities in Hyderabad.

1*a*. E.R.: A Reddi Woman.

1*b*. A Mala Woman.

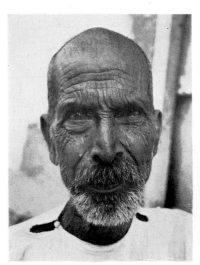

1*c*. A Muslim.

1*d*. Middle-aged Man from a clean caste.

2a. Mother and Son.

2b. A Mala Untouchable.

2c. A Madiga Untouchable.

2d. Village Barber.

CHAPTER ONE

The Setting

I. THE SETTING

SHAMIRPET is a village situated at a distance of about twenty-five miles from the twin cities of Hyderabad and Secundra-bad in the Deccan plateau of India. Culturally it lies in the region known as Telangana, which is itself a part of the wider culture-area of Andhra-desa. Telangana is a country of fertile fields and barren rocks; a land of temples, tanks and lakes. It is estimated that there are over twenty thousand lakes and tanks in this region, which covers an area of more than 42,000 square miles. Shamirpet is located by the side of one of these tanks and lies on the road that links the capital city of Hyderabad with Karimnagar, the headquarters of the northern district of that name.

The picturesque landscape of the village is truly characteristic of the Deccan plateau. The soil is in part black and in part red, and is suitable for the cultivation of rice, millet, castor and other oil-seeds, pulses and tobacco. An endless series of barren rocks formed of gneisses and granites dominates the land. Tall palmyra trees stand magnificently and imperiously against the often-clear sky, evergreen shrubs circle the rock formations and tamarind trees grow here and there near human habitation. In the country-side surrounding Shamirpet the average annual rainfall is about twenty-five inches. From Indian standards, the climate is moderate and knows no extremes either in winter or in summer. The days during the summer season are rather hot, the temperature often touching 112° F., but the evenings and nights are always cool and pleasant. In some winter nights the temperature drops to 45° F. There is little forest in the country immediately surrounding

17

Shamirpet and the neighbouring cluster of villages. However, villagers are able to collect some fuel as well as small quantities of edible and marketable minor forest produce from the local scrub jungle. In this type of landscape little game is to be expected. Tigers from the forests fifteen or twenty miles away are occasionally seen, but panthers, in search of stray goats, calves and dogs, are more frequent visitors to the village. Wild pigs are plentiful and always do very considerable damage to the crops. Spotted deer make an occasional appearance in the surrounding areas, while hares which abound in the shrubs are very often shot or hunted with dogs trained for this purpose. Wild ducks come seasonally to the large tank near the village, and green pigeons and partridges are among the other feathered game found in the vicinity of Shamirpet.

It has been pointed out that Shamirpet is only some twenty-five miles from Hyderabad and Secundrabad, which rank fourth among the cities of India in respect of population and size. It is only fifteen miles from the Bolarum cantonment and twelve miles from the military aerodrome of Hakimpet. A regular bus service plying between Hyderabad and Karimnagar touches Shamirpet, and there are about twelve buses running in both directions on this road every day. From this it should not be assumed, however, that Shamirpet is just a suburban extension of Hyderabad. Although it is in regular and constant touch with the capital, it is an independent village with an organization of its own.

No village in India can be singled out as being typical of the country as a whole, but Shamirpet possesses most of the characteristics which are common to the rural communities in middle and peninsular India. As an independent socio-economic and ritual unit it enjoys partial self-sufficiency in several aspects of community life. In the wider organization of the rural community it possesses partial autonomy. Its component units are mostly the occupational castes which are integrated into the structure of the village. Finally, it has a semi-judicial village council composed of caste elders and other influential persons. This council administers justice in socio-religious cases involving breaches of the traditional norms of society. The village as a unit of social organization performs several significant functions which form an important agency of social control.

THE SETTING

2. THE PEOPLE

According to the census of 1951, the total population of Shamir-pet, which included the two neighbouring hamlets of Babuguda and Upparpalli, was 2,494, with a total of 508 houses. The following table shows the distribution of the population according to religion:

1. Hindus. A. Clean castes 1,434
            B. Untouchables or Scheduled castes . 680
2. Muslims 340

The predominant language in Shamirpet is Telugu, the main language of Telangana and Andhra-desa. It is known as 'the Italian of the East' and is praised for its sonorous and lyrical qualities and possesses a vast literature, both classical and modern. However, the dialect of Telugu, which is spoken in Shamirpet, and generally in the countryside, is criticized by the more sophisticated Andhras for its harshness and rustic accent. In the census of 1951, 2,008 persons in this village were recorded as speaking Telugu, while 340 persons were recorded as speaking Urdu, which was until 1948 the official language of Hyderabad administration. These figures are, however, misleading, and make reference only to the mother-tongue. In practice most men in the village are bilingual; those whose mother-tongue is Telugu have at least a smattering of Urdu, and of the 340 Urdu speakers at least half possess a working knowledge of Telugu. As a generalization it may be stated that knowledge of the mother-tongue alone is confined only to women, although several women among both the Hindus and the Muslims are also bi-lingual.

Thus the two major divisions in the population of the village may be distinguished on the grounds of religion and language. Culturally also the Hindus and Muslims stand in marked contrast to each other.

The Hindus of Shamirpet can be classed under three broad divisions:

1. Cultivators.
2. Occupational castes, with traditional crafts and professions regarded as clean and respectable.
3. Depressed classes, subsisting by humble and lowly callings.

In the first group we can place the following castes: the Reddi, the Muttarasi, and their subdivisions. These groups are often

19

referred to as 'the Kapu' or agricultural castes. As this name suggests, they derive the major part of their subsistence by tilling
the land, although individuals from any of these groups may
engage in trade and commerce or may take up urban occupations.

In the second group we can place the following: the Brahmin
(priests), the Komti (traders), the Kummari (potters) and the
Golla (shepherds). The five sections of the Panch Bramha group
of artisan castes, that is, the Wadla (carpenters), the Kammari
(blacksmiths), the Ausula (goldsmiths), the Kase (workers in
bell-metal) and the Kanchari (sculptors), also belong to this group
—although they claim separate identity and are rather exclusive.
The Sale (weavers), the Gaondha (toddy-tappers), the Sakali
(washermen) and the Mangali (barbers) also follow their traditional occupations; and although in the hierarchy of caste organization their place is a little inferior to the castes mentioned above,
they belong to the second group for the purpose of our classification. The position of the once-tribal but now largely assimilated
Vaddar (stone-breakers) and the Erkala (hunters and basket-
makers) is slightly different, for although they are not untouchables their position among the clean castes is the lowest.

There are only two untouchable or depressed castes in Shamirpet, the Mala and the Madiga. Of these two, the Malas consider
themselves superior to the Madigas, by whose touch they are
polluted. However, it should be pointed out that the Indian constitution has abolished untouchability. The untouchable castes
can draw water from the public wells and can without discrimination share the public utilities with the clean castes. Their children
now freely attend the common village school. But social conserva-
tism dies hard and legislation alone cannot overnight change the
deep-rooted complexes of thought and behaviour which are the
heritage of many generations of a caste-ridden social system.
Caste still retains its endogamous character, and traditional rules
prohibit inter-dining with persons of lower castes. Thus in these
two spheres at least the untouchable castes have still to confine
themselves to their narrow circles. While in the cities the clean
castes are no longer sensitive to the touch of a person belonging to
these castes, in the countryside an untouchable still cannot
approach too close to clean-caste people lest they be polluted by a
chance physical contact. Some progressive-minded untouchables

resent this disability, but nevertheless they recognize the value of realizing their own limitations and continue to conform to the traditional norms of behaviour.

The people of Telangana and Andhra-desa belong to the great family of Dravidian-speaking people who developed a great civilization in the south and have materially contributed to the final make-up of Indian civilization as we know it to-day. Racially they represent a mixture of several elements. In physical types also the people of Shamirpet show great variation. Most of the Muslim inhabitants of Shamirpet are the descendants of local converts and do not therefore greatly differ in physical characteristics from the local Hindu inhabitants, but the few immigrants whose arrival dates from recent times present a marked contrast with their more delicate features and fairer skin colour.

In point of dress and ornament the Hindus and Muslims differ widely. Muslim men and boys wear loose trousers of thin white cloth called *pyjama*, and a vest or a shirt. Out of doors they put on the more conventional long coat buttoned up to the neck known as *sherwani*. They invariably wear a red fez cap or a black cap made of sheepskin. Muslim girls wear a tight *pyjama* and a long, loose tunic which often touches the knees. Round the shoulders and thrown round the back they wear a thin white or coloured scarf known as *dupatta* or *odhni*. On festive occasions these clothes are very colourful. Married Muslim women usually wear a blouse or bodice, and a *sari*—a wide piece of cloth, some five or six yards long, which is tied round the waist to form a skirt that nearly touches the ankles. It is tied in such a way that one end of the cloth is taken over the chest to one shoulder and then passed behind the neck to the other shoulder. Married Muslim women are obliged by the rules of their religion to observe *purdah*, i.e. veil themselves in the presence of all but their closest relations. Whenever they leave their houses they wear this veil known as *burkha*, a garment which falls from the crown of the head to the ground. The Hindu mode of dress is quite different, and varies greatly according to the financial status of the different families. Among the poorer classes, infants remain naked, but occasionally a few rags are tied round their waists; and in childhood they go about in these tattered rags. Boys wear a vest or shirt and a *dhoti*. Girls wear a skirt (*lahanga*) and a blouse. Among the poorer classes these clothes are almost always dirty, for within a few days of their purchase they lose their new look; and although they are periodic-ally washed, soap or soda-ash is rarely used and consequently they appear to be stained and soiled. In families which are financially better placed, and among those who have received some degree of education or who have been influenced by urban friends and rela-tions, the children's clothing is markedly superior in quality and cleanliness. Boys wear shirts cut in modern style and *dhotis* or occasionally *pyjama*. Girls wear either a blouse and skirt or frocks bought ready-made from the city stores or made by the local tailor. Men wear a vest or shirt and a *dhoti*. Influential and well-to-. do persons put on a coat when leaving their houses, particularly when going to the city. Women wear a *sari* and a bodice, the latter invariably embroidered. The favourite colours of the women in the countryside appear to be the deeper shades of red, yellow and green. The village shepherds have a distinctive dress. When they go out to graze their herds of goats and sheep they always have a locally made black blanket on their shoulders, even in the hottest season.

The people of Telangana, particularly the women, are ex-tremely fond of ornaments. The commonest types are those made of metal which include ear-plugs and ear-rings, nose-pins and nose-rings, rings worn on the fingers and toes, bracelets, anklets, several types of light and heavy necklaces and belts worn round the waist. Among well-to-do people ear and nose ornaments as well as necklaces are generally made of gold; the rest of a woman's ornaments are of silver. However, very few people can afford ornaments of a metal as expensive as gold, and most people have a few silver pieces, the rest of their ornaments being made of cheaper metals and alloys. In addition to the metal jewellery all Hindu women except widows wear a number of glass bangles on the wrists. The Muslim women's choice of ornament differs from that of their Hindu neighbours, and such jewellery as they wear often comes from the shops in the city and is not made according to the designs of the local goldsmith.

3. THE VILLAGE

Shamirpet cannot claim to be a village of any great age. No historical records relating to the actual founding of the village are available, but the elderly people have some information regarding its past history 'as it was passed on to them by their forefathers'. The village of Shamirpet owes its present shape to the construction of the large and beautiful tank which lies some three furlongs north of the village site. Before the construction of this tank there was a tiny hamlet on the present site which consisted of a few households and was known as Shahpur. Some three hundred and fifty years ago Ibrahim Quli Qutub Shah, then ruler of Hyderabad, wishing to perpetuate his name, ordered the construction of a huge tank which, he expected, would be called after him. This tank is the hyphen linking the city of Hyderabad with Secundrabad. However, according to the legend, the people associated it with the name of the engineer Hussain Khan and called it 'Hussain Sagar'. So the ruler decided on the building of a second tank, and chose the site of Shamirpet. But the Shamirpet tank was his second disappointment. On the completion of the tank, he is believed to have come to the site and asked the people, 'Whose tank is this?' The people unwittingly answered, 'It is Shah Mir's tank.' The people's tribute to the man whose brain had created the project did not satisfy the Qutubshahi ruler. He ordered a third tank to be constructed at a different site some thirty-five miles away, and it is this tank which now commemorates his name and is known as 'Ibrahimpatan Sagar'. The second of these tanks, constructed near the hamlet known as Shaepur, changed the fortunes of that tiny settlement. The people who had worked on the construction of the tank settled permanently in the vicinity of the hamlet and were joined by more settlers attracted by the irrigation facilities provided by the tank, so that the village gradually grew to a considerable size. Because of its association with Shah Mir's tank, the hamlet was given the new name of Shah Mir Pet, which became gradually corrupted into Shamirpet.

In the year 1798 H.E.H. the Nizam of Hyderabad (until 1948 the feudal ruler of Hyderabad) granted this village together with several others as *jagir* (feudal estate) to one of his nobles, the late Fakhrul Mulk Khan Khanan. On his death the estate was inherited by his son Nawab Nizam Yar Jung, also known as Nawab Ehsan-ul-Mulk Khan Khanan. The last in the line of the Jagirdars of Shamirpet was Kemal Yar Jung. He constructed a beautiful summer house, which is now in ruins, adjoining the tank, as well as several office buildings in the village which house the post office, the school, the police station and the village granary. After

the death of Kemal Yar Jung the property came under the administration of the Court of Wards. In the meantime, vast changes
were taking place in Hyderabad. After the Police Action of 1948,
Hyderabad became an integral part of the Indian Republic.
With the inauguration of the democratic order the Nizam has
become a constitutional ruler and the feudal system within the
State has been abolished. In consequence Shamirpet now comes
under the jurisdiction of the normal district administration.

Shamirpet is situated at a distance of about a furlong from the
north-bound road which runs between Hyderabad and Karimnagar. An unmetalled road links the village with the main road,
from which some of the houses in the village are clearly visible.
Between the road and the village there is a flat and fairly level
patch of ground, and in the centre of this ground there is a tree
around which the Muslims bury their dead. At the junction of the
main road and the diversion leading to the village there is a small
shelter for passengers awaiting the buses, built in stone and lime.
A little way down to the north stands the Inspection Bungalow
of the State Public Works Department. It is intended for the use of
touring government officials, and can also be used by occasional
visitors, who have to make a small payment for its use. Further
north, at a distance of about two and a half furlongs, is the tank,
which in its setting of barren rocks and tall trees provides a beautiful landscape. Between the tank and the road now lie the ruins of
the 'summer house' which was built on the tank-bund by the last
feudal landlord of the village. In his time it was provided with an
electric generator, pipe lines and modern sanitary fittings, but
after the Nawab's death it was deserted and is now a melancholy
but romantic sight.

The village itself is not built according to a definite plan. A
wide main street lies in the centre and runs almost parallel to and
roughly a furlong away from the main road. As we proceed north-
wards down this street we find on the right a number of white-
washed stone buildings housing the various government offices,
and on the left there are a number of small tea and betel shops.
On the right there are also the residential quarters of the sub-
inspector of police who is in charge of the police station, a government granary, living quarters of the police constables, the village
dispensary, the school and the post office. Lanes branch off both
right and left from the street, and on either side of these lanes are

built the residential houses of the people belonging to the clean castes or to the Muslim community. The house of the Deshmukh, or the village headman, is the very first house and stands a little to the right of the unmetalled road that joins the main road to the village. It has a very high compound wall made of locally available stone and looks more like a small fort than a dwelling-house. In the main section of the village that sprawls to both sides of the main road it is difficult to discern any clear and systematic caste 'quarters' in which only members of one caste live. There is an unmistakable tendency among some castes, as for instance the Sakali (washermen), the Vaddar (stone-workers), the Golla (shepherds) and the Kummari (potters), to occupy houses in compact blocks on contiguous patches of land, but in close proximity are situated the houses of people belonging to other communities. In no sense can the individual clean castes be said to live in separate colonies, nor is any one caste in exclusive possession of any clearly marked out area. In many cases people live outside their own caste 'blocks'. The houses of the clean castes are built so close together that it is clear that considerations of caste distinction do not materially affect their choice of sites for the construction of houses. A Hindu may live in the immediate neighbourhood of Muslims, and often people belonging to quite different castes are one another's neighbours. It is probable that in the beginning the different castes marked out different blocks for themselves on the proposed site for the settlement. People coming later to the village either found a place to construct their houses in their caste block or had to choose a plot elsewhere. However, there are some communities which live in separate colonies or *wada*. To the east, a narrow strip of land separates the main settlement from the *Malawada*, or the colony of the Mala untouchables. Further east, and separated from the houses of the Malas by another narrow strip of land, is the colony of the Madigas. Distinct from both these groups, and situated to the north-east of the main village, there is a small colony of Erkala hunters, whose small circular huts stand out in marked contrast to the houses in the rest of the village.

It has already been pointed out that there is a school, a dispensary, a post office and a police station in the village. The school is at present ill-housed; it has five classes meeting in two small rooms and only two masters, who teach both Urdu and Telugu as well as the other subjects of the primary school curriculum.

Children of all communities now go to school, and the old prejudice against admitting untouchable students is dying out. In recent years some Mala and Madiga boys joined the school, but most of them attended only in name, playing truant so consistently that they derived little benefit and eventually stopped going altogether. The school is ill-equipped, having some miserable-looking furniture, a few charts and maps and the inevitable blackboard. The master still wields his stick, and among other reasons this explains perhaps the lack of enthusiasm on the part of the lower-class children and their parents for the school.

The dispensary is housed in a small room and its adjoining verandah. The rest of the building is used as living-quarters by the Medical Officer. This small dispensary was started by one of the Jagirdars, and has had a succession of Medical Officers who had no qualifications for the job. The present incumbent too is not properly qualified, for he is not even a medical licenciate. He is paid Rs. 45 per month and is supplied with a small quantity of drugs by the Medical Department of the Hyderabad Government. As a result of contact with the cities, the villagers have developed a great liking for injections, expecting them to work like magic and provide quick and certain cure for all ailments. The Medical Officer, although he is not authorized to give injections, does so in the course of his limited private practice. People go to the dispensary only for the treatment of common ailments, such as scabies, cough and malaria. For want of proper equipment and a qualified medical practitioner, the dispensary at Shamirpet has very few patients. In addition to the allopathic dispensary there are several elderly people in the village who administer herbal preparations according to Indian indigenous systems of medicine. Magic and divination are also employed to a considerable extent by all sections of the people. 'Where herbs and medicines do not work, proper chants and spells do not fail us', the people often say. Indeed, for certain categories of disease and difficulties recourse to divination is often regarded as the only proper remedy. It must be added that increased contact with the cities and the influence of education have greatly enhanced the value of modern medicine in the eyes of the people. There is now practically no prejudice against vaccination, although some people are still afraid of plague and cholera inoculations because they cause pain and fever. A minority of the villagers take advantage of the qualified doctors who practise in Secundrabad and Hyderabad, and a few even go to the well-equipped hospitals for prolonged treatment of difficult and persistent diseases. However, for the majority of the population the only medicines used for ordinary ailments are the inexpensive indigenous herbs and drugs which are locally available.

The local post office, under one of the village schoolmasters, serves Shamirpet and a large number of adjoining villages. The system of mail distribution in the countryside is very defective. Often the village postman takes a month or even more to reach a village on his periodic rounds. Letters are generally delivered personally to people who come to the post office for them, or they are handed to a co-villager who happens to visit the post office, for further transmission.

The police station at Shamirpet is in charge of a sub-inspector and has a strength of two head constables and twelve constables. This force is responsible for the maintenance of law and order in the villages under its jurisdiction. The police keep an eye on all doubtful characters, organize regular patrols of the villages and through the subordinate officials keep themselves informed of local developments. Their official records register all births and deaths, which must be reported by the inhabitants of the village.

As the tank is more than a mile from the village, the people use well water for domestic purposes. In respect of wells, Shamirpet has been very unlucky. Out of a total of thirty-three wells within the village limits, there are only three which yield good, drinkable water, the water of all other wells being brackish and unpalatable. Most people are therefore able to use sweet water only for drinking and cooking, whilst clothes and household utensils are washed in brackish water. The outlying wards of the Malas and Madigas are more fortunate in this respect, for their wells, situated at a distance of about half a mile from their respective colonies, yield 'sweet' water. In the summer months there is often an acute scarcity of drinking water in the village, and at this time large crowds of women gather at the few sweet-water wells waiting patiently to fill their many brass and earthen pots. This time of enforced waiting is spent in gossiping, in exchanging news and often in relating the latest scandals.

The sanitation of the village is the responsibility of the Yetti Madigas, whose traditional duty it is to sweep the street and lanes; in return for the service, the government grants them the use of certain rent-free lands. Moreover, every morning the womenfolk of each house sweep and clean that portion of the lane which lies directly in front of their own house, sprinkle it with water or water mixed with cow-dung and often decorate the entrance with designs drawn with millet or rice flour. Notwithstanding this, the lanes are not always very clean. The reasons for this are many. The Yetti Madigas do not sweep the village very regularly; and the women, when they have finished their housework, often throw the refuse into the public thoroughfare. Thirdly, very few people have latrines in their houses, and even those who have them are inclined to make their children ease themselves at the side of the road. However, the pigs kept by the Erkala caste as well as the large number of dogs in the village are good scavengers and help to keep the village clean.

4. THE HOUSES

The dwellings in Shamirpet can be classified into three main groups: the Bhawanti, the Penkutillu and the Gudse.

The Bhawanti. This is a large house with stone walls and tiled roofs; it generally stands in its own compound, which is surrounded by a wall, and invariably has five to six rooms. The following account of the house of I.R., a woman with considerable local influence and a good-sized agricultural holding, will illustrate this type of house. As we enter the gate in the compound wall we find ourselves in front of an open space which constitutes the courtyard of the house. On one side of this courtyard there is a cattle-shed, the end of which is partitioned off as a store-room for fuel-cakes made of cow-dung. Opposite the gate across the courtyard is a verandah running the whole length of the house; at one end of this verandah there is a small room in which agricultural implements are kept. The main door of the house leads into an inner court which is open to the sky. In the centre is a stone-lined sink, known as *gachhu*, which can be drained and cleaned, and here, sitting on small wooden stools, the women of the house bath. The inner court is surrounded on three sides by rooms; on one side there are two inter-connected rooms, the first being used as a dining-room and the second as a kitchen. Opposite this, running the whole length of the inner court, is a long room, while opposite to the main house door and across the inner court is a door which

28

leads into the room used for the storing of grain and various household goods. At the end is a small room, and here are lodged the gods and deities of the household.

Although small variations are sometimes seen in the internal arrangement of this type of dwelling, the principles of construction are generally everywhere the same. The walls are made of local stone, which is available at very cheap rates; the doors and their frames are fashioned by the local carpenter and are often decorated on the outside with carvings of geometrical designs and occasionally human or animal figures. The walls are plastered with mud and washed with coloured earth. Almost all the rooms have mud floors; the roofs are always tiled. The Bhawanti type of house is the house of the well-to-do cultivator as well as that of the more substantial people belonging to the occupational castes. Although the houses of the Muslims, both cultivators and traders, as well as of Hindus with urban contacts, conform to the general pattern of the Bhawanti, they show certain marks of sophistication which are obviously the result of urban influences. Such houses have whitewashed walls and stone floors, and many, especially those of the Muslims, have pit-latrines in the backyards. The outer walls are often decorated with motifs borrowed from the city.

The furniture in this type of house is very meagre. In some houses there are a few hard wooden chairs, crude benches and stools or perhaps folding chairs with canvas seats. A popular item of furniture is the wooden *takht*, a large, portable wooden platform, rectangular in shape and supported on four legs. It is about two feet high and seats four to eight people. The other common article of furniture met with in the village is the bedstead, on which the meagre bedding is spread. Rich people have a large framed bedstead which is often ornamented. It is known as *palang*. But poorer people use the small-framed *charpoy* or *khat* woven with locally made thin hemp ropes.

It has been pointed out earlier that the average rural house of this type is often embellished with carvings on the doors. Moreover the walls are generally decorated with designs or human or other animal figures. Cheap prints of Hindu gods and goddesses or family photographs taken by street photographers in the city decorate the walls in some of the houses. The more educated people and retired petty officials sometimes possess clocks, but these are generally out of order and are used rather as decorations than to tell the time.

Household utensils are generally made by the local potter. But shining brassware, including a few large pots for storing water, are a mark of respectability. Food is served on brass, bell-metal or aluminium plates. Water is drunk from metal mugs or brass beakers. In some houses a couple of china cups and saucers and a few glass plates are also to be seen.

The Penkutillu. This type of house is smaller and less ostentatious, and is built by average cultivators with small holdings, who are neither rich nor poor according to village standards. These houses also have a courtyard and possibly a backyard; a verandah and two or three rooms which are used for various purposes. The walls are of stone, the floor of mud and the roof is tiled. The cattle-shed is generally close to the living-room and there is neither latrine nor bathroom in the house.

This type of house is also decorated with carvings on the doors, and designs are painted on the wall. In such houses furniture is regarded as a luxury; there may be a few bedsteads, some small wooden stools and possibly a crude chair or two. People with city contacts decorate the walls of their houses with commercial calendars or coloured magazine covers. The household utensils in this type of house are, except for metal plates used for serving food, of earthenware, even water being stored in clay pots. Yet respectability demands that such a house should have at least some brass utensils. These are greatly coveted by the ambitious housewife.

The Gudse. These are the commonest type of dwellings found in Telangana, and are indeed the most numerous in Shamirpet. The walls of these huts are either made of mud or they are made of wattle-screen and plastered with mud. The roof is always thatched. The hut is built in a small enclosure and has generally only one room, from which the kitchen is partly partitioned. These huts have very little furniture and all household utensils are the wares of the local potter. The few metal utensils which the family possesses are among the most treasured parts of the household property.

All the three types of village dwellings have some features in common. Almost all of them have some open space either at the front or at the back. This is generally enclosed. Here women bath and in times of emergency, such as illness or other incapacity, it may also be used as a latrine. During the rainy season it is used for the growing of vegetables, specially fruit-bearing creepers, and throughout the year it is used by the household fowls. Similarly, in most of these houses the cattle-shed is very close to the main living-room. Hardly half a dozen houses in the village have latrines; the majority of the people go out into the fields or behind the rocks for answering the call of nature. Notwithstanding some variety, the decorative designs found on all the houses follow a generally established pattern. The floors are swept twice every day in almost all the houses. The mud floor is periodically smeared with cow-dung mixed with water and the walls are washed annually with lime or coloured earth. Grain and provisions are stored in large receptacles made either by the potter and well burnt to a vermilion red or by the Erkala in their traditional styles of basket-work.

All the houses in Shamirpet can be classed into one of these three types. The Gudse-type huts of the Erkalas are, however, a class by themselves. These small, circular huts, made from sheets of weed-matting, are about twenty feet in diameter and are often only six feet high. The interior is unpartitioned and serves as bedroom, dining-room, living-room and kitchen. Pigs and poultry are housed in similar but smaller round huts built in the immediate vicinity of the dwelling-hut.

From time to time groups of families belonging to the nomadic castes come to the village. These have their low, portable huts, which are mostly made of folding bamboo screens. Almost every month some group belonging to this category makes its appearance in Shamirpet and after a stay of a week or so moves off with its huts, dogs and pigs.

5. THE NEIGHBOURHOOD OF SHAMIRPET

The nearness of Shamirpet to the cities of Hyderabad and Secundrabad has been mentioned. People holding small government posts or having urban relations make periodic visits to the city. Others, especially young men, cycle down to Secundrabad or Hyderabad to visit the cinema or to look at the shops.

In the broad social sense, however, Shamirpet's more intimate ties are with the villages in the neighbourhood. In the events and developments of these villages the people of Shamirpet are very keenly interested. The hamlets of Babugura and Upparpalli are in fact entered as parts of the village of Shamirpet in government records, and in a sense they are; nevertheless, on a restricted scale they enjoy considerable autonomy. The elders of the hamlets try, as far as possible, to decide the hamlet's minor disputes without referring them either to the headman or to the village council of Shamirpet. They say, 'We are poor inhabitants of a small hamlet. Our resources are limited. The people of Shamirpet are prosperous; they have adopted the ways of the city. If we refer our cases to them, they will impose such fines that our necks will break.' Yet there are many cases in which one of the disputing parties, dissatisfied with the judgement of the elders and possessing the necessary financial resources or influential support, will refer the case to the Shamirpet village council. In all such cases one or two elders and influential people from the hamlet in question are summoned to attend the proceedings of the village council at Shamirpet. Similarly, for all the ceremonies organized jointly by the people of Shamirpet as a whole it is customary to send invitations to Babugura and Upparpalli and it is expected that they will be represented by at least some of the village elders. When the people of the village as a whole are summoned on government business to the district or subdivisional headquarters, the residents of the two hamlets have also to accompany the people of Shamirpet, for all the three settlements are, according to government records, component units of one village. However, the distance between Shamirpet and the two hamlets is an effective barrier to the pursuance of a common social life. And from this point of view the two hamlets are as independent as two self-contained small villages.

The area surrounding Shamirpet is quite densely populated. It is not unusual to find a village or a small hamlet every three to six miles, and Shamirpet is surrounded by a number of villages, some large and others small. With most of these, Shamirpet, as a village, has very little to do. However, individual residents remain in constant touch with friends and relations in the surrounding villages. Ceremonies connected with the major crises of life, i.e. birth, marriage and death, often take people out of Shamirpet to the neighbouring villages, or bring people from there into Shamirpet. For a more or less well-defined block of villages the different castes have their respective caste councils, to which matters concerning the caste only are taken.

3a. Shamirpet from a hill outside.

3b. The Village Well.

4. Men Making Stakes.

THE SETTING

Three miles to the north on the Hyderabad–Karimnagar road there is another village, about as large as Shamirpet. It is called Aliyabad. It has some rich and influential Muslim and Hindu agriculturists among its residents who share with those of Shamirpet the waters of the Shamirpet tank for irrigation purposes. This system is not very satisfactory and the two villages have numerous complaints against each other. There is a keen rivalry between the two, and every two or three years the tension and passions of the people rise to such an extent that there is danger of a breach of peace and of rioting. The residents of Shamirpet do not think much of the people of Aliyabad, and the latter heartily reciprocate their dislike.

People living in different villages have very few occasions on which to meet each other as a whole. There are no common ceremonies and functions in which several villages participate. To a certain extent caste ceremonies provide opportunities for inter-village meetings; but the most common meeting-places for people belonging to the nearby villages of the same area are the markets and fairs.

CHAPTER TWO

Social Structure

To understand the social structure of an Indian village it is necessary to examine the various units through which the village community is organized. The basic and primary unit of the society is the elementary or joint family. Every family belongs to an exogamous division of a caste and several such divisions constitute an endogamous caste or an endogamous section of a large caste. Only excommunication or a change of religion can alter the position of the individual in any such social units. On the other hand, every family belongs to the community with whom it shares a settlement site, be it a village or a hamlet attached to a village. In socio-religious affairs, control of the individual is threefold—that of his family, his village and his caste. Often it is only the independent, endogamous division of the caste which takes cognizance of offences and penalizes erring members, and not the caste as a whole. On the other hand, very serious cases or matters concerning more than one village may be heard and decided by a larger judicial organ, comprising members of all the constituent villages. The structure and organization of the family, as well as the criterion of status differentiation in the community, can best be described in a separate chapter; here we shall examine the division of the community into castes, and follow it up by an analysis of the internal organization of the village with special reference to authority and the machinery regulating the administration of justice in the village.

I. CASTE IN THE VILLAGE COMMUNITY

The Hindus and the Muslims constitute two distinct sections in the population of Shamirpet. Although long residence and close association have brought them in close contact with each other and their cultures are in certain fields inter-related, the two communities retain their own socio-religious identities. The Muslims are in a minority in the population of the village; but they are a close-knit group in socio-religious matters. All Muslims belong to the Sunni division. Among them there are no great inequalities of wealth and possession, and consequently there is, within the Muslim community, no evidence of class distinction. In matters affecting their socio-religious life they act as a separate and self-sufficient group, rarely seeking the help, assistance or advice of their Hindu neighbours. One of the remarkable characteristics of the predominantly Hindu rural society of India is that non-Hindu communities have also been influenced by the caste-hierarchy of Hinduism. Even the non-Hindu groups have had to fit somehow into the rigid framework of the caste-dominated social system; and while they have always remained outside it, never having been regarded as Hindus, they have nevertheless acquired a quasi-caste status in accordance with their general social, economic and political position. As Hyderabad was formerly ruled by a Muslim, his co-religionists had a privileged position in the affairs of the State. Their social status in the rural areas has always been more or less equal to that of the agricultural castes; although from the point of view of religion the Hindus have always regarded them as inferior. Nevertheless, a clean-caste Hindu can sit down with a Muslim, and the less orthodox can even touch them without having to take a subsequent purificatory bath.

The Hindu social system, founded on the division of society into 'castes', presents a social framework of great complexity. The traditional *varna* system, modified in the course of the evolution of Indian social polity, divides Hindu society into five major groups. The first three of these, viz. Brahmins (priests and men of learning), Kshatriyas (rulers and warriors) and Vaishyas (traders) are regarded as *dvija* or 'twice born'. According to Hindu ritual only they are allowed to undergo the *upanayana* ceremony which symbolizes their spiritual re-birth and entitles them to wear the sacred thread. The fourth group is composed of numerous occupational castes who are relatively clean and are not classed as untouchables. Finally, in the fifth major group we can place all the untouchable castes. This classification is accepted by the Hindus all over India. The relative positions of the different groups,

SOCIAL STRUCTURE

ascribing order of precedence and social superiority or inferiority,
are recognized everywhere. The legitimate occupations to be
followed by people in these major groups (*varnas*) are defined by
tradition. Within each group there are several sub-groups (*jati* or
castes), which can again be arranged in a hierarchical order within themselves. Inter-relations, between both major groups and
their sub-groups, are largely governed by traditional rules, and
all major forms of contact, viz. touch, inter-dining and sexual
intercourse, come under the purview of these elaborate rules.

Within this general frame of the *varna* system, in the different
regions and territorial units of the land, there are several socially
autonomous castes, each fitting into one of the five major divisions
but otherwise practically independent in socio-religious spheres of
life. These castes often share a common generic name and title with
castes of comparable status in other regions; but often they do
not inter-dine, whilst inter-marriage between them is prohibited.
Each caste is further subdivided into several sub-castes which are
endogamous and are for all practical purposes independent
groups by themselves.

The organization of the Hindu castes and their relative positions
in the traditional caste-hierarchy require a detailed and careful
examination. From the point of view of caste superiority the different castes in Shamirpet may be grouped in the following order:

'TWICE-BORN' CASTES
Brahmin (Priests)

Komti
(Traders)

OCCUPATIONAL CASTES
Agriculturists, Workers and Labourers

Kapu—Reddi (Agriculturists)	*Kummari* (Potters)	*Golla* (Shepherds)
	Kapu—Muttarasi (Agriculturists)	
Sale (Weavers)		*Gaondla* (Toddy-tappers)
Sakali (Washermen)		*Mangali* (Barbers)
Vaddar (Stone-workers)	*Erkala* (Hunters and Mat-makers)	*Pichha-Kuntla* (Minstrels narrating caste and clan legends)

36

SOCIAL STRUCTURE

Mala
(An untouchable caste)
Madiga
(An untouchable caste)

The above table does not include the Panch Bramha group. In point of religion they are Hindus, but their position in the caste hierarchy is rather uncertain. This group comprises five divisions: The Wadla (carpenter), the Kammari (blacksmith), the Ausula (goldsmith), the Kase (carver of figures in wood and stone) and the Kanchari (worker in bell-metal). Of these only the first three sections are found in Shamirpet. Inter-dining and inter-marrying, these sections constitute a distinct group of their own. In the local caste hierarchy they should be placed below the Kapu-Kummari-Golla group, but it cannot be said that they rank equal to or below the Sale-Gaondla group.

Among Hindus the Brahmin holds the highest place. He officiates at the ceremonies of all castes, except those of the Vaddar, the Erkala, the Pichha-Kuntla, the Mala and the Madiga. However, he is consulted by these castes also regarding the auspicious timing of agricultural operations or to perform marriage ceremonies; and his astrological calculations are eagerly sought by all people. All castes, except the Panch Bramha group, will accept food at his hands, but being 'pure and high-born' he cannot accept food from the hands of any but his caste fellows.

The Komtis rank next to the Brahmins. They are mostly traders and money-lenders, keeping small shops where they sell grain and general provisions. All castes except the Brahmin and the Panch Bramha group accept food at their hands, but they do not take food from those castes whose social position is lower than their own, and thus can only accept food at the hands of the Brahmins.

The Reddi sections of the Kapu (agricultural) group, the Kummari and the Golla castes are of equal caste status. Although each is an endogamous caste, they will freely inter-dine with each other, and social contact between them is on a basis of equality. The position of the other Kapu section, viz. Muttarasi, is a little lower. The first Kapu section as well as the Golla will eat at their hands, but the Kummari will refuse food which they have touched.

On the next level are the Sale and the Gaondla, who enjoy a

more or less similar position but are both endogamous and do not
inter-dine. They accept food at the hands of the castes higher than
themselves but not from those which are lower. Similarly, the
Sakali and the Mangali have a similar caste status, but they
do not inter-marry or inter-dine. But again, both the Sakali
and the Mangali will dine with the Sale and the Gaondla and
all the other castes higher than themselves. The Vaddar and
the Pichha-Kuntla will eat with neither the Sakali and the Mangali nor with the untouchable Malas and Madigas, but they can
take food at the hands of all castes higher than themselves. The
Erkalas will eat from the hands of all castes except those of the
Mala and the Madiga. The Sakali and the Mangali do not accept
food from the Erkala. The Erkala and the Pichha-Kuntla will
accept food from the Vaddar, but the Vaddar will not accept
food from the Erkala and the Pichha-Kuntla. Finally, the Mala
and the Madiga will eat at the hands of all the higher castes, but
the Mala, considering himself superior of the two untouchable
castes, will refuse food touched by a Madiga.

The position of the Panch Bramha group is peculiar. They
constitute a consolidated and self-sufficient group. They do not
accept food at the hands of any other castes, nor do any other
castes accept food touched by them. Here the position differs
vitally from that found in north India, where the carpenter, the
blacksmith, the worker in bell-metal, the goldsmith and the carver
of images constitute different endogamous castes which do not, as
they do in this area, inter-marry and inter-dine. Their social
status is neither very high nor very low. Everywhere they rank
lower than the 'twice-born' *varnas* of Brahmins, Kshatriyas and
Vaishyas, but they are not regarded as impure and their status
is infinitely superior to that of the untouchables. In the area under
study while the Panch Bramha group is regarded as 'clean',
even the untouchable Mala would refuse food touched by them,
and it is only in recent years that the Madigas have started to eat
from their hands. 'Their very touch poisons the food. How can
we accept it?' the people are often heard to remark when they are
asked to explain their refusal of food touched by any of the Panch
Bramha castes. The Panch Bramha castes wear the sacred thread
of the twice born and refuse food even from the Brahmin. It is
probable that their social exclusiveness reflects an attitude which
was developed in ancient times when a great fusion of Aryan and

non-Aryan groups was taking place in Indian society and Hinduism was consolidating itself. The highly organized craftsmen's guilds of those days may perhaps have succeeded in maintaining their integrity and exclusiveness for a long time, but had ultimately to yield; yet the tension created by their resistance remained, and even when they were absorbed into the fold of Hindu society they were not admitted as equals to the groups of comparable social status and in consequence probably continued to maintain their age-long exclusiveness.

All the castes whose relative positions in the caste-hierarchy have been shown in the accompanying table are endogamous. There is a permanent social distance between them; the individual is born into a caste, and a subsequent change in status is, except to the very lowest strata of society, equally impossible upwards or downwards.[1] In general it may be said that people accept food at the hands of all castes occupying a higher level in this hierarchy, the only exception being that of the Vaddar, who do not accept food from the highly placed Sakali and Mangali. Without exception people on a higher level refuse food from those on a lower level. Each caste has a traditional occupation sanctioned by religion, and these monopolies should not be infringed upon, except in the case of agriculture, which all may pursue.

Mention should here be made of the Jangam and the Katike castes, of each of which there is one family in Shamirpet. The Jangam are a semi-priestly caste ritually attached to the Baljas, for whom they tie the 'lingam'—a phallic symbol representing Shiva —and function as priests on the occasion of weddings. On the days of *Pitra Moksha Amavasya*[2] and *Shivaratri*,[3] they visit Hindu houses, particularly of those peasants who follow the Shaivite[4]

[1] When a person is excommunicated or out-casted he is not down-graded and pushed into a lower caste; he is merely denied the privileges of equal participation in the socio-religious life of the community.

[2] The night of the New Moon in the Hindu month of Bhadrapada (August– September).

[3] The day on which Shiva is believed to have drunk the world's poison, retaining it in his throat, and thereby saving mankind from possible harm from this poison.

[4] Of the great gods of the Hindu 'trinity' Brahma is not worshipped because of his sinful infatuation for his own daughter, whilst Vishnu and Shiva are worshipped. Those who principally worship the former, usually in his incarnations as Rama and Krishna, are known as Vaishnava; those worshipping the latter as Shaiva or Shaivite. Cf. Dowson, *A Classical Dictionary of Hindu Mythology* (London, 1950), pp. 56–59, 296–300, 360–362.

faith, and beg from them. In Shamirpet, however, there is only
one Jangam, who, being an old woman and having no Balja
clients in the village, tours in the neighbouring villages in order to
beg sufficient for her needs. In point of social status the Jangam
can properly be placed a little above the Komti. With the exception of the Brahmins, the other castes, including the Shaivite
Komti, eat at their hands. The Katike, who are Hindu butchers,
slaughter goats and sheep and sell the mutton to the village folk.
In status the Katike is equal to the Kapu-Kummari-Golla group,
and he inter-dines with all of them. As all the non-vegetarian
Hindu castes including the respectable Reddis eat the meat of
animals slaughtered by the Katike, the status of his group is so high.

Most of the castes enumerated above are further subdivided
into endogamous divisions which for all practical purposes are
themselves independent castes. The Brahmins of Andhra-desa are
divided into two main groups—Vaidiki and Niyogi; each of these
sections is further subdivided into a number of branches (*shakha*).
These *shakha* are endogamous. There is only one family of Brahmins in Shamirpet and it belongs to the Yajurvedi section of the
Vaidiki Andhra Brahmins.

The Komtis are divided into six endogamous divisions: Yegina,
Yepa, Doodi, Bandur, Neti and Poga. Of these only Yegina Komtis live in Shamirpet.

The Reddis have four major endogamous divisions—Motati,
Gudati, Gone and Paknati. All the Reddis of Shamirpet belong to
the Gone division.

The Muttarasi have three sections—Muttarasi, Ediga and
Besta. In Shamirpet there is no representative of either the Muttarasi or the Besta sections.

The Kummari caste is also divided into four endogamous divisions. They are Balije, Bandar, Cheluka (also known as Setti)
and Dandu, of which only Cheluka Kummari live in Shamirpet.
It may be noted that with the exception of the Balije section all
the other sections of the Kummari caste inter-dine but do not
inter-marry. The Balije abstain from meat and drink and on these
grounds regard themselves as superior to the other sections of the
Kummari caste, with whom they do not inter-dine.

The Gollas have seven endogamous subdivisions: Erra, Paka-
nati, Do-guita, Muda-Sarla, Pooja, Mushti and Paddanapu; an
eighth and inferior division of the Gollas who weave blankets is

known as Kurma. The Pooja Gollas do not follow the traditional caste occupation of shepherds, and they neither eat meat nor drink liquor. With the exception of the Pooja Golla, from whose hands all sections accept food, and the Kurma, at whose hands no sections do, all the other sections inter-dine but do not inter-marry. In Shamirpet there are only two sections of the Gollas, Erra and Paknati.

The Sale in Telangana have no endogamous subdivisions. They call themselves Padmashali to distinguish themselves from the Mala Sale, who are akin to the untouchable Malas in social status but who also follow the profession of weaving.

The Gaondlas are divided into two major sections on the basis of their faith: Vibhuti-darulu, following the Shaivite, and Tiru-mani-darulu, following the Vaishnavite faith. However, these sections both inter-marry and inter-dine.

The Sakalis have three endogamous groups—Sakali, Bondili, and Turuka, between whom inter-marriage and inter-dining is not permitted.

Among the Mangalis there are only two divisions, Siri and Konda. Inter-marriage between these groups is not permitted. All the families residing in Shamirpet belong to the Siri section.

The Vaddar have two sections: the Rai Vaddar work with stone, and the Gampa Vaddar work with earth. They are mutually exclusive groups, both inter-marriage and inter-dining being prohibited. In Shamirpet there are a few houses each of both these sections.

Similarly, the Erkala have two divisions—Kunche and Tatta-gulla, the latter only being represented in Shamirpet.

The Pichha-Kuntla too have two sections—Burra and Ganta. They are mutually exclusive from the point of view of inter-dining and inter-marrying. The one Pichha-Kuntla family in Shamirpet belongs to the Burra group.

Traditionally the Malas believe that their community is divided into twelve and a half sections, but no Mala in Shamirpet was able to give the names of all the twelve sections or to give any explanation for the half section. The section residing in Shamirpet describes itself simply as Mala.

Finally, the largest untouchable caste of Telangana, the Madiga, is divided into six major sections. These are Madiga, Nulka Sandayya, Baindla, Sindu, Mashto and Dakkal. The only section living in Shamirpet is the Madiga. The various sections of the Madiga community have their own special functions which are of great significance for the social life and culture of the caste. The Nulka Sandayya are said to be the descendants of Jamavanta,[1] who is believed to be the founder of the entire Madiga caste. The Baindlas are the marriage priests of the Madigas. Of the Sindus, the men are the minstrels of the Madigas and have the function of reciting the sacred caste legends and enacting them in the form of folk-drama; while the women are the prostitutes of the community. The Mashto earn their living by giving acrobatic displays. The Dakkal are the lowest of all Madiga sections and are distinguished by their customary refusal to take food from any non-Madiga. The Brahmin, who is at the apex of the caste-hierarchy, refuses to partake of food at the hands of anyone with a social status lower than his own, in effect from any but his own caste-fellows. And it is a juxtaposition that the lowest of the low castes refuses food from all communities of the higher levels, including the Brahmins.

Each independent endogamous division is divided into exogamous *gotram*; these in turn may be further subdivided into numerous *vansham*. The main function of these divisions is the regulation of marital unions. A person cannot marry in his own *gotram*; he must marry in some other *gotram* bearing a different name. Different *gotram* may have a number of common *vansham*, and as marriage between persons of the same *vansham* is forbidden, one must marry not only outside one's *gotram* but in a different *vansham* also. If a person of one's own *vansham* dies, one must observe ceremonial mourning for ten days. These subdivisions seem to perform no other special function. The enumeration of the various *gotram* and *vansham* is difficult and would only result in long and tedious lists running to forty and fifty names, and will not here be given.

The diagram shown opposite will illustrate the organization of the endogamous sub-castes *gotram* and *vansham* within the wider social unit of caste in the area under study.

In the diagram each sub-caste is endogamous; and as such a person born in unit 1 must marry within that unit, and so also persons in units 2, 3 and 4 must confine their marital relations to their respective units only. But each of these units is divided into a

[1] A conspicuous figure playing a significant role in the epic of *Ramayana*.

SOCIAL STRUCTURE

number of exogamous *gotram*, and it is necessary that one must marry outside his own *gotram*. A *gotram* may be further subdivided into a number of *vansham*. In some cases the *vansham* units in the different *gotram* have common names, and this necessitates a further precaution: not only should a man marry in a *gotram* different from his own, but he must also see that he does not marry into his own *vansham* although it belongs to a different *gotram*. Thus, a person belonging to sub-caste 1, *gotram* 'A', *vansham* 'a', must marry within sub-caste 1, but he can choose a spouse from *gotram* B, C and D subject to the condition that he does not marry anyone belonging to *vansham* 'a' and chooses the spouse from *vansham* b, c or, for that matter, a *vansham* having any other name.

Gotram, for all practical purposes, are like exogamous clans. Each *gotram* bears a distinctive name, which is either derived from

CASTE

1	2	3	4
A B C D	A B C D	A B C D	A B C D

abcdabcdabcdabcd abcdabcdabcdabcd abcdabcdabcdabcd abcdabcdabcdabcd

1, 2, 3, 4 . . Sub-castes
A, B, C, D . . *Gotram*
a, b, c, d . . *Vansham*

a sage of ancient India or is totemic in nature. The term *vansham* is derived from Sanskrit and means a lineage. Sociologically, in the context of patrilineal societies, if we define a lineage as 'an association of people of both sexes comprising all the recognized descendants by an accepted genealogy of a single named ancestor in a putatively continuous male line',[1] we can regard *vansham* as a lineage. Each *vansham* bears an individual name which is either derived from or is in some way associated with the common mythological ancestor of the sub-group. At the death of a person belonging to one's own *vansham* formal observance of ritual impurity and ceremonial purification are necessary even when one has no kinship or afinal ties with the deceased. A girl belonging to one's own *vansham* is a sister, a boy a brother, and that is why

[1] Meyer Fortes, *The Dynamics of Clanship among the Tallensi* (London, 1945), p. 30.

43

sexual union of any type between the two is regarded as a kind of incest. It has already been pointed out that these units have no functions beyond those mentioned above and have no common organization, authority or ceremonial distinctively belonging to them.

Although in general we can regard Shamirpet as fairly representative of Telangana villages, some Telugu-speaking castes which play an important part in rural Telangana are not to be found in the village; and it will be perhaps advantageous to make a passing reference to some of these castes here. The Velma are a rich agricultural caste more or less equal in status to the Reddis. The Kamma are another caste of the Kapu group who inter-dine with the Reddi, but they are regarded as equals of the lower clean caste groups. The Balja traders are Shaivite Hindus whose status is regarded as being a little higher than that of the Komti. The Gandla works the oil press, and his status is similar to that of the Sale and the Gaondla. The Yenadi, who in some parts of Telangana act as village guards, are in status equal to the Erkala. The Lambada provide a colourful though somewhat alien element in the population of Telangana. In language, dress and ornament they stand out from the rest of the people of Telangana. Their northern origin is clear both from their physical appearance and from their language. The dress of the Lambada woman is picturesque. Her multi-coloured skirt (*lahanga*), tight bodice (*choli*) and upper covering (*odhni*) are elaborately embroidered and worked with appliquéd mirror. Her ornaments are heavy and distinctive, and their tinkling sound lends an air of romance to the dusty roads of the countryside. There is a Lambada settlement some six miles from Shamirpet and they are a common sight on the nearby road.

Mention should also be made of three wandering caste groups— the Balsantanam, the Sharda-galu and the Dasari. The Balsantanam live in small, low, portable huts and move from village to village. They weave mats, sing songs and legends, and beg from village cultivators. The Sharda-galu are professional story-tellers and earn their livelihood by reciting the legends of their vast repertoire. Similarly, the Dasari are country dramatists who contribute towards the entertainment of the villagers by performing folk plays. Members of many of the castes mentioned above make occasional appearances in Shamirpet.

SOCIAL STRUCTURE

2. INTERNAL ORGANIZATION: AUTHORITY AND MACHINERY OF JUSTICE

In the internal organization of Shamirpet two different units can be clearly delineated. The socio-religious organization of the village with its independent set of office-bearers and functionaries is quite distinct from the administrative organization of government and semi-government officials.

The following diagram will illustrate the internal organization of the village in socio-religious matters:

Deshmukh   *Panchayat*
(Headman of the village)   (Village council)

Ganadi
(Organizers of village ritual)

Kulam-pedda
(Headmen of the different castes)

Peddamanshi
or
Inti-pedda
(Head of the family)

The Deshmukh is the hereditary headman of the village. He is the richest person in the settlement and has very considerable landed property. His forefathers became the headmen of the village some three hundred years ago, and since then the family has retained the title and office. By virtue of his wealth, position and the contacts he maintains with powerful government officials, the Deshmukh is a pivotal figure in the village and enjoys a position of great influence. Although his word is no longer law, he still wields very great influence in the village and is always given a place of honour at all village ceremonies. Village disputes of any importance are always referred to him, and his decisions and wishes are seldom disregarded. However, the Deshmukh takes very few decisions on his own authority and initiative. He seeks the help of the *panchayat*, which can be regarded as the central council for the village as a whole. Of course, the Deshmukh takes a prominent part in the deliberations and discussions of the *panchayat* and often guides it in such a way that his wishes in the matter are carried out.

The *panchayat* or village council consists of the headmen of

45

all the major communities living within the village and in addition several other rich and influential persons. It necessarily includes the headman of the village and the three organizers of village ritual. In May 1951 the *panchayat* consisted of twenty-seven persons: four village officers (one Deshmukh and three Ganadis), seventeen heads of different communities resident within the village, and six other rich and influential persons. Of the seventeen heads of different communities, eight are inactive members of the village council. They only attend its meetings on formal and ceremonial occasions and not when it meets to consider ordinary business. Two of these eight inactive members do not attend because they complain that the prejudice of some of the members prevents due consideration being given to their views and hence their participation in the deliberations would be useless. Others do not attend because they are 'too occupied with their own affairs' and do not want 'to get involved in local politics'. However, representatives of these six persons stand for the community in the meetings of the *panchayat*. The six members from the category of rich and influential persons are: V.P.R.—a substantial Reddi cultivator; B.R.—a rich toddy-tapper; N.B.—a Madiga cultivator; K.M.—a Muslim pensioner and brother of an influential village official; K.G.—a well-to-do shepherd; and B.N.—a substantial Mala cultivator.

Thus the *panchayat* of the village is formally composed of the mportant village officers, the heads of various castes and religious groups in the village and a few other people of influence. But it has been observed that, for one reason or the other, many of the caste heads do not attend its meetings. In most cases they do not have the necessary personality traits and do not mind if someone else volunteers to represent them. More talkative and influential persons gradually replace such inactive members, first temporarily, then permanently. Members of cliques wielding some influence in the community and others with some nuisance value have often been appeased by being invited to the *panchayat*, for this appeals to their sense of vanity. This recognition of their importance in some cases develops in them a greater sense of social responsibility.

The *panchayat* performs several important functions. It hears and decides minor disputes which do not ordinarily go to the courts of law, criminal or civil. It fixes the details of the ceremonies to be organized by the village community as a whole. If smallpox, cholera or plague is reported in any nearby village or from Shamirpet itself, it has to fix the day on which the whole village shall perform religious worship in order to ward off the epidemic. It fixes the contribution which should be made by the different families to any communal undertaking. In any undertaking concerning the village as a whole the initiative often comes from the *panchayat*. For example, if a temple or shrine has to be constructed or a tank or well has to be repaired, the matter would be placed before the *panchayat*. This body would plan the measure and then proceed to fix all the details. It will determine the amount of the contributions to be raised, and collect it from each family. If it is necessary to approach the government for financial help in the matter, the *panchayat* would first thoroughly analyse the subject and examine all the possibilities. Only after such a discussion would it determine the precise steps to be taken. Similarly, if a complaint has to be made against any government official, the matter is first discussed by the *panchayat*.

In the village community there are several groups and factions; the various cliques often hold divergent views. However, at the meetings of the *panchayat* the minority almost always yields to the majority—mostly without any grumbling. But once the *panchayat* has risen a protégé of the dissenting clique may be instigated to defy the decisions of the council. With the emergence of several factions within the community, and the tacit encouragement given by some of the minority groups to certain offenders to ignore its decisions, the authority of the *panchayat* has been slightly weakened. In consequence, even when the *panchayat* has heard them and given its verdict, some cases drag on in a state of indecision. From time to time they come up for reconsideration, but two or three years often elapse before a final decision is made. Some long-drawn-out cases are decided by the active intervention of the Revenue or Police officials. But such cases are few. Only a comparatively rich person can defy the *panchayat*, for unless he is able to bribe one of the minority cliques, he cannot enlist their sympathy and support in the lengthy proceedings. In most of the ordinary cases the decision of the *panchayat* is binding and final.

It has been pointed out that the *panchayat* includes all the headmen of the different caste-groups as well as of the Muslim community. These headmen do not merely represent their respective castes; they are expected to do much more. In fact, a caste headman is the link between the residents of the village belonging to his own caste and, on the one hand, the common organization of the village as a unit, and, on the other, the wider caste organization of the entire neighbouring region. When the caste *panchayat* of the entire block constituting the regional community holds its meeting it is invariably the caste headman who participates in its deliberations on behalf of his village caste group. The office is hereditary, passing from father to son. But if the son has not attained maturity at the time of the death of his father, and is consequently not in a position to take over the responsibility, one of the brothers of the deceased may exercise the authority on behalf of the minor. In some cases even after attaining maturity the son remains only the nominal head, while his uncle continues to be the *de facto* chief. The general consensus of opinion regarding the function of the caste headman appears to be that 'he should keep his people under control' and 'not allow them to stray from the traditional ways of life'. 'If boys of my community do not behave themselves, the *panchayat* reprimands me for not keeping them under control. The village headman says that I must check them, but what powers do I have?' remarked one caste headman. With regard to his functions there is a general unanimity. 'Under a good caste headman boys of the caste obey established authority, respect is shown to the elders and quarrels are not often heard from houses in his jurisdiction.' All this he must do by the sheer force of his personality, for the nature of his authority is not well defined. 'He must be strict and firm, and also considerate and helpful. If he is only strict he will not be able to get the willing co-operation of his people. If he is too lenient nobody will pay any heed to what he says.' It has been pointed out earlier that some of the caste headmen are only nominal members of the *panchayat* and that at its meetings others speak on behalf of the caste. With one exception, these caste headmen lack the above qualities, and in general their caste people do not have much regard for their views. At least two of the hereditary caste chiefs are regarded with scorn by their own people and with ridicule by the villagers. Among the successful caste headmen, E. D. R., the leader of the Kapu (agriculturist) group, may be mentioned. He is in his late thirties, but even older people listen to him. If a son does not show due regard to his parents or a husband and wife quarrel too often and too publicly;

48

if one of his caste fellows fails to fulfil the terms of his obligations
or in any other way brings dishonour to the caste; if boys get un-
manageable or girls earn an evil reputation for easy virtue, he
effectively enters the scene, gives suggestions and advice, admon-
ishes people if they do not seem amenable to persuasion, and in the
case of adolescents and young boys may even inflict light corporal
punishment. In his dealings with people E. D. R. possesses some
dramatic qualities which make him something of a hero to his
people. With his great influence in the counsels of the village he
commands obedience from his own caste fellows as well as from
many others. V. P. R., in a sense E. D. R.'s rival, has also a strong
personality, and although he is not the recognized head of the
caste he exercises considerable control over 'his area of influence'.
Because of his influence he is one of those who are invited to
participate in the deliberations of the *panchayat*. However, the
two men exercise considerable tact in dealing with each other,
and so far there has been no effective challenge to the position of
E. D. R. The position of the head in a caste is what its holder
chooses to make it. Ambitious rivals can steal some of his light and
authority. If he proves unsuitable he may for all practical purposes
be superseded by someone who is abler or more ambitious and
aggressive.

The structure of the family and part played by the 'head' in its
affairs will be analysed in a subsequent chapter. It will suffice here
to point out that the type of family organization in Shamirpet
and the neighbouring rural areas is patrilineal and patrilocal.
Joint families are regarded as ideal, although there is a tendency
for sons to separate after marriage, and brothers almost always
separate some time after the father's death. The eldest male is
generally regarded as the chief of the household, and, according
to tradition, he must benevolently dominate the scene. Younger
members of the household must show respect to him and his
wishes. In his turn the head of the family should treat his brothers
or sons equally, 'as alike as his two eyes'. A serious socio-religious
offence committed by one member of the family would result in
the excommunication of the whole family. As such the head of the
family must watch the actions of all the members of his household
and advise, warn or admonish them according to the necessity of
the situation. The head of the family is answerable to the caste and
the village councils for the members of his household, and this

entitles him to maintain a controlling hand in domestic affairs. In the case of the head of the family also, much depends on the character and personality of the individual concerned. An irresponsible head who becomes a liability to the members of his family forfeits his claim to their obedience and respect, and in such cases the sympathy of the village people is generally given to the dissenting members of the family. Even after separation it is good form to treat the elders with courtesy and respect. On the occasions of family reunions, such as those connected with the crises of life or with the annual offering of water to the spirits of the deceased, it is the eldest member of the family who occupies the dominant position. In general, even after separation his help is sought in cases of disease and difficulty, and in all matters involving priority of one or the other, preference is always given to the elder. The exact position of the head of the family would, however, vary according to the equations of different families, with which we propose to deal later.

The Deshmukh also figures at the head of the government or semi-government village officials, whose relative positions can be arranged in a tabular form as follows:

DESHMUKH	Sub-Inspector of Police
[Combining the offices of Mali Patel and Police Patel]	Head Constables
	Masters
	Constables

Patwari

FOURTEEN VILLAGE MENIALS

i. Kawalkar	viii. Kammari
ii. Talari	ix. Kummari
iii. Majkuri	x. Sakali
iv. Neerudi	xi. Mangali
v. Begari	xii. Ausula
vi. Yetti	xiii. Dappu
vii. Wadla	xiv. Kommu

The Deshmukh is the recognized headman of the village. Two hundred and ten acres of rent-free land, the normal revenue of which would have been Rs. 556/6/-, have been granted to him by the State. He also formally holds the offices of Mali Patel and Police Patel; in the former capacity he assists the government officials in the collection of land revenue, in the latter he helps the police in the maintenance of law and order. The Deshmukh used to cultivate the rent-free land earmarked by the government for persons working in these two capacities, but he had delegated his powers and functions to agents who acted for him. Now he gets a certain percentage of the total revenue collected in the village in lieu of the rent-free land. Thus, theoretically, the Deshmukh is both Mali Patel and Police Patel; but in actual practice these duties are carried out by his agents. In his capacity as Mali Patel of the village the Deshmukh takes steps to ensure the speedy collection of land revenue after each harvest and remits it to the district treasury. The Patwari can seek his assistance in matters connected with the land records and revenue of the village. For this he gets annually 5% of the total land revenue collected in the village. As Police Patel the Deshmukh is entitled to receive another 5% of the revenue collected during the year. In this capacity he has to send regular reports to the police regarding the occurrence of any crime in the village, keep an eye on the 'bad characters' and watch the activities of suspicious strangers. He maintains records of births and deaths in the village. It is his duty to assist the police in all possible ways in their investigations regarding criminal offences in the village. The other officials, such as the sub-inspector of police, head constables, constables and schoolmasters, are not a permanent part of the local population, and as such they do not generally get mixed up in local politics and other affairs. The police officials enjoy both prestige and power and are, in general, greatly feared by the people.

The Patwari, in spite of the fact that he is a petty revenue and land records official, occupies a pivotal position in the village and plays a very significant part in local politics. Being in charge of the land records, he can manipulate things both to the advantage and disadvantage of landowners, who often consult him and ask his advice. Of Patwaris in general it is said, 'What will they not do for a consideration? Give them money and they will prove their own father a bastard.' The present Patwari of Shamirpet is, for one in his position, a man of more than average intelligence and is himself a careful and substantial cultivator who owns some 247 acres of land jointly with his brother. He receives no salary from the government, nor does he have any rent-free land, but a certain percentage of the total land revenue is fixed by the government as his remuneration for the work.

All villages in Hyderabad State, as do most of those of middle and peninsular India, have a number of village menials. Their functions in the internal organization of the village are of two kinds: routine duties in the everyday life of the village and special duties connected with the arrangements which have to be made for touring government officials arriving in the village. The division of work among these village menials follows in the main the traditional occupations of the different castes. Payment for their work is often nominal. Some of them are paid small monthly salaries; others are granted small fields free of land revenue; while still others supplement their earnings by collecting their 'dues' from the agriculturists of the village at the time of harvesting.

Of the fourteen *kamgars* or village menials, six persons holding four different categories of posts are paid a salary of Rs. 3 per month. The rest enjoy small fragments of rent-free land in return for their part-time government duties. The Kawalkar is responsible for keeping a watch on the village and for patrolling it at night. He must assist the police and the Police Patel in the prevention and detection of crime. He should immediately bring to the notice of the Police Patel any criminal act, epidemic and births and deaths that occur in the village. When required by officers he must carry government mail and revenue remittances. In general it is his duty to assist the touring government officials in their work. He is aided in these tasks by the Talari and the Majkuri. These two menials perform similar functions. The Talari must fetch water for touring officials. The Majkuri must report all relevant matters to the police and to the Deshmukh. The present Kawalkar belongs to the Reddi caste, and the Talari is a Muttarasi. Both the Majkuris are untouchable Malas. The work of carrying government correspondence and money remittances as well as that of patrolling the village falls to the lot of these two Majkuris. At present there are three Neerudis in the village, two of whom are Malas and one a Madiga. It is their duty to look after the tank bund, particularly to keep a watch on the flood-gates and report any damage or suspected foul play. They should also periodically check the water-level in the tank and keep the superior village officers informed. The three Neerudis hold together seven acres of rent-free wet land granted to them by the government. The present Begari belongs to the Mala caste; and besides holding this petty menial position, he is a grave-digger by profession. His main duty is to keep clean the village rest-house, which is used by occasional travellers and officials of low status. He is expected to light fires there during winter evenings, and generally sleeps there at night. Dogs, cats and donkeys dying in the village have to be disposed of by him, for the Madigas only deal with dead cattle and will have nothing to do with other carcases. The Yettis in Shamirpet are from the Sakali and the Madiga castes. The Sakali Yettis do most of the superior kinds of menial work, such as carrying the baggage of touring government officials who would not allow their luggage to be carried by the untouchable Madigas; while the Madiga Yettis have to do all sorts of odd jobs of an inferior nature. They may be required to patrol the village, to keep watch on government buildings and to sweep and clean the village occasionally. They are also required to bring fuel for the use of touring government officials. The Yettis are not paid any salary for their work, and the nominal payments made to them by touring officials bear no proportion to the work done by them. The rest of the village menials are occupational caste groups, also performing some semi-government duties. The Wadla, for example, must repair the flood-gates of the tank, attend to the repairs of furniture and other woodwork in government offices, repair the central flag post in the village and supply free of charge or on nominal payment the pegs required for fixing the tents of touring government officials. When required the Kammari do iron work for the government officials. The Kummari has to supply earthen pots for use on public occasions or for the use of touring government officials. The Sakali cleans the kitchen utensils and plates of touring government officials, washes their clothes and carries their baggage to the next camp. The Mangali lights the lamps in the village rest-house, shaves touring officials and massages their bodies if they require this service. The Ausula has the duty of examining, when required to do so, coins which are believed to be counterfeit. He has also to help the police in weighing stolen ornaments and in making estimates of their approximate market price. Finally, the Dappu and the Kommu, who are both Madigas, play their drums and pipes respectively on public occasions. They make all public announcements by the beat of drum and are, like the Yetti, often required to do other menial work as well.

3. INTER-CASTE AND INTER-VILLAGE ORGANIZATION

The village is a territorial unit, the smallest but most significant among territorial groups in the social organization of the village communities. Persons belonging to several different castes are united by some common values and obligations in this unit. But caste as a unit of social organization cuts across the narrow boundaries of the village and extends to a fairly wide geographical region. The *varna* system or the fivefold division of Hindu society is an all-India phenomenon, but in the different geographical and linguistic regions these *varnas* are divided into numerous castes (*jati*) which are practically distinct from and independent of comparable castes in other areas. Thus in South India, in the Tamil, Malayalam and Telugu-speaking regions respectively, there are separate groups of Brahmins who constitute independent castes. There are numerous restrictions on inter-dining, and inter-marriage between them is not permitted. All these groups will be designated by the generic term Brahmin; but in actual practice they are each a separate caste characterized by endogamy and distinctive local traditions. It has been pointed out earlier that culturally Shamirpet lies in the area of Telangana, which is a part of the larger culture-area of Andhra-desa. Most of the castes in the village confine their social intercourse to Telangana itself, a few extending it to other parts of Andhra-desa. The Muslims, being converts to an alien religion, are not obliged to observe this rule and can freely inter-marry with Muslim immigrants from other parts; but among them also marriage between people already having some blood ties is preferred. For Hindu castes it may be said that in actual practice a number of neighbouring villages constitute for them a quasi-independent local group within the wider regional community. In analysing one hundred and twenty family case-histories, it was found that out of three hundred and eighty marriages over 68% were confined to a group of villages (and the cities of Hyderabad and Secundrabad) within a radius of approximately thirty-five miles from Shamirpet; 30% to other villages within sixty miles of the village; and only 2% in still more distant villages or towns. In no case was a marital union entered into with a non-Telugu caste, even with a similar caste name and social status in another linguistic or geographical area. Thus the horizontal ties of caste extend to the whole culture area, but active social relationships are generally confined to a cluster of neighbouring villages.

Two types of inter-village organizations deserve to be noted. They are councils of the different castes and inter-village councils.

According to the caste composition of the villages and existing social bonds between them, people belonging to one particular caste will have their own *panchayat* for a group of villages. Thus in the case of some castes ten to twenty villages have their own caste *panchayat*, while in the case of others thirty to forty villages together have a common council of this type. In some cases endogamous sub-castes have their own *panchayats*; but in many others the wider caste group comprising many sub-castes has a composite council of its own. Caste headmen representing each constituent village are the members of this council—although in actual practice other wealthy and influential, as well as vocal and assertive, persons also gradually come to occupy a seat in it. Serious breaches of the norms and traditions of the caste, as well as important intra-caste disputes, are heard and decided by these caste *panchayats*. Cases of divorce, failure in fulfilling agreements made before finalizing marriage arrangements, serious sexual lapses, and of breaches of the social norms of the caste, such as incest, breaches of the rules of endogamy and exogamy, eating forbidden food and pursuing a 'lower' occupation, etc., would be under the jurisdiction of such a caste *panchayat*. But it must be pointed out that there is no clear-cut distinction between the powers and functions of the caste *panchayat* and the village *panchayat*. For example, when a serious case of incest comes to their notice both these *panchayats* take action independently. Similarly, if a person belonging to one of the Hindu castes kills a cow or is found to have eaten beef, simultaneous action is likely to be taken by both the *panchayats*. In general, however, it can be laid down that matters of a primarily local interest are brought to the village *panchayat*, while those having a bearing on specific caste customs fall under the jurisdiction of the caste *panchayat*. A large number of marginal disputes may be heard by either, and often the local tradition defines their respective jurisdictions. As the *panchayat* in Shamirpet is sufficiently aggressive it has arrogated to itself a considerably wide range of powers.

While all villages and nearly all castes have their own *panchayats*, inter-village *panchayats* are formed from time to time when they are demanded by a special situation. They function as *ad hoc* arbitration committees. Conflicts between two villages, or between two parties belonging to different villages (and not drawn from one particular caste), often necessitate an inter-village *panchayat.* In this the elders of the two villages which are parties to the dispute as well as the elders from an agreed number of villages from the neighbourhood sit together, hear the dispute and give their verdict. Of course, they have no authority to enforce their decision, and these days such cases often go to the courts of law established by the government.

CHAPTER THREE

Economic Structure

I. CASTE IN VILLAGE ECONOMY

THE functional basis of the Indian caste system is generally well understood, but the integration of the different castes into the economic pattern of the rural community organization of India is not so well known. The occupations and functions of the different castes are not wholly exclusive, but the economic system of rural India is founded mainly on their functional specialization and interdependence. For example, agriculture is mainly the task of the Kapu group of castes, but all other castes—both high and low—can cultivate land, if they have any, besides following their traditional occupation. Similarly, trading was originally the function of the Komti caste, but now several other castes have also taken to it. However, a large number of crafts and occupations in rural India still remain the monopoly of different castes. A non-Brahmin cannot officiate as a priest for any of the higher castes. No one other than a Kummari will follow the profession of a potter. The Mangali alone would do the barber's work. Carpentry and working in metals are the monopoly of the Panch Bramha group of castes in Telangana. Only the Madiga will dispose of dead cattle and undertake to do leatherwork. Castes other than the Sakali would not think of doing the washerman's work. Tradition has given to each group a definite position in the structure of the community, and with that position also goes a definite economic function which is the major source of livelihood for that group. As agriculture is the mainstay of the rural economy of India, the crafts and occupations of the countryside are generally integrated with it. A brief analysis of the economic role of the different castes would give us a clear idea of the

57

economic system of the community and also of the place occupied in it by the various castes.

Most of the castes have a major craft or occupation which is their traditional monopoly. Besides this they are free to exploit certain other subsidiary sources of livelihood also. The Brahmin, besides functioning as the village priest, may also cultivate his land. The potter, the barber and the washerman occupy themselves mainly with their respective professions, but there is nothing to prevent them from accepting occasional work as field labourers. In fact, during the busy agricultural season, when there is a heavy demand on the limited labour supply of the local group, efforts are made to persuade the artisan caste to send their womenfolk to work in the fields for daily wages. Notwithstanding this, a caste is identified with some occupation or other, and established social usage largely governs the modes of practice of this particular occupation.

In the chapter on Social Structure mention has been made of the fourteen village menials who work as semi-government functionaries, generally in return for the grant of a piece of rent-free land by the government. Their work lies mainly in the fields of their caste monopolies. It comprises personal services to touring government officials, as well as certain routine duties for the village as a whole.

A closer scrutiny of the economic system and its consequent bonds of mutual obligation and expectation reveals four major types of economic dealings and obligations within the caste network into which the community is organized. These are:

(i) Obligations to render to the agriculturists occupational services having a direct bearing on their agricultural activities. No immediate payment is expected for services of this kind. The agriculturists get their ploughs and other implements repaired by the carpenter every year as a matter of routine. Periodically the carpenter supplies new implements. In return for this, twice every year the cultivator gives a share to the carpenter when the crops are harvested. Services of an agricultural nature are generally expected and rendered on this basis. The extent of both the service and the payment is generally fixed by tradition, and depends very much on the size of the holding which the agriculturist is cultivating. Some castes offer their occupational services, even of a non-agricultural nature, to the agriculturists on the tacit understand-

58

ing that they too will have their share after the crops are harvested. Thus, the potter periodically supplies the agriculturist with earthenware and pots for his normal requirements. The barber does the hair-cutting and shaving of the members of the agriculturist's family on this basis. The washerman, too, follows this rule in so far as established cultivators of the village are concerned.

(ii) Obligations to render some occupational services, to the agriculturists as well as to many non-agriculturists, having a bearing on their socio-religious life. Castes such as the barber, the washerman, the carpenter and the potter, and the Madiga have definite functions in the rites and ceremonies connected with the major crises of life. These are performed by them as a matter of routine, without any direct negotiations regarding the wages that they may expect in return for their services. Convention has fixed the basic minimum, and in the course of ritual duties, at different points, a part of this payment has to be made. Depending on their status and financial position, people pay something more for these services at the completion of the ceremony.

(iii) Obligations to render some occupational services to other occupational castes in return for their traditional services. As an example, it may be pointed out that a barber will attend to the grooming of hair and shaving of the members of a weaver's family to which he is attached. No cash payment is either expected or made. However, every year the weaver will give him a few yards of cloth and possibly a *sari* or two for his wife.

(iv) Occupational services rendered with an expectation of cash payment in return for the work. Casual visitors to the village can get the services of the barber only when they pay cash. For making a bullock cart, or for preparing timber for use in the construction of a house, a carpenter would first settle his wages and then undertake to do the work. In this respect he would not make an exception even in the case of established cultivators to whose households his family may have been attached for several years, even for decades. The Vaddar stone-workers also usually undertake an assignment only when the obligations on both sides are settled.

For most of the castes economic dealings falling in category (iv), described above, are of a casual nature, though their economic returns through them may be quite substantial. With a few exceptions, most of the castes have to accept a basis of reciprocity in discharge of their functions. Tradition approves of such an arrangement, and mutual trust and inter-dependence ensure its continuity. Where this arrangement is accepted, a system of attachment of some families to certain other families naturally follows. Agriculture being the most important activity of the countryside, the number of agriculturists is naturally the largest in the village population. These constitute the bulk of those who require and accept the occupational services of small caste groups offering them. Even the occupational castes stand in need of one another's services, although the number of families from each caste offering them within a village community is of necessity small. Each family will, therefore, attach itself to a number of families in the village and offer them services both in agricultural pursuits and socio-religious rites and ceremonies. Among the occupational castes themselves also there is a system of family attachments in operation. In Shamirpet some family affiliations date back to the time of the foundation of the village. Later immigrants either secured the services of some of the established families of the occupational castes, or they made arrangements with some of the newcomers to the village belonging to those castes.

This sytem is both complex and delicate. It is not easy for an agriculturist to remove a family attached to his household and secure the services of another. For example, A, a barber, is attached to the family of B, an agriculturist. If for any reason B is greatly dissatisfied with the services of A and wants those of another, he cannot abruptly dismiss A. His difficulty will not be in dismissing him, but in finding a substitute. Each of these castes has its own inter-village council. Occupational castes have a developed trade unionism, and their code of professional ethics and etiquette too is very rigid. The dismissed person will be protected by this professional etiquette. No one else would be willing to act as a substitute, for fear of being penalized by the caste *panchayat*. It may even be difficult for a number of families to join together and import a family belonging to that occupational caste from a different village. First, under these conditions of tension, an outside family would not come for fear of social pressure and ultimate ostracism for such an action. And if they do come, the caste fellows already in the village will make things very difficult, even unbearable, for them. In the course of our investigations, we recorded three cases of protracted antagonism between a group of employing families and the occupational caste families employed. In one of them the dissatisfied employer agreed to retain the family on its promise of doing better work in the future. In another the caste people arrived at an amicable settlement by attaching another family to the employer, and attaching the dismissed caste member to a newly-settled family in the village. The third one dragged on for a little less than four years, and, yielding to the pressure and persuasion of the village elders, the caste agreed to give a substitute. The employer in this case was a hot-headed farmer, but he was a man of some wealth and considerable influence, and as such he could secure the effective intervention of the village elders in his own favour.

According to our informants 'the system to-day is not what it was a decade or two ago'. Many attribute this change to the spirit of individualism which is now manifesting itself in several walks of life in the countryside, and is bringing about changes in the established patterns of life. 'In former times,' said an agriculturist, 'these low classes knew their position and behaved themselves well. If they worked satisfactorily they were treated by us very well. In fact, with the passage of time, our relations became more and more intimate. I remember those days when a barber's son would come into the courtyard, offer salutations to us and say "Uncle, the headman has called you" or "Mother, the ceremony in the neighbour's house is about to start and they are awaiting you." In many cases they were just like the members of our family, and although both parties maintained the traditional caste distance, we could always take each other into confidence even on matters of a delicate nature. But now things have changed. Those boys don't want to work here. They want to go to the city. They are not satisfied with the traditional arrangements of payment; and so there is difficulty.' However, the system still continues more or less in its established, traditional form. Urban contacts, education or attraction of something better or more lucrative, may distract a young man, causing him to refuse to replace his old or deceased father's services with a family to which they were attached, but one of his poorer and less ambitious brothers or cousins will always be willing to take up the work.

We shall now examine the main economic functions and activities of the major caste groups in the village.

ECONOMIC STRUCTURE

THE BRAHMIN

There is only one Brahmin family in the village. The head of this family enjoys considerable local prestige owing to the fact of his birth, and also because he is a substantial landowner. He is the local priest as well as an astrologer. People consult him regarding the suitability of proposed marriages, and when negotiations are completed they seek his astrological calculations regarding an auspicious date and time for the wedding itself. He officiates at the marriage ceremony among the higher castes. On childbirth he is consulted about the planetary position at the actual time of the baby's birth, and its astrological implications for the child as well as for the parents and the other members of the family. If the reading indicates any difficulty, the Brahmin is often commissioned to offer special worship and perform the necessary rituals to ward off the evil. Similarly, after a death the Brahmin is consulted. If it is found that the time of death was inauspicious the members of the household may be asked to leave the residence temporarily, for a period of three to six months, according to the advice of the Brahmin. These consultations on the occasions of birth and death are generally sought only by the people of higher castes and by those who are well-to-do. Prescribed fees have to be paid to the Brahmin in cash for these consultations. Indirectly, the Brahmin contributes also to the agricultural activities of the community. He advises the agriculturists on when to start sowing at the beginning of the agricultural year. He is also consulted regarding the auspicious dates for starting weeding and harvesting. The date of the New Eating ceremony for the different families in the village is fixed by him. For these consultations no one pays him in cash. He visits the houses of his agriculturist clients fortnightly or once a month, especially in the harvesting season, and is customarily given a certain quantity of grain by each family.

THE KOMTI

The Komtis are traders. They also function as village moneylenders. They keep a permanent small shop at some central point in the village, and also attend the weekly markets in the neighbouring villages. They generally sell provisions for cash, although things may also be bought on credit by those who are known to the shopkeeper and are willing to pay slightly higher prices. They advance money to the people for buying bullocks and agricultural implements. A mortgage is not insisted upon in all cases, but the rate of compound interest which they charge is often exorbitant. The Komtis also advance seed grain to the people. For this, too, they charge a heavy interest. Loans are often taken by people against the mortgage of land or a part of the crops, depending upon the sum of money which they borrow. In Shamirpet the Komtis seem to be the only caste whose monopoly has been seriously affected by the change of times. To-day Shamirpet has in all thirteen shops. If we do not take into account some of the petty shops, four of these belong to Komtis, two to Muslims, two to Toddy-tappers and one to a goldsmith. Even in the field of advancing cash and seeds for agricultural purposes, the Komtis have to face the competition of some of the comparatively rich Reddi and Muslim cultivators.

THE KUMMARI

In Shamirpet there are five families of potters, with fourteen people actually working at the wheel. Each family is attached to some agriculturists in the village, and it periodically supplies them with a certain number of earthen pots for domestic use. Every two or three years they also supply the agriculturists with large baked earthen bins for storing grain. For this they do not expect a cash price. At the time of harvesting the potter visits the fields of the family to which he is attached, and is given *bheek-bali*, that is his share of the new crop. The quantity of grain that is given away depends on the size of the land cultivated, and also partly on the owner's financial circumstances. On the occasion of rituals connected with birth, marriage or death a supply of new pots is expected from him. Tradition has prescribed the minimum payment required for these services, although on happy occasions people often give a little more. If he can arrive at an agreement with the other occupational castes, such as the barber, the washerman and the weaver, he will offer them his services in return for their occupational services to his family. The details are fixed by the parties concerned, and often considerable haggling and making of charges and counter-charges against one another go on. Notwithstanding this, the system works quite satisfactorily, for out of forty-four cases of such mutual arrangements studied very closely at Shamirpet only in six were the relations finally broken off on account of dissatisfaction to either or both parties. Non-agriculturists and such occupational castes as do not have arrangements with the potter buy their requirements from him for a cash price. The Kummari families of Shamirpet have more clients and customers in some of the neighbouring villages which have no potters' families living in them.

THE GOLLA

The shepherds occupy a block of their own in the village. Some of them cultivate small land-holdings, but the major source of livelihood for all of them is their traditional occupation of keeping herds of goats and sheep. They may keep one or two cows and buffaloes besides these herds which are their livelihood. They have an elaborate lore regarding these animals, and they are experts in caring for quite large herds. They train country dogs to help them in this, and with their aid prevent the goats from going astray when they are taken out for grazing in the forest. By turns the Golla families in the village contribute goats or sheep for sacrifice in the village ceremonies. For this they are not paid. With this exception, they carry on all other transactions with the village people in cash. When people buy goats and sheep, the owner of the animal is always paid in cash. For goat's milk they expect spot payment, but arrangements for weekly or monthly payments may be made in the case of regular buyers. However, in one respect they may also enter into an agreement with the agriculturists which may entitle them to a small share of each harvest. After the harvest, when all the crops have been reaped, the agriculturists ask the Gollas to graze their herds on their fields and keep them penned in during the night. As there is very little fodder in the fields, the shepherds take the goats and sheep out for grazing in the nearby forest, and during the night keep them in the field. The urine and dung of the herd is believed to be good manure, and as such this service is much in demand by the agriculturists. The shepherds often fix days with the agriculturists, and each one has his turn only on a limited number of days. According to the nature of agreement between the cultivators and the shepherds, the payment is either in cash or the latter collect their dues from the fields at the time of harvesting.

64

THE SALE

The Sale consider themselves superior to the other artisan castes. Nowadays they no longer work on the basis of affiliation to the village agriculturists. According to an old informant, 'In the good old days when the Sale used to spin their thread in addition to weaving cloth, they also entered into a definite arrangement with the agriculturists, as most castes do to-day. They supplied us with a certain length of cloth every year, and in return we gave them some grain at each harvest. But now times have changed. They buy yarn manufactured in the mills, weave fancy cloth and sell it for cash.' The weavers have now practically abandoned the traditional system. Only with certain occupational castes do they arrive at a working arrangement under which, in return for their services, they give them an agreed length of cloth. In the course of our investigations we found that such arrangements existed between weavers on the one hand, and potters, barbers and washermen on the other.

THE GAONDLA

The villagers in this area are very fond of *sendi*, or fermented palm juice. The Gaondla shops are the centre of attraction in the evenings for men—young and old—as well as for many middle-aged and old women. This caste has the monopoly of tapping the different kinds of palm trees, and also of selling the fermented juice, and has admirably succeeded in maintaining it, notwithstanding the introduction of the system by which government leases trees to the highest bidders irrespective of their caste. In Shamirpet, so far, there has been no challenge to their monopoly; although occasionally the Madigas and other poor people steal juice from the pots tied to the trees by the Gaondlas. The Gaondlas first mark out the trees to be tapped, then actually tap them in the afternoons and evenings, and tie pots at the points where each tree has been tapped to collect the dripping juice. Early next morning they go round to these trees again, climb up, and bring back to the village all the juice collected during the night. This is kept by them in large earthen pots and retailed to customers on demand, expecially in the afternoon and in the evening. One of the Gaondla families in the village has a government contract for other liquors and intoxicants. In addition to the fermented palm juice, that shop also sells several other varieties of liquor obtained from distilleries in Hyderabad. Payment is generally in cash, and only in exceptional cases may a credit account be maintained.

THE PANCH BRAMHA GROUP

In an earlier chapter mention has already been made of the group of artisan castes who designate themselves as Panch Bramha and maintain a certain degree of exclusiveness from the other Hindu castes. Out of these, two groups, namely, the Wadla (carpenter) and the Kammari (blacksmith), enter into relations of permanent affiliation to the agriculturists. Under this system, they have to supply new agricultural implements periodically, and look after their maintenance and repairs. In return for these services they get a share of the crops which they have to collect from the fields when harvesting is in progress. In addition to this, they practise their own occupation independently. All their services to non-agriculturists, as well as their services of a non-agricultural nature, must be paid for. The carpenter makes the wooden marriage-post required for several of the rites of Hindu weddings. For this he is paid a small fee prescribed by tradition. The blacksmith repairs and periodically supplies new iron agricultural implements, but in this case the agriculturist concerned has to supply the iron, charcoal and a labourer to work the bellows. The other three groups, that is the goldsmiths, workers in bell metal and carvers of images, specialize in fields which have little or almost nothing to do with agriculture; and as such they carry on their crafts independently.

THE SAKALI AND THE MANGALI

The barber and the washerman have no direct contribution to make to the agricultural pursuits of the landowners, but their services are required so often by the agriculturist, especially in their socio-religious ceremonies and rituals connected with birth, marriage and death, that the agriculturists find it more convenient to have families from these castes permanently affiliated to their households. For their normal services all the year round, that is for shaving and hair-cutting, or for washing clothes, they collect their share after each harvest. Other services, especially those connected with socio-religious activities, are generally provided for in the rituals themselves, for at several points in their progress these castes have to be given something, either in cash or in kind. In the course of a long ceremony, two or three times they may get money, twice or thrice some grain or a few brass or bell-metal utensils, and ultimately a set of new clothes. Like the other castes, the barber and the washerman also work independently outside the system of these traditional arrangements.

OTHER CASTES

Before describing the system of family affiliation between the Madiga untouchables and the agriculturists, brief mention should be made of the other castes in the village.

There is only one family of Katike (Hindu butchers) in the village. In point of social status this family ranks equal to the Kapu group. The head of the family slaughters goats and sheep and sells meat to the villagers. The Muslims slaughter their goats and sheep separately or buy their requirement of beef from the market in the city. Shamirpet is largely a Hindu village, and partly out of regard for the sentiments of the majority community, and partly to avoid trouble, the Muslims do not slaughter cows in the village.

The solitary family of the Darzi (tailor) with an old sewing machine is obviously a new addition to the population of the village. Even by modest city standards the abilities of this tailor in his craft must be regarded as rather crude. Yet he has a fairly good business in the village. Except for the well-to-do people, and a few others who maintain regular contact with the city, all others either buy cheap ready-made clothes, or they get their tailoring done by this man in the village, who also attracts considerable custom from nearby villages.

The families of Vaddars (stone-workers) always have sufficient work, either in Shamirpet itself or in some of the neighbouring villages. Those who can afford a house of a superior type have it built of stone. Use of bricks is very rare in this part of the country and thus practically all substantial houses in the village are of stone. The rocky surroundings of the village provide an ample supply, and the Vaddars, adept in the traditional technique of breaking and shaping stone, turn it into a useful building material. Because of their crude technique the work of the Vaddars is very hard indeed and entails considerable physical exertion. Payment for this work is generally on the basis of piece wages. In the busy agricultural season the Vaddars accept other work also for extra wages.

The Erkalas earn their livelihood through a variety of means. The menfolk are hunters. They are also adept in the use of snares and traps. They train hunting dogs and use them effectively for chasing and tracking wounded animals. When they succeed in getting some game, they retain a part of it for their domestic consumption and sell the rest to the villagers. The women beg in the countryside by singing songs and narrating legends. They also do some fortune-telling. Family earnings are supplemented by basket-making, a task at which both men and women work. They also rear pigs.

THE MADIGAS

The Madigas are the lowest caste in Shamirpet. Economically they constitute the poorest section of the community. While the Malas, who are also untouchables but a degree higher than the Madigas, either cultivate their own land or work as farm labourers for daily wages, the Madigas affiliate themselves to the households of the substantial agriculturists in the village. According to the size of the land-holding of the cultivator, one or more Madiga families permanently attach themselves to him. At every stage of agricultural operations during the year the attached Madiga, and his wife and children, work in the fields of their master. They are not paid any daily wages. After the crops are harvested they have to go and 'beg' in the master's fields or threshing grounds. The conventions of the community have prescribed the rates of payment, mostly on the basis of the area of land under cultivation and the yield during the particular harvest. Thus for a certain area a basic minimum must be given; but if on account of good crops the yield has been high it is expected that the affiliated Madiga family would be given a proportionately larger share. In former times there used to be considerable compulsion, and, being in no position to protest, the Madigas had to slave for their masters, who could be quite ruthless. If the master was kind and considerate, they regarded it as their good luck. On the whole it was advisable for them to tolerate even a bad master, for any protests or refusal to do the allotted work on their part would eventually have meant their being forced to leave the village. Now, of course, conditions have changed, and Madigas do not any longer put up with indignities, unreasonable harshness in behaviour or rough handling. Payments differ on the basis of the quality and quantity of work they turn out, and also partly on the nature and temperament of the employer. Slow and lazy workers are paid the barest minimum, while the experienced and the efficient earn much more. In the words of a Madiga, 'If we do not work well, who will pay us? If we do very little work and that too badly, we get what we deserve in the end. If we do not work well we cannot afford to be sensitive; we have to be thick-skinned to stand the abuse of our master. But if we work hard and earn our wages by the sweat of our brow, the master has to treat us well.' To quote another informant: 'Some masters are large-hearted. They make us work hard, but they feed us well. Others expect us to work like oxen, but when it comes to feeding us they dole out mere handfuls as if we were little calves. They always grumble and curse, but when it is time for making payment to us they seem to forget that we too must have a morsel to fill our bellies and a yard of cloth to cover our bodies.' In addition to what the Madiga families get by 'begging' at the time of harvesting, during the busy agricultural season they are fed once a day by the master. According to convention, the master should give a new cloth once every year to each individual from the attached Madiga family who has worked in his fields.

Very few Madigas possess any land worth mentioning, and therefore independent cultivation by them is almost negligible. But they have several other additional means of subsistence open to them. They have to dispose of the dead cattle in the village. As they do not refrain from carrion, this constitutes one source of food supply for them. They are also entitled to get one half of the hide of the dead animal; the other half belongs to the owner. From the owner's share of the hide the Madigas have to make for him such leather articles as he may require for agricultural purposes. Several Madiga families cure hides and work in leather; others earn a part of their living by playing drums and pipes at ceremonial occasions.

2. AGRICULTURE

The settled area of Shamirpet, including the two neighbouring hamlets, is spread over an area of 58 acres. Out of this Shamirpet proper occupies 31·4 acres. In the land surrounding the settlement,

ment, classified in government land records as belonging to this village, approximately 20·4 acres are covered by streams and small rivers, 25 acres by unmetalled roads and footpaths and 61 acres by irrigation channels. Thus apart from the 58 acres which provide the site for the village and the two hamlets attached to it, 106·4 acres are covered by these footpaths, channels and streams. The total land area of the village according to government records is 5,777 acres. Out of this 2,012 acres are uncultivable; 162·8 acres being covered with rocks and shrubs. In all 3,765 acres are under cultivation in the village: 3,339·5 acres are classed as 'dry land', for this area is irrigated entirely by the rains; and 425·6 acres are classed as 'wet land' as extra irrigation is available. Although the dry land occupies a proportionately wider area, it is much less productive than the wet land. In 1951–52, out of the total village land revenue of Rs. 9,137 (Hyderabad currency) only Rs. 3,982/4/- were derived as revenue on dry land, the rest came from wet land. The wet land is further classified into ābi, tābi and do fasla land. In the ābi land seeds are sown in the rainy season (June to July) and harvested in mid- or late winter (November to January). This type of land occupies 131 acres and yields a revenue of Rs. 1,332 per year. In the tābi land sowing is done in winter (October to November) and the crops are harvested in summer (April to May). Tābi land covers 162·4 acres in the village and yields a revenue of Rs. 1,868/12/0 per year. Finally 63·5 acres are classed as the much prized do fasla or two crop land. As the very name suggests, crops are sown and harvested on this land twice every year. Notwithstanding its small area this land yields a revenue of Rs. 1,208/12/0. All this wet land is irrigated by channels from the Shamirpet tank. Mention may also be made of another 68 acres, which are irrigated by small privately owned tanks and wells and bring to the government a revenue of Rs. 745/12/0 per year. Wet land is very much desired by the cultivators because of its high productivity and requirement of comparatively low investment. According to current valuation average wet land sells at Rs. 1,000 to Rs. 1,200 per acre.

It would only be natural to expect that in a primarily agricultural community the number of professional cultivators and others directly dependent upon agriculture should be the highest. Table I shows the number of people who are wholly agriculturists, partly agriculturists and partly field-labourers, and partly agriculturists and partly dependent for subsistence on other crafts and professions.

TABLE I

Number of Families and People Depending on Agriculture as the Main Source of Livelihood.

Nature of agricultural work	Total number of families	Total number of persons	Men	Women	Children	Number of people actually working
1. Agriculturists (depending only on the cultivation of their land)	129	713	226	231	256	336
2. Partly agriculturists and partly field-labourers	154	803	249	271	283	493
3. Partly agriculturists and partly dependent on other crafts and professions	59	305	89	105	111	170

From the above it will be clear that 336 people actually employed whole-time in agriculture maintain 129 families consisting of 713 people. The other class is more numerous. In it 493 people working together maintain 154 families comprising in all 803 people. These partly cultivate their own fields and partly work as labourers with other agriculturists. The third category includes those who are partly agriculturists, and derive a part of their subsistence from some other craft or profession: 59 families having in all 305 people constitute this group.

The remaining fraction of the village population consists of people who contribute indirectly to agriculture or who have a function in some other field of community life. Table II gives the number of families and people in other occupations.

The figures in Tables I and II are for the main village of Shamirpet and do not include the agriculturists and occupational castes from the hamlets of Babugura and Upparpalli, which are regarded, in land records, as parts of Shamirpet.

Out of a total of 3,765 acres of land under cultivation, the residents of Shamirpet are cultivating approximately 3,000 acres.

TABLE II

Craft or profession	Total number of families	Total number of persons	Men	Women	Children	Number of people actually working
1. Potters	5	21	6	7	8	14
2. Carpenters	4	15	5	5	5	5
3. Blacksmiths	4	28	8	11	9	8
4. Washermen	7	31	7	8	16	18
5. Toddy-tappers	16	99	29	34	36	53
6. Shepherds	21	108	31	42	35	69
7. Barbers	2	11	2	4	5	8
8. Goldsmiths	2	13	4	6	3	4
9. Stone-breakers	3	16	5	5	6	10
10. Erkala hunters	5	16	6	6	4	11
11. Traders and Shop-keepers	13	81	22	22	37	27
12. Government servants	46	211	70	60	81	90
13. Others	7	33	10	12	11	14

An analysis of the pattern of land-ownership in the village reveals the following:

i. A fourth of the land is owned by 1 family having 800 acres.

ii. A fourth of the land is owned by 8 families having 100 acres each.

iii. A fourth of the land is owned by 20 families having 40 acres each.

iv. A fourth of the land is owned by 160 families having 5 acres each.

The headman of the village is the biggest single land-owner. He belongs to the Reddi caste which is the dominant section of the group of agricultural castes in this area. The second category includes, besides the Reddis, two Muslims—one of whom is the Patwari of the village. Even in the third category approximately 40% of the land is held by the Reddis; the rest being shared by other castes, especially the Brahmins, the Komtis, the toddy-tappers and the shepherds, as well as the Muslims. This category also includes two Malas and a Madiga—all three belonging to untouchable castes. The land in the fourth group belongs to several different castes. However, many of these families possess only small fragments of dry land which are quite inadequate for their needs and can in no sense be described as 'economic holdings'.

The above figures have been taken from government records. While the possession of land sold to persons outside the kin-group is given after the completion of the necessary legal formalities, the division of shares from the family land does not necessitate this and in consequence we find that the land shown in the name of one person in the official records may actually be in the possession of several families. This may be illustrated by two examples. E. D. R. has four acres of dry land and six acres of wet land recorded in his name in government registers. The dry land and three acres of wet land are under his exclusive possession. This land is cultivated by him; and the entire harvest belongs to him. But the other three acres of wet land are divided into four pieces. One of these fragments is cultivated by E. D. R. himself, one by his cousin S. R. who is E. D. R.'s father's elder brother's son. The other two fragments are cultivated by E. R. and N. R. whose position is a little unusual. In the life-time of E. D. R.'s grandfather they 'came to his house' for suitor service. After serving the family for a stipulated number of years they were married to the daughters of the family, but continued to live there to assist the old man in his cultivation. After the death of E. D. R.'s grandfather they established separate houses of their own, and are now in exclusive possession of these fragments of land which belonged to E. D. R.'s family. From the above it is clear that although the land records show the land as being in the possession of E. D. R. alone, it is in fact possessed by four different families. The Madiga untouchables were given two acres of land as a reward for the services which they render to residents of the village and touring government officials. Official records show this land as being in the possession of one family: in point of fact, it is shared by as many as seven families.

Seceding members of a family get a share of the family's ancestral land. Fragmentation follows this division of ancestral property. For many years, however, the land continues to be in the name of only one member of the extended family in the government records. The division of land, cattle and effects takes place under the supervision (and with the advice) of some of the village elders, and the terms and conditions agreed upon at this time are generally respected by the seceding units of the family. In the course of our investigations only three cases came to our notice in which inconvenience was experienced in the working of arrangements thus made. This necessitated the entry of the division into legally valid documents and government records. Thus, it is clear that while government records show only 189 families as owning land, actually the number of those who possess their own fields is larger. If we do not take into account the houses in the two neighbouring hamlets, Shamirpet proper has 380 houses. Each house represents a family, elementary or joint. Out of these, 240 families have some land of their own, although from among them 60 families possess only tiny fragments. Among the other families some have only dry land, some have very little wet land, while some have highly fragmented land which often lies in many different corners of the village. This still leaves nearly 140 landless families. From these we can eliminate about 20 government officials who are not a part of the permanent population of the village; and about 10 others who have an occupation or calling which gives them a sufficient income to maintain a reasonably comfortable life according to prevailing rural standards. Eliminating these, we have some 110 families that are landless. These are in addition to an equal number of families who have insufficient or uneconomic holdings.

Those who have no land, as well as those who have very little land, are left with the alternatives of either working as whole-time agricultural labourers or of cultivating land taken on lease (*kaul*). Persons choosing the second alternative, either pay the owner of the land a fixed sum of money every year, or they give him a quarter or one-third of the produce. Absentee landlordism is almost negligible in Shamirpet, and those who own the greater part of the village land themselves want to cultivate their best fields. Thus only inferior quality land can generally be had on lease. With hard work and financial investment this land can be improved, but unfortunately this is impeded by several factors. If the same person continues to hold the lease for certain fields for

74

a number of years, according to law he acquires semi-proprietary rights over them. The landlord does not want this to happen, and so with a view to safeguarding his own interests he leases out his land to different persons in different years. A short-term lease is naturally not conducive to land improvement, for the person cultivating the land does not risk any investment in it. If he does improve it, in one of the following years the landlord may lease it out to someone else who offers to pay more than the person who improved the land. Secondly, those who hold most of the agricultural land in the village are interested in maintaining a supply of cheap agricultural labour, without which it would be impossible for them to cultivate their extensive fields. They benefit more by cultivating their land with the help of this labour, than by leasing out their land. If they leased out all their surplus land the cheap labour supply would appreciably diminish, and for want of competition wages of those who were still available would rise. To avoid this they choose to leave some of their land uncultivated, and thus we have the paradox of having in the same village many land-hungry families and several hundred acres of uncultivated land.

The land belongs to the family, and normally the head of the family exercises control over it. On the death of the father, the land and other agricultural property—such as tools, implements and livestock—are distributed equally among the brothers. Provision is made for the marriage of unmarried daughters as well as for the maintenance of the minor sons of the deceased. In very special cases, with the consent of all the brothers, a widowed sister is also given a small share. But this is a gratuity rather than a rightful share.

The agriculturists have considerable sentiment for their land and cattle. If adversity compels them to sell some of their fields or cattle, the day when this is done becomes a day of semi-mourning for the household. The hour of transfer is indeed a sad one, and the farmer will complete the necessary formalities with a heavy heart. For several days the family atmosphere remains overcast with gloom. The womenfolk may even wail and shed tears of real grief. In the sentiments of an Indian peasant, the Earth occupies a mother's position and parting with a fragment of it is nearly tantamount to separation from the mother. It is surprising how cattle become almost members of the agriculturist's family, and how

ECONOMIC STRUCTURE

their separation by death or selling causes so much sorrow among the peasants.

Land is indeed the most precious and coveted possession of the village people. With the exception of women's ornaments, land and cattle are almost the only property they have. With the overall increase in general price levels in recent years, the price of land has also risen. The following table will give an idea of the average prices of different grades of land in 1939 and in 1950.

TABLE III

Prices of Land in 1939 and 1950

Type of land	Price per acre in rupees					
	1939 Grades of land			1950 Grades of land		
	A	B	C	A	B	C
1. Dry land	60	40	18	220	170	75
2. Wet land	250	150	90	1,200	800	480
3. Garden land	300	240	110	1,500	1,200	550

I propose to examine the standards of living, and relative earnings and expenditure of the different levels of the population in a subsequent chapter. But a consideration of the economics of agriculture will not be out of place here.

The two major crops grown by the people of Shamirpet are rice and millet. Table IV gives the averages per acre of gross income, total cost and net income, in the cultivation of millet, particularly *jawar*. Tables V and VI give similar figures for paddy, for single crop and double crop lands respectively. The figures have been worked out from a survey of a 50% sample of village families cultivating the three different categories of land. Figures are given to the nearest whole number.

TABLE IV

Average Cost and Yield per Acre in the Cultivation of Millet

Grade of land	Gross income	Total expenditure	Net income
A	Rs. 140	Rs. 64	Rs. 76
B	„ 82	„ 40	„ 42
C	„ 62	„ 30	„ 32

76

ECONOMIC STRUCTURE

TABLE V

Average Cost and Yield per Acre in the Cultivation of Paddy (One-crop Fields)

Grade of land	Gross income	Total expenditure	Net income
A	Rs. 420	Rs. 180	Rs. 240
B	,, 310	,, 160	,, 150
C	,, 200	,, 120	,, 80

TABLE VI

Average Cost and Yield per Acre in the Cultivation of Paddy (Two-crop Fields)

Grade of land	Gross income	Total expenditure	Net income
A	Rs. 530	Rs. 220	Rs. 310
B	,, 420	,, 200	,, 220
C	,, 380	,, 190	,, 190

If we work out the averages for the different items of expenditure incurred in agricultural activities, we find that the expenditure on seeds is the most important single factor, accounting for nearly 60% of the total amount spent. Land revenue, wages for hired labour, maintenance or hire of plough and cattle, and interest on loans and capital investments are the other important items of expenditure. Manure and land improvement between them account for only about 7% of the sum spent. Table VII gives the averages of expenditure on the items mentioned above, according to our field survey.

TABLE VII

Item of expenditure	Percentage of total expenditure
1. Seed	58
2. Land revenue	9
3. Hired labour	6·5
4. Maintenance and/or hire of plough cattle	5·5
5. Interest on loan and capital investments	4
6. Manure	3·5
7. Agricultural tools, repairs and field improvement	3·5
8. Miscellaneous	1

In the pages that have preceded, the position of land as a factor in village agriculture has been briefly examined. Some general observations have already been made about labour, and I shall return to it presently. Here a passing reference should be made to the factors of capital and organization.

77

Analysis of the family budgets of the agriculturists in the village revealed that 10% of them were surplus, 24% were balanced and the rest were deficit budgets. Exact figures regarding the extent of indebtedness could not be obtained as the people invariably sought to conceal information on this subject. According to our rough estimate, 55% to 60% of the families are indebted. As relatively few persons can get agricultural or land improvement loans from the government at a reasonable rate of interest, and as there is no co-operative society in the village, most people have to take recourse to the money-lenders either in the village or, preferably, in a neighbouring one. Petty loans may be obtained from well-to-do shopkeepers and peasants. The rate of interest varies greatly. For large loans a mortgage is generally insisted upon, and anything between 6% and 12% compound interest is charged. For petty loans interest is charged at the rate of 2 annas per rupee per month. If ornaments or other valuables are pawned, the rate of interest is reduced even for the smaller loans. Borrowing in kind also takes place. Seeds are often obtained on loan, and are returned after the harvest with 25% interest. In several cases the indebtedness of the family could be attributed to over-spending in socio-religious ceremonies and litigation rather than to agricultural needs.

The organization of agricultural pursuits rests mainly on the head of the family, although grown-up sons—if they are living with the parents—are also consulted. When buying or selling land the advice of the elders of the extended family is always obtained. This has to be done before mortgaging family property against loans. The scope for individual initiative and innovations is very limited, for the system of agriculture still largely follows the traditional patterns and is governed to a great extent by the agricultural lore passed from generation to generation through oral tradition.

Most agriculturists can manage the cultivation of their fields with the help of family labour. The traditional system on inter-caste relations secures for them the specialized services of the occupational castes. The more well-to-do landowners have Madiga families attached to them. However, the migration of some Madiga families and concentration of considerable areas of land in the possession of a few families make it almost essential for many agriculturists to employ additional labour. In the busy season even

ordinary cultivators have to employ casual labour. The rates of
daily wages have now increased considerably. In 1939 a male
labourer was paid 3 to 6 annas a day, while a woman was paid
2 to 4 annas. In 1951, men were paid between 1 rupee and 1
rupee 8 annas per day, while the women got 8 to 12 annas per
day. Rich landowners employ labourers on the basis of an annual
contract also. Rates of payment vary with the age, ability and
experience of the person employed; and also partly with the
financial position of the employer. According to our statistics
wages differ from Rs. 280 to Rs. 120 per year, and may be paid
in cash or kind. Depending on the agreement the employee may
be paid a cash monthly salary, or he may be paid a part in cash
and a part in grain. Very often the agreement includes the following in the wages for the year: an agreed sum at the end of the year,
one or two meals a day or a specified quantity of grain every week,
and a set or two of new clothes and footwear or a blanket. As a
rule advances are drawn from time to time, and when they exceed
the stipulated sum the labourer has to agree to work the following
year also to repay the debt.

3. THE AGRICULTURAL YEAR

The agriculturists in Shamirpet follow the local almanac. Most
of their moves in farm activity depend upon the position of the
stars in the sky. According to this almanac a month is divided
into two *katis*, each with a duration of approximately fifteen days.
Each of these divisions bears a name which indicates a particular
position of the stars. According to the traditional agricultural lore
of the people the different *katis* are suitable for different kinds of
agricultural activities and provide the agriculturist with a schedule
for the different stages of his work in the field. Of course, he also
takes into consideration other natural factors, such as the possibility of rainfall in the immediate future; but in general his moves
follow the time-tested schedule of the Hindu calendar. Muslim
agriculturists too follow this calendar and share with their Hindu
neighbours their agricultural folklore.

In late summer (i.e. the end of May) the agriculturists keep
their fields clear for ploughing in anticipation of a light shower of
rain. Invariably there is some rainfall during this period which
softens the ground and makes it possible for them to start ploughing. With the advent of this eagerly awaited drizzle the farmers

can be seen carrying their wooden ploughs and driving their pairs of bullocks to the fields. No time must be lost, for the hardening of land may render ploughing difficult and this may eventually result in late sowing.

About this time they go to the Brahmin to fix an auspicious day for planting vegetables and creepers in their backyards. The Brahmin consults his almanac to find out a day on which the stars of the person and the constellation in the sky match, for such a day is believed to be most suitable for sowing vegetables. Fortified with these astrological predictions, the Hindu agriculturists make initial preparations for planting these backyard crops. Muslims and poorer Hindus do not avail themselves of the services of the Brahmin priest. Beds and pits are kept ready well in advance, and on the appropriate day suggested by the Brahmin (or fixed by the family if the priest has not been consulted) seeds are sown. In the rainy season almost everyone grows some vegetables and creepers, and these are in most cases the only vegetables regularly eaten in any part of the year. The favourites among these vegetables are: runner beans, snake-gourds and pumpkins. Bottle-gourd and sponge-gourd are planted a few days later. Okra, bringals and some other green vegetables are also grown.

Later, when more showers have fallen, the agriculturists hasten to sow maize and millet in the fields. A late variety of rice, locally known as *samber*, is sown in carefully made beds to be transplanted into regular fields later.

In the first two weeks of June operations started in late May are continued. Light showers at this time are further utilized to complete the ploughing. Sowing of maize is also continued. Late varieties of paddy are now directly sown into the fields. Fifteen to twenty days after sowing they visit the fields to remove the weeds.

In the second half of June the rainfall is generally regular and satisfactory. During this time people must complete their sowing of *kharif* crops such as maize and millet. Ground-nut, linseed and other oil seeds are also sown during this period. All these crops are grown on dry land as they do not require any extra irrigation.

For a month and a half after this the sowing of paddy is continued. At this time mostly coarse and medium varieties are sown. These include two mixed strains developed by the Department of Agriculture, Hyderabad State, and are locally known as paddy nos. 12 and 19. A month after the sowing, weeds are removed from the fields. Labour is usually hired for weeding the wet fields, but in the fields on dry land this is done with a forked plough designed and used specially for this purpose. Immediately after the weeding they proceed to manure the fields. Many people now use an artificial fertilizer known as 'paddy mixture', which they buy from the Agriculture Department of the Hyderabad State government. On wet land some people sow fine and sweet-smelling late varieties of rice also.

The harvesting of the *kharif* crops, as well as the other first crops, has to be completed by October or early November. This is indeed the busiest season for most cultivators. Between the harvesting of these crops and the sowing of *rabi* crops (such as gram, castor, etc.) and the second crop of paddy the interval must be as short as possible. They have to expedite the former, in order that sowing for the new season may not be delayed. As a general rule the sowing of *rabi* crops precedes the second sowing of paddy in the wet-land fields.

With the slow advent of winter the village witnesses considerable agricultural activity. The *rabi* crops, i.e. gram, castor, chillies, mustard, tobacco, *til* (sesame), onions, garlic, coriander, *methi* (fenugreek) and several varieties of oil seeds are now sown. All these are dry land crops. With the exception of chillies, onions, garlic, tobacco, coriander and *methi*, which are sown near wells and are irrigated roughly once a week by the Persian-wheel, or by large leather buckets raised by bullocks, the other crops do not require any irrigation. Most of these crops are ready for harvesting in three to five months. Mustard, gram and coriander are ready in three months. Castor, chillies and tobacco take four months. The oil seeds take longer and may be harvested in the fifth or in the beginning of the sixth month. With the completion of the sowing of these crops, agriculturists take in hand the sowing of the second crop of paddy. Fields are flooded with water from the irrigation tank, ploughed and kept ready for sowing well in advance of the actual sowing time. If the flooding of the fields is not possible on account of the low water-level in the tank, showers of winter rains are awaited. For the second crop an early variety of paddy is generally chosen. This crop ripens in three to four months and does not make heavy demands on the limited irrigation facilities available in the village.

As these crops become ready for harvesting, the annual cycle of agricultural activities comes very near to completion. When the harvesting is over, the farmers get a brief spell of rest and leisure. Now and then they go round the fields and remove the weeds and other wild plants. Their work during this part of the year does not necessitate hard manual labour. In a leisurely way they take in hand activities of a preparatory nature which are a prelude to their major agricultural work of the rainy season and winter. Manure from cow-dung pits is carried to the fields and is evenly spread there. Grass and other wild plants growing in the fields are removed. The land is kept ready for ploughing in a month's time. In a few days the signs of approaching rains compel them to cast off their lethargy. The preparations for ploughing inaugurate a new circle of annual agricultural activities, and the advent of late summer rains sends them back once again into the fields.

4. CATTLE AND DOMESTIC ANIMALS

Agriculture in the village still largely follows the age-old pattern. Even to-day old style bullock-drawn wooden ploughs are used by the agriculturists. In such a system the value of draught cattle is very great indeed, for efficient farming under these conditions depends to a very great extent upon the availability of good bullocks. Some agriculturists use male buffaloes for ploughing the fields, but bullocks continue to be their favourites. Cows and she-buffaloes are kept for milk. The shepherds keep large herds of goats and sheep. Some Muslims as well as Hindus, with the exception of the Brahmins and the Komtis, may also keep a few goats. Pigs are kept only by the Erkalas. Among domestic pets, dogs are popular with every section of the village population. The number of cats in the village is fairly large, but they are not kept as pets. Some people keep parrots in cages, and teach them to utter a few words. Three Muslims have domesticated partridges. A Hindu shopkeeper has a tiny blackbird in a cage hanging in front of his shop. Poultry is kept by all sections of the village population, except the Brahmins and the Komtis. In addition to the usual fowls, four families have ducks and turkeys also.

In connection with this study a survey of village animals was undertaken in May 1951. The result of the survey is summarized in the following tables:

TABLE VIII

Cattle in Shamirpet

Type of animal	Bovine	Bubaline
1. Work animals, over three years of age	285	75
2. Animals in milk	7	17
3. Milch animals gone dry	18	71
4. Animals under one year of age; both male and female	152	69
5. Cows not fertile or heifers	186	8
	648	240

TABLE IX

Goats and Sheep

Animal	Number		
	Age up to 1 year	Age between 1 and 3 years	Age over 3 years
1. Goats (a) male	9	21	9
(b) female	5	149	1
2. Sheep (a) male	13	85	5
(b) female	11	297	2

TABLE X

Pigs and Poultry

Type	Number
1. Pigs	58
2. Fowls (a) male	52
(b) female	232
(c) chickens	105
3. Ducks	14

From Table VIII it will be clear that for the 3,000 acres of agricultural land there are only 360 plough animals in the village. As cattle work in pairs for ploughing there are only 180 units available in the village for this purpose. Each unit has to plough a little more than 16 acres, and this is really too much for the animals which are, according to the report of the Veterinary and Animal Husbandry unit working with our team, 'in a poor condition—weak, emaciated, ill-nourished, ill-housed and uncared for'. In recent years liver fluke and fascioliasis have impaired the health of the cattle and exposed them to attacks of various other diseases. Plough cattle are on the whole better looked after. But the neglect of the cow, traditionally regarded as 'the mother', is indeed pathetic. Absence of good breeding bulls and lack of grazing grounds further account for the poor condition of the cattle. In the absence of a good pedigree bull, scrub bulls of no particular description are allowed to move freely among the cows. According to village land records there are 1,482 acres of pasture-land in the area surrounding the settlement; but this land is almost always auctioned to contractors from outside the village. As these pastures are not available for grazing to the village cattle, they roam about the shrubs and rocks around the village and eat whatever fodder is available there.

The shortage of draught-cattle is a serious handicap to the prosperity of average peasants in the village. The well-to-do agriculturists always have a sufficient number of cattle to meet their own agricultural requirements. But the average and poorer peasants find great difficulty in tilling their fields in time with the limited number of their own or hired cattle. Dependence on the monsoons obliges them to make certain variations in their agricultural schedule to fit in with the uncertainty of the rains. Some of their operations must precede the first rainfall; others must follow it almost immediately. For some days during the busy season this causes great pressure on available resources in men and cattle. The cultivators who depend on hired cattle or who practise co-operative lending and borrowing of cattle cannot take the best advantage of the first rains, and this enforced wait results in untimely sowing and poor crops.

The absence of good milch cattle affects the nutrition of the people. In May 1951 the total daily yield of milk in the village was about 14 lb. only. Earlier it has been pointed out that most people in the village keep poultry, but in general its quality is poor, and the production of eggs is estimated to be in the neighbourhood of 1,400 a year.

5. OTHER ECONOMIC PURSUITS

Before we pass on to the other occupations brief reference should be made to some common exploitative activities of the people.

Hunting is done regularly by a very limited number of people. Only the Erkalas have adopted it as a part of their profession.

They mostly hunt small game, and are adept in the use of traps, snares and dogs. At the time of these investigations there were six guns in the village; and occasionally their owners went out shooting. Similarly, fishing is done by very few people, mostly by some young Muslim men. They do not use fishing nets and traps, and practically the only method employed by them for catching the fish is that of using the rod, hook and bait. The large tank in the vicinity of the village could afford a good supply of fish, but the absence of the fishing caste in the village population leaves this possibility almost unexplored. Fishermen from the neighbouring villages, however, periodically come to the tank.

The surroundings of Shamirpet offer very few opportunities for the collection of wild food. Around the village there are not many fruit-bearing trees. Mango and *jamun* (rose apple, *Eugenia jambolana*) fruits are mostly eaten while they are still unripe by the village boys. Parties of children and young people periodically go to pick wild berries when they are in season. These are mostly eaten on the spot. When wild figs are ripe children collect and eat them. Another item of food eagerly sought by everyone is the *chikur*—tender tamarind leaves. These leaves are curried, as well as pickled and preserved. Honey is collected by some men of lower castes and inferior social status, whenever they can spot a comb. Medicinal herbs, roots, tubers and barks are collected according to need.

Utilization of forest resources is not open to everyone now. From the surrounding scrub jungle villagers can collect only a limited quantity of fuel, as this—as well as getting timber—is regulated by the Forest Department of the government, and permits can be obtained only by making scheduled payments.

Different kinds of coloured earth used in washing walls and decorating the interiors of homes, as well as the ordinary requirements for the construction of houses, can be freely collected by the people. The Vaddars can break and shape stones without having to pay for them.

6. NON-AGRICULTURAL OCCUPATIONS

In an effort to explain the broad outlines of the economic organization of the community, the traditional occupations and functions of the different castes have already been described. With reference to the inter-relations between the agriculturists

and some of the occupational castes, four different types of economic dealings have been mentioned: a system of family affiliation
under which the family of the occupational caste attaches itself
to a family or families of agriculturists for rendering to them
services in their agricultural pursuits, similar affiliation for performing definite functions in connection with socio-religious rites
and ceremonies, barter of professional services between occupational castes, and finally the rendering of services within the domain of caste monopolies for cash payment. Six occupational castes
assist the agriculturists by rendering them services within the
field of their functional specialization. It will be interesting to
analyse the exact contribution made by each of these four types of
economic dealings to their total earnings. The averages in the
following table have been calculated from family budgets of the
different castes in question. Where the number of families was
small, such as among potters, carpenters and blacksmiths, 100%
sample was taken; in others a 50% random sample was taken.
However, it is necessary to point out that the budgets were made
mostly on the basis of verbal estimates of the families. Only substantial payments received during a period of three years were
checked. In making these calculations income from the cultivation of land belonging to the family as well as from agricultural
labour lying outside the occupational specialization of the family
have not been taken into account.

TABLE XI

Caste	Percentage of income from:				
	Traditional system of family affiliation	Services at socio-religious ceremonies	Barter of occupational services	Services for cash payment	Miscel-laneous
Potter	18	3	1	78	–
Carpenter	60	1	2	36	1
Blacksmith	60	–	2	37	1
Barber	40	12	2	43	3
Washerman	30	10	2	55	3
Madiga	50	8	–	40	2

From the above table it will be clear that the carpenters, blacksmiths and barbers derive 63%, 62% and 54% respectively of
their total income from one or more types of traditional arrange-

ment. As all the Madiga families in the village are not affiliated to the agriculturists, in these calculations their average income from these sources comes to only 58%, although a few decades ago, when the traditional system worked better, it must have been considerably more. The potters earn much more by selling their earthenware in the markets than by their traditional arrangements with the families of agriculturists. Similarly, some of the washermen have now a clientele in the city. Twice or thrice every month they collect clothes from them, delivering at the same time the previous washing. The barbers have a limited number of clients in the neighbouring villages. All the castes in this group derive an appreciable portion of their total earnings from private work done outside the system of traditional arrangements.

The economy of the village is only partially self-sufficient. The traders, both Komtis and Muslims, buy their goods wholesale from the city and retail them in their shops in the village. People often buy their requirements from the city if they happen to go there. They frequently visit the weekly bazaars also. The weavers buy their spindles from Hyderabad wholesalers, and depend for the sale of their cloth on the cluster of several nearby villages. The customers of the goldsmith are also distributed in several villages of the neighbourhood. The Gaondla produces all the fermented palm-juice required in the settlement from the trees around the village, but he has also to keep a certain quantity of liquor distilled in the city for such customers as may order it occasionally. The occupation of stone-breaking takes the Vaddars to several villages in the neighbourhood where there are no members of their caste. Finally, Madiga families acquiring a reputation for their skill in curing and tanning hides, or in their leather-work, are also commissioned by outsiders occasionally to do some work for them.

CHAPTER FOUR

Ritual Structure

1. THE CHARACTER OF RELIGION

A TEXT-BOOK knowledge of the religious lore of India, and an acquaintance with her ancient classics and their modern expositions will hardly give us a true picture of the actual religious beliefs, thoughts, feelings and practices of the people now living in the countryside. A classification of their religious beliefs and ritual is not an easy task. Folklore and myths, religious teachings of saint-poets, and contacts with persons having knowledge of scriptures and popular religious books have all influenced their religious ideology, and consequently their religion is a mixture of animism, animatism and polytheism, with the occasional appearance of monotheism also. To these must be added a living faith in spirits, ghosts, demons, witches and magic. The complex of all these diverse factors constitutes the picture of the supernatural world as it is understood by the people in the countryside. Tenets of classical Hinduism having an all-India spread are mingled with the regional religious beliefs and forms of worship current among the Hindus of the Deccan plateau. Several cults and worships of a purely local nature add further to the complexity of the beliefs and ritual system of the community. A wide variety of cults is observed by the family, some by the village as a whole; and still others by individual caste groups.

What is the attitude of the individual towards religion in general? And what is his attitude towards the rituals and cults organized by the different units of the community? An attempt to answer these questions will greatly help our understanding of the character of religion as accepted and practised by the people.

Shamirpet is predominantly a Hindu village. The Muslim section of the population belongs to the Sunni sect and follows the religious pattern laid down in the Koran as interpreted by the founders of this sect. A devout Muslim is expected to offer prayers five times a day. In Shamirpet this would be the exception rather than the general rule. Some of the Muslim elders offer prayers twice a day, some only once and the rest are contented with their weekly prayers on Friday. The Mulla, the Muslim priest in the village, is the only person who offers the prescribed prayers every day. Fasting during the month of Ramzan is undertaken by a very large number of Muslims, but those maintaining it without a break until the end of the month would not total even a quarter of that number. The Muslims have a high degree of community-consciousness, but in Shamirpet it does not find expression in the form of intense religious devotion among the adherents of the Islamic faith.

With the exception of the Brahmin and the Komti castes, the Hindus have no fixed time for daily worship. The number of people who visit a temple or shrine every day is negligible. But festivals and ceremonies are observed with unfailing regularity. Otherwise the gods are remembered only at times of disease or difficulty. As a rule, only some of the elderly people devote themselves to 'the daily duty of remembering the creator'; the younger people 'have much else to do'. They participate in ceremonies, partake of the festival feasts, and assemble to listen to the reading of the holy books and to the recitation of mythological legends by professionals when they happen to visit the village. The tasks of remembrance and repentance are postponed for old age. Among both men and women, only the elders seem to talk about 'the change of times' and 'the decline in the religious attitudes and ethical standards of the people'. In the everyday thought and speech of the younger generation there is very little of religion; and little conscious effort at seeking any deep religious experience or thrill is to be found among them. In the life of the community under observation, we noticed only two exceptions to this. One of these is the *Urs*, a semi-religious fair, commemorating Jalal Miyan, a local Muslim divine with some reputation for being a holy man. This fair is sponsored by the Muslims but is largely attended by the Hindus also. The second is the annual worship of a village goddess organized by the village. On both these occasions several people are temporarily possessed by the spirit of Jalal Miyan or by one of the goddesses. Going into a trance these people speak for the spirit which possesses them. The other people who are present there make offerings to them, seek solutions of their pressing problems and difficulties, and request them to remedy their ills and worries. Considerable enthusiasm is in evidence among them at this time. With these exceptions there is very little religious thought, talk or worship in normal life.

However, both Hindus and Muslims have a degree of fatalism and demonstrate a spirit of resignation towards predestined facts ordained for them by the supernatural forces of the world beyond. People can often be heard to remark, 'If it is written in our fate, we must submit to it. Human effort cannot alter the will of God. What is predestined must have its course.' But this fatalism makes its appearance only when the people have tried their best to solve the problem and having spared no effort still find themselves no nearer a solution. Coupled with this concept of fate is the Hindu doctrine of *karma*. According to this concept, which takes for granted the phenomenon of the transmigration of the soul and its re-birth, our actions in the past life determine the character of our present life, and our actions in this life will determine the character of our future life. The village people clearly reconcile and synthesize these two views into a practical precept: the course of our present life is largely predestined on the basis of our acts in the past life, but by acting 'rightly' in this life we can materially influence the course of our life after death.

The rural ethic lays great emphasis on 'acting rightly', that is on the observance of traditional norms; because it is the only way to achieve happiness and prosperity in this life, and more than that to ensure the destiny of the soul after death. The problem of the future plays a very significant part in the ordering of life. Both Hindus and Muslims believe that death is not the end; there is something beyond it. Both attach great importance to the destiny of the soul after death. While the Muslim expects to remain in his grave until the Resurrection, when on the Day of Judgement he will be assigned to heaven (*jannat*) or hell (*jahannum*) according to his deeds, for the Hindu life is practically an unending process. After death one either goes to heaven (*swarga*) or to hell (*narka*), or one takes re-birth. Depending on one's actions in the past life, one may be born into one of the castes higher or lower than one's caste in the previous life, or even into some other lower species of the animal kingdom. One should therefore endeavour to go to heaven or to secure re-birth in a respectable caste and good family. In the course of our investigations we found very few people who had even a hazy notion regarding the higher Hindu concept of *moksha* or salvation which secures the emancipation of the soul from all worldly obligations and ensures that it shall cease to take birth again and again in different shapes and forms. But the desire to go to heaven or to ensure a better birth is universal. From one's childhood, one keeps on hearing, often colourful and dramatic, accounts of heaven and hell. 'We shall have to account for our actions before God. We can deceive our family, our village, our caste, and even the established authority, but we can never deceive God. He has the record of every little thing that we do, and after death His agents will decide whether we go to heaven or to hell', is the refrain in the talk of most of the people when they are asked to explain their belief regarding the future of man after death. Descriptions of heaven and hell are vivid and imaginative. 'In heaven you have only to desire a thing and the next moment you find it there', said one of our informants. 'There is peace and plenty in heaven. All people live in luxurious palaces where an army of countless servants looks after all their comforts. There you have the choicest foods, and the best of everything,' explained a Reddi cultivator. A Madiga's picture of heaven was somewhat different. He said, 'When you go to heaven you have a comfortable house fitted with chairs, soft beds and velvet cushions. And you get all the rice that you want to eat, and all the sweets. And you can do what you like for there are no administrative or village officials to curse you and abuse you.' The descriptions of hell are fairly standardized. 'Hell is an awful place. It has several compartments, each one worse than the other. In one compartment roaring fires are kept eternally burning, in another there are deadly snakes, scorpions and crocodiles; then there is a large tank—several miles long—filled with pus and foul-smelling blood, swarming with maggots and hideous insects; and there are hundreds and hundreds of such compartments each with a different torture and punishment awaiting the sinners. According to the nature of their sins, wrong-doers are thrown into one of these sections to suffer the penalties for what they have done. They cry and scream and weep, but the warders in God's prison are merciless. The more the sinners cry, the more they are tortured.' The above account represents a fairly typical description of hell which one often hears in the village community. Through conversation, folktale, myth and legend these ideas are implanted fairly early into the minds of the village children, who start life with a fear of sin. But by the time they reach the age of undertaking wild adventures these fears are diluted, and the gruesome accounts of hell no longer hold their spell of horror over them. As old age approaches, bitter memories of failures and frustrations accumulate and the flesh does not have the energy to undertake fresh adventures; people slowly begin turning their attention to thoughts of life after death. As an illiterate informant pithily put it: 'While youth lasts, passions rule the actions of man. While property lasts, the glitter of gold makes a man blind. But in old age, man laments for what he did in his youth. With his dim vision, he can no longer see the maddening glitter of gold. Then his thoughts turn to religion.'

The concept of *dharma* is also important, as it covers all the phases of the human life-cycle and fixes several details of intra- and inter-group life. *Dharma* has often been translated by Western writers as 'religion', but this translation hardly conveys the original meaning. It will perhaps be more appropriate to describe it as '*the* way of life' or 'that which is right'. Acceptance of caste traditions and the general rules of piety, observance of fasts and feasts, rigidly following the norms governing the *rites de passage* and undertaking pilgrimages to places of worship or for bathing in holy rivers, can generally be said to constitute the *dharma* of the people. Special worship and rituals may be performed to attain certain special ends. It is through *dharma* that one can look forward to shaping one's destiny. The concepts of *pap* (sin) and *punya* (merit), and of ritual pollution are fundamental to the wider concept of *dharma*. Certain things must not be done by any member of the community irrespective of his caste because they are sinful. Murder, extreme cruelty and violence, and incest can be placed under this category. There are certain other things which must not be done by certain castes, or by certain individuals in particular conditions. Sexual relations or inter-dining with a person of lower caste will lead to impurity. A woman in menses or a family immediately after childbirth and death remains in a state of ritual impurity for a specified period. After certain bodily excretions such as those of fæces, urine or semen, a prescribed bath or wash is necessary to remove the impurity caused by the act. Non-observance of these rules will have a polluting effect; and according to the nature and degree of pollution purificatory rites will have to be undertaken.

Belief in ghosts and spirits is universal. They are feared and propitiated. Strange mystical power pervading certain objects is recognized, and fetishes and amulets are eagerly sought. Witchcraft is often suspected, and three or four people in the community are believed to possess magical powers.

Clearly, Hinduism as it is practised in the village is not the Hinduism of the classical philosophical systems of India, for it possesses neither the metaphysical heights nor the abstract content of the latter. It is a religion of fasts, feasts and festivals, in which prescribed rituals cover all the major crises of life. Worship and propitiation of gods and spirits follow the annual round of festivals and the ritual of the human life-cycle. Disease and difficulty may also necessitate invoking assistance from these sources.

In early childhood religious instruction through legendary tales and anecdotes exercises its influence on the developing mind of the child in whose thoughts and world of fancy these ideas linger on. Youth brings in its wake a more worldly and materialistic outlook towards life and its pleasures. Thoughts are turned to religion when the evening of life approaches, partly to postpone the final moment of departure as long as it could be, and partly to ensure the future lying beyond the point of death. Analysis of life-histories reveals that spiritualism cannot be said to be the keynote in the life of the community; far from it the religion appears to be a practical one. It strengthens and fortifies the individual and the group in situations where technical competence and practical intelligence are of no avail, and at the same time acts as a bond of cohesion for maintaining the structural unity of the society.

2. BELIEF: GODS AND DEITIES

The Muslims believe in one God, and follow the way of life laid down for them by their Prophet. They all belong to the Sunni division, and as such differ from the Shias and other splinter divisions of Islam in respect of the interpretation of their holy book as well as in several details of belief, ritual and ceremonial. Almost all the Muslims of Shamirpet have been converted to Islam from

RITUAL STRUCTURE

Hinduism in the course of the last four or five generations. They do not believe in any of the gods of the Hindu Trinity, nor in any of the later incarnations; but they share with the Hindus a living faith in the existence of malevolent ghosts, spirits and witches. They participate with the rest of the community in village ceremonies and sacrifices. To ward off cholera, plague and smallpox, they too think that it is necessary to propitiate the local deities and goddesses.

Village Hinduism is not easy to describe. It is an extremely elastic religion, and within its all-India framework admits of a considerable degree of regional and local variation. In his *Religion and Society among the Coorgs of South India*, M. N. Srinivas has introduced the useful concept of 'spread', and split up village Hinduism into 'All India Hinduism', 'Peninsular Hinduism', 'Regional Hinduism', and 'Local Hinduism'.

The people of Shamirpet worship all the major gods of the Hindu pantheon, but many of their cults distinctly belong to the complex of ritual that can be regarded as peculiar to peninsular India. Some of these observances present variations which are confined only to this particular village.

The Hindu concept of a Trinity, comprising three manifestations of divinity—Brahma, the creator; Vishnu, the sustainer; and Shiva, the destroyer—has an all-India spread, and in common with the Hindus of the other parts of India the residents of Shamirpet principally worship either Shiva, or Vishnu and his numerous incarnations—particularly Rama and Krishna. The concepts of soul (*atma*), of the reckoning of an individual's actions and their consequences on his present and future life (the concept of *karma*), of laying emphasis on the right ordering of life and on doing what is just and moral (concept of *dharma*), of heaven and hell, and finally of the transmigration of the soul and its re-birth also have such an all-India spread; although there are significant regional and local variations in their details. Finally, the nature of rituals connected with the human life-cycle has been very considerably influenced by the Sanskritic ritual of all-India Hinduism, but it still continues to be characterized by some distinctive regional peculiarities.

All over India some rivers are regarded as sacred, and legends and cults grow around them. The Godavari is among the rivers whose sanctity and importance have been enhanced by prominent

94

mention in Hindu scriptures. Being the most important river of the Deccan region its significance is very great to the Hindus of this area.

Along with the great gods of all-India Hinduism the people also continue to observe cults associated with regional and local deities and goddesses. The nature and characteristics of these goddesses differ widely in the different culture-areas of the land. Some of the goddesses listed below are commonly found in the Telugu-speaking areas, particularly in the Telangana districts of Hyderabad. Their main characteristics according to the residents of Shamirpet have also been mentioned.

They are:

1. Pochamma—goddess of smallpox.
2. Mutyalamma—goddess of chickenpox.
3. Balamma—goddess of fertility whose wrath causes sterility in women.
4. Mahakalamma—goddess of cholera.
5. Durgamma—goddess presiding over the destinies and welfare of the village.
6. Maisamma—goddess protecting the village boundaries.

Besides the above, certain other goddesses are also worshipped. Important among them are Ellamma (for the cure of boils), Pinamma (when naming a child after one of his deceased grandparents), and minor goddesses of the fields who protect the crops. To these must be added several other named and unnamed deities and goddesses whose worship is confined only to the village of Shamirpet.

All the characteristics of Hinduism having an all-India spread, described above, are in evidence in the religion of the people of Shamirpet. There is a small Shiva temple near the house of the Brahmin; another with several images on a hillock by the side of the Deshmukh's house. There are two platforms in the village on which the monkey god Hanuman[1] is lodged. In many clean caste houses there are images or pictures of some of these gods. Those

[1] Hanuman, the 'Son of the Winds', was one of the monkey helpers of Rama in his search for Sita when she was abducted by the demon Ravana (according to the epic poem *Ramayana*). Modern tradition seeks to interpret the Monkeys and Bears of this story as the aboriginal inhabitants of the Deccan at the turn of the Christian era.

who have images of deities bathe them every day and make offerings of food. They are often described as 'family' or household gods. The pictures are worshipped on the occasions of festivals. In the neighbouring village of Aliyabad there is a temple of Rama. Besides these, there are several shrines of the village goddesses. Eight of these are important. Two shrines are dedicated to Maisamma—the *Gadi Maisamma* protects the house and dependants of the village headman, and the *Katta Maisamma* lodged near the tank protects the village boundaries and presides over the agricultural prosperity of the community. Pochamma too has two shrines—one near the houses of the Vaddars and another between the living quarters of the Madigas and the Erkalas. The shrine of Dugamma near the village post office is also important. There is one shrine each for Mahakalamma, Mutyalamma, and Pinamma.

People eagerly take the opportunities of attending religious fairs, and of going to holy places for a dip in one of the sacred rivers. The major centre of pilgrimage in the Telugu-speaking parts of Hyderabad is Bhadrachalam where there is an old and impressive temple by the side of Godavari. Those who can afford to and have the inclination go to the other places of pilgrimage having country-wide recognition, such as Allahabad (Prayag) and Benares (Kashi).

3. THE RELIGIOUS YEAR

Three major types of religious ceremonies and festivals are observed in the community; family ceremonies, village ceremonies, and caste ceremonies. The Muslim section of the village population has its own family festivals and some communal ceremonies. As pointed out earlier, they participate with their Hindu neighbours in the observance of common village ritual.

HINDU FESTIVALS

Feasts and fasts form an important part of Hindu religious life. Festivals are spread evenly over the whole year. Apart from village ceremonies, agricultural ritual, and special worships organized by some castes individually, there are several festivals which may be observed by most Hindu families, irrespective of their caste and social status. Important among these are: *Ugadi* (Telugu New Year's Day), *Rama Navami* (birthday of Rama; also regarded as his wedding anniversary), *Toli Ekadashi* (fast in honour of Vishnu), *Nagula Panchami* (worship of the cobra), *Rakhi Purnima* (day for the renewal of the sacred thread), *Krishna Ashtmi* (birthday of Krishna), *Chauti* (birthday of Ganesha, son of Shiva), *Petramasa* (day for offering water to the spirits of the ancestors), *Dasara* (celebration commemorating Arjuna's victory, with the help of Krishna, over the Kauravas), *Deepavali* (celebration commemorating the defeat of the demon king Narkasura at the hands of Krishna), *Til Sankranti* (day of the winter solstice marking the change of season, when days start gradually getting longer), *Shivaratri* (fast in honour of Shiva), and *Holi* (bonfires to commemorate the burning of Kamadeva, the god of love). In addition to these there are some festivals which are observed only by the higher castes, more particularly by the Brahmins, Komtis and Reddis. Important among these are: *Neela Gauri* (worship of Gauri, wife of Shiva, observed by Brahmins only), *Narsimha Jayanti* (day of Vishnu's incarnation as Narsimha—part human and part lion god, observed by Brahmins only), *Shravana Somwar* (Mondays in the Hindu month of Shravana, when Brahmins and Komtis observe a fast), *Ananta Chaturdashi* (the day when Vishnu incarnated himself as Ananta; observed only by Brahmins), *Kartika Purnima* (day for the worship of Gauri, observed only by Brahmin, Komti and Reddi women), *Vasant Panchami* (worship of household gods by Brahmins only), and *Rath Saptami* (worship of the Sun by Brahmins only). Two important agricultural rites observed by the families of cultivators are the First Sowing and the New Eating (Kottalu); each observed twice every year to inaugurate sowing operations and commencing the eating of grain from the freshly harvested crops. Ceremonies organized by the village as a whole are: the *Pochamma* festival (in honour of the goddess of smallpox), the *Batkamma* festival (in honour of Gauri; observed by village women) and the *Maisamma* festival (in honour of the goddess protecting the village boundaries). The different caste groups residing within the village have several caste festivals and ceremonies. For example, on the Dasara day the occupational castes worship their implements; the Gollas—caste of shepherds—have the festivals of Saudamma, Mallamma and Maude-Pochamma, all connected with their traditional occupation, and the untouchable Madigas have cults and related folk-plays concerning Jamavanta, their legendary hero and founder of the caste.

I do not propose to give minute ethnographic details regarding the festivals enumerated above. The brief accounts that follow are intended to illustrate the nature of the festivals and their place in the annual round of activities in the community. The mythological background of these festivals has been recorded from oral tradition and not from Hindu scriptures. Hindu months, according to the Western calendar, would be:

Hindu Month	Corresponding English Months	Hindu Month	Corresponding English Months
Chaitra	March–April	Ashvina	September–October
Vaishakha	April–May	Kartika	October–November
Jyeshta	May–June	Margashirsha	November–December
Ashadha	June–July	Pushya (Pousha)	December–January
Shravana	July–August	Magha	January–February
Bhadrapada	August–September	Phalguna	February–March

The festivals are described in their chronological order:

Ugadi. Ugadi, the Telugu New Year's Day, is an important festival. It is observed on the first day of the Hindu month of Chaitra. Although it is observed by all the Hindu castes generally, its significance for the Brahmins, Komtis, Reddis and the Panch Bramha group is greater.

The day previous to Ugadi the Panch Bramha groups worship their implements and renew their sacred threads, which they alone wear, apart from Brahmins and Komtis.

On the Ugadi day itself people get up early in the morning. Women sweep the courtyard, sprinkle cow-dung mixed in water, and then draw decorative designs with flour or coloured powders. Men go out to collect mango leaves and *neem* (margosa tree, *Azadirachta indica*) twigs; make festoons (*toran*) by stitching these together in a long string, and decorate the front portions of their houses with them. The potters supply each household with two earthen pots: one large, another small enough to act as a lid for the larger. Each family expects these pots from the potter attached to it. All members of the family, except the sick, take their bath on this day, and gather together inside the house. In the room where the gods of the household are lodged the earthen pots are placed in a central position. The large pot is filled with a sweet drink made by mixing jaggery, tamarind pulp, slices of raw mangoes, grated coconut and other spices. It is topped by the smaller pot.

An earthen lamp is lighted and kept near the pot. Vermilion and turmeric paste are applied to the pots. The assembled members of the household then bow down before the images of the gods and pray to them for the prosperity and well-being of the family. If the family does not possess any images, the ceremony is generally performed in the main room of the house and people bow down in front of the pots 'with the thought of the gods in their minds'. A special kind of bread, with a sweet stuffing inside, is made in all well-to-do homes. Among the poorer occupational castes and the untouchables this is not done. Instead they visit the houses to which they are attached and are given a portion of the sweet bread and the drink.

The Brahmin family observes the festival in a more elaborate way. The images are bathed and dressed. Along with these the holy books in the possession of the family are also worshipped.

In the evening people gather together in front of the Desh-mukh's house. All the responsible village elders are expected to be present on the occasion. Also the families of other major agriculturists are represented by one or more persons. The Brah-min consults his almanac and makes predictions for the year. Should they expect bumper crops this year? Or do the stars indi-cate scarcity and famine? Will the year be good for the health of the residents and their cattle? Or is there any apprehension of epidemics? What will be the general price-level in the market? Is there any fear of accidents—of snake-bite, drowning, lightning, etc? These and allied questions are covered by the priest in his forecast. Other questions of popular interest are referred to the Brahmin who tries to answer them on the basis of his astrological calculations. People soon break up into small groups, talk in a reminiscent mood about the years that have gone by, and com-ment upon the shape of things to come as indicated in the Brahmin's predictions.

Rama Navami. This festival is celebrated on the ninth day of the Hindu month of Chaitra. It is observed only by the Brahmins and Komtis, and by a few other enthusiasts belonging to some of the upper castes. Adults keep a 'fast' on this day; but this fast does not necessitate total abstention from all food. Fruit, milk-prepara-tions, sago and cooked tubers can be eaten after the midday wor-ship of Rama. In a fast like this it is necessary to abstain from cereals, lentils, everyday vegetables and common salt. In general

only the adults are expected to observe this fast; but the novelty
of the food which is given to all those who are fasting induces many
children also to undertake it. At midday an image or picture of
Rama, standing in a clean, central part of the main room is worshipped for a short while; offerings of the special food cooked for the
day are placed before it, and all members of the family bow down
to it asking for forgiveness and blessings. Most people break their
fast in the evening to partake of a special meal comprising rich
dishes and delicacies.

Neela Gauri. The observance of this festival is confined only to
Brahmin women. On the third day of the Hindu month of
Vaishakha, a large earthenware pan is filled with several kinds of
soil—such as black earth, red earth, earth from an ant-hill and
manure, and nine different grains are sown into it. The sprouts
are supposed to represent Gauri, wife of Shiva, and are watered
and worshipped daily for a month. Offerings of jaggery and gram
soaked in water are made every day.

Narsimha Jayanti. This festival is observed in honour of Narsimha
—an incarnation of Vishnu in a half-lion, half-human form—on
the fourteenth day of the Hindu month of Vaishakha. In Shamirpet it is observed only by the Brahmin family. Some members of
the family observe a fast on this day. At midday an image or
picture of Narsimha is worshipped and offerings of jaggery and
gram sprouts are made to it.

Toli Ekadashi. Brahmins, Komtis and some Reddis observe this
fast on the eleventh day of Ashadha in honour of Vishnu. In the
Brahmin family all adults are expected to observe this fast; among
others only a few responsible people keep it. Although foods permissible in fasts can be eaten on this day, some people make it a
total fast and do not take any food or water until the evening.
Images of Vishnu and his incarnations are worshipped at home
and at the village shrines; and offerings of coconut, dates and a
preparation of gram and jaggery are made.

Nagula Panchami. On the fifth day in the month of Shravana, this
festival is observed by the Brahmins, Komtis, Reddis and some
other higher castes. On this day *all* Hindus are expected to observe
the taboo which forbids the use of an iron girdle (*tawa*) for making
bread. Even those who do not observe the festival itself refrain
from using one on this day. In the families observing this festival,
generally one adult member of the household fasts until the com-

pletion of the worship of the cobra which takes place some time in the afternoon. Coconut, puffed rice, milk and a preparation of gram and jaggery are all arranged on a plate, and taken to an ant-hill by the person observing the fast. The ant-hill is supposed to be the abode of the cobra. There he lights a lamp and makes an offering of small quantities of the food brought on the plate. While returning home he keeps on dropping a grain or two of puffed rice all the way. A special sweet dish of rice and milk is prepared for the principal meal on this day.

Rakhi Purnima. Observed on the full-moon day in the month of Shravana, this festival has special significance for the Brahmin, the Sale and the Gaondla. All castes wearing the sacred thread change their old threads and wear new ones on this day. Some of the occupational castes, especially the Sale and the Gaondla, tie multicoloured threads to their professional implements. Normal economic and occupational activities are stopped on this day, and a feast comprising some sweet and rich dishes is a special feature of it.

Shravana Somwar. A half-day fast is observed on Mondays in the month of Shravana by the Brahmins and the Komtis. Those who are especially keen may observe a similar half-day fast on Saturdays also. The evening meal on such days almost always includes a sweet dish.

Krishna Ashtami. Observed on the eighth day of the dark fort-night of Shravana, this festival resembles in all essentials that of Rama Navami described earlier. The principal worship takes place at midnight, the hour when Krishna—an incarnation of Vishnu—is believed to have been born. A sweet preparation consisting of jaggery, spices, and herbs—similar to one given to women after childbirth—is distributed at this time among those who attend the midnight worship. On the following day a fast is observed, and is followed by a feast in the evening.

Chauti. Chauti, observed on the fourth day in the month of Bhardrapada, is an important festival. This ceremony is observed in honour of Ganesha, the son of Shiva. On this and the three days that follow there is considerable festivity in the village.

With the exception of the untouchable Malas and Madigas and the semi-tribal Erkalas, in all other Hindu castes this day is celebrated with considerable enthusiasm. Those who can afford to, buy images of Ganesha from the shops in the city; those who cannot, make clay images at home. These idols are placed prominently in the front or central part of the house. The Brahmins and Komtis first clean the place where the idol is to be lodged, besmear it with cow-dung, then spread some soft sand over it. On this sand they place some leaf-plates, spread rice on them and cover the rice with a new cloth. The idol is placed on this cloth. Among the other castes the idol is placed either on a bunch of mango leaves kept on the floor, or else on a wooden seat. A sacred thread is put on the image, and finally it is marked with vermilion and turmeric. With this it comes to possess life as the deity starts residing within it.

A little lamp is lighted and kept burning in front of the image. At the time of the principal worship which differs in various families, flowers of several varieties are placed on and around the image, vermilion and rice (the latter made yellow with turmeric) are sprinkled on it, and *laddus* (little sweet balls of gram fried in syrup) specially made for the day are offered to the deity. When this is done all members of the household bow down before the idol. Many people express their wishes, which they then expect will be fulfilled with the blessings of Ganesha.

The image is allowed to remain in its place for three to twenty-one days, and is worshipped every day. When it is removed from its place, it is taken to the village tank and immersed in water.

Two special features of this festival deserve to be noted. First, some of the occupational castes worship their tools and implements. For example, the washerman applies vermilion and turmeric pastes to the large earthen pot in which he boils the clothes, and also to the stone on which he beats them clean. The barber does the same to his razors and scissors. The weaver worships the paraphernalia of his caste occupation. Secondly, it is believed that seeing the moon on the Chauti day is inauspicious, for anyone who does so may be falsely implicated in theft. But if anyone does see the moon, it is not difficult for him to undo its harmful effects. If he is abused by someone, the ill effect of his having seen the moon can be cleared. Thus in order to be abused by others people seeing the moon on this day indulge in practical jokes and cause offence to them in various ways. In return they are favoured with the abuse which expiates their sin.

Ananta Chaturdashi. Ananta Chaturdashi is observed on the fourteenth day of Bhadrapada by Brahmins only. On this day Vishnu is worshipped. Incense is burnt by putting *ghee* (clarified butter) on a fire in front of Vishnu's image. Two red threads are tied by the Brahmin, first to the arms of the image, and a little later, after being removed therefrom, to his own arm.

Petramasa. The last day of the dark fortnight in the month of Bhadrapada is dedicated to ceremonies in honour of the ancestors and the deceased members of the household. In fact the whole fortnight preceding this day is occupied by this activity, for water must be offered to the dead on the *tithi* (the lunar day corresponding to that of their death). Among the higher castes, if the family can afford it, the Brahmin is invited to officiate at these rites. Those who cannot afford it, and people of the lower castes, manage it themselves. On the Petramasa day itself cooked rice, curds and several other preparations are offered to the deceased members of the lineage. Gifts of money, grain and vegetables are made to the Brahmin and the Jangam.

If there was a death in the family in the preceding year, during the Petramasa fortnight on the lunar day of death, an elaborate rite is performed to call home the spirit of the deceased and lodge it with other ancestor-spirits in one corner of the house. For these rites different branches of a family gather together under one main roof.

The Malas and Madigas as well as Vaddars and Erkalas do not have an elaborate observance. However, the first two make small gifts of money to the Jangam in honour of their dead, if the Jangam visits their houses.

Dasara. This festival is observed in the village both individually and collectively. All Hindus bath early in the morning. The Brahmin and the Komti worship a bunch of *shami* (*Prosopis spicigera*) leaves along with the images of gods; others worship only the deities. Observed on the tenth day of Ashvina, Dasara is regarded as a non-vegetarian festival. With the exception of Brahmins and Komtis, who are vegetarians, the other non-vegetarian castes make it a point to cook some meat dish on this day. At midday people worship the gods in their houses.

In the afternoon the Brahmin visits the Deshmukh's house, and worships a bunch of *shami* leaves and the headman's ancestral weapons. In the meantime a flag is hoisted on the central flag post near the police station. Madigas beat their drums and people start collecting. When all the responsible village elders assemble there the procession starts in the direction of the Hanuman shrine outside the village. The Madiga drum-beaters are at the head of the procession. At some distance from them are the Deshmukh, the Brahmin and the other elders. These are followed by the other villagers. At the shrine the Brahmin worships the *shami* leaves and the goddess Durga. When the worship is over people snatch the leaves. Then follows the important social act of exchange of these leaves and a friendly embrace. Between castes of equal social status and between persons of equal kinship and age status within the caste itself, the exchange is on a basis of equality. For example, A will take a few leaves from B; and B will take a few from A. The two will then lock each other in an embrace for a few seconds. On the other hand, people of high caste will give some leaves to those of the low and untouchable castes; and the latter will respond by bowing down to touch the feet of the former. In the case of the untouchables this is a symbolic gesture, for they touch the earth near the feet of their superiors and not the feet. Within the caste itself the nature of this exchange is determined by the age and kinship status of the persons concerned. As a general rule elders and persons with a recognized superior status give some leaves to the juniors; and the latter, in their turn, bend down to touch the feet of their elders. On this day people are expected to forget their quarrels of the last year, and to meet each other in a spirit of friendship. In fact, many petty differences are forgotten, and several people who were hitherto not on speaking terms resume normal friendly relations again.

Deepavali. Deepavali or the 'festival of lights' is one of the most important Hindu festivals and is observed throughout Hindu India. The celebrations extend to two days—the fourteenth and fifteenth days of the dark fortnight of the month of Ashvina. On the first of these two days, known as *Narka Chaturdashi* or *Bhogi*, Hindus get up very early and have their bath. Women in the higher castes, especially among Brahmins, Komtis and Reddis, take lighted lamps on a plate and, waving them before their husbands, perform the *arati* rite otherwise reserved for gods. This has to be completed before the break of dawn. Later in the day images of gods and deities in the house are worshipped and specially cooked dishes are offered to them. In the evening a large number of little earthen lamps are lighted and arranged in front of the house; in other parts of the house, too, one or more of these lamps are kept. Some people worship Lakshmi, the goddess of wealth, on this night; others do so on the second day. The Komtis, who are a trading caste, regard this worship as the most important in their religious year.

The second day is the day of Deepavali itself. Hindus wasn their cows and bullocks, and put multi-coloured decorative marks on their bodies. Tinkling bells and other decorations are tied round their necks. A gruel is made and served to the cattle on this day. In the evening rows of lighted earthenware lamps are arranged in front of each house; some also being put in other parts of the house. In some families Lakshmi is worshipped on this day.

On both these days delicacies and rich sweet dishes are prepared. There is no fasting, for Deepavali is regarded as a festival for feasting.

Kartika Purnima. This is observed on the full-moon day in the month of Kartika, mostly by the Brahmin, the Komti and some women of other higher castes. Women keeping the fast take their bath early in the morning, apply turmeric paste to their bodies and wear yellow clothes. Later in the day they worship the sacred Tulsi plant (basil) and offer it twenty-one threads, twenty-one flowers (each of a different kind, if possible) and twenty-one garlands. In well-to-do homes the Brahmin priest is invited to officiate at this worship.

Til Sankranti. Sankranti (winter solstice) inaugurates the gradual lengthening of days, and is celebrated by all sections of the Hindu population of the village. While Brahmins, Komtis and Reddis observe it as a *lomulu* (*vrata*) or an occasion for special worship, in the other castes it is just an occasion for feasting.

In the higher-caste families observing special worship on this day, the women take their bath early in the morning. They apply turmeric paste to their bodies. For the worship itself two things have to be done. On a spot swept, cleaned and smeared with cow-dung, five new earthen pots are put. These contain sweet balls of *til* (sesame), pieces of sugar cane, country plums and other available fruit. Nearby, four lumps of cow-dung are placed, forming the corners of a rectangle which are then joined by new thread. Inside the rectangle a fire is lighted, and on it some milk is set to boil. This milk is allowed to overflow, and the direction of overflow is carefully noted. If it flows in a northern or eastern direction it is regarded as auspicious. Later some quantity of rice is cooked in this milk, and a sweetening—sugar or jaggery—is added to it. Small portions of this preparation are offered to the five earthen pots, and to the household gods and ancestor spirits.

In families which do not have this elaborate worship, women cook rice in milk, which is later offered to the household gods. Sweet balls of *til* are made and distributed by all families of means. Meat-eating sections of the population consider it essential to have a rich meat dish on this day. In fact some lower castes, such as the Vaddar, the Erkala, the Mala and the Madiga, do no more than have a meat preparation for their principal meal.

Vasant Panchami and *Rath Saptami*. Observed on the fifth and seventh days respectively in the month of Magha, these festivals have a special significance only to the Brahmins. On *Vasant Panchami* day the images are carefully cleaned and dressed in new clothes. The main worship on this day is that of Shiva. On the *Rath Saptami* day, on the other hand, the Sun is the principal god to be worshipped. In addition to the Sun, Vishnu and the Tulsi plant are also venerated.

Shivaratri. With the exception of a few Reddis, all Hindus in Shamirpet observe this festival in honour of Shiva on the four-teenth day of the dark fortnight of Magha. A day prior to the festival the Hindus clean their houses. On the Shivaratri day itself they get up early in the morning. Men take their bath, women sweep the courtyard, sprinkle on it water mixed with cow-dung and make decorative designs with flour or coloured powders. After finishing this they too have their bath. Clothes and household linen are also washed. Those who can afford to, put on new clothes on this day.

This is an important fast. Those who observe it are not supposed to eat or drink anything until the worship, which takes place late in the afternoon at about 4 p.m., is over. For this worship most of the clean castes go to the village shrine where there is a Shiva *lingam*. Each family is represented by one or two responsible adults; women go only when there is no male member in the house. They take with them, on a plate, a coconut, a cucumber, boiled sweet potatoes and a preparation of gram and jaggery. These are offered to Shiva at the shrine. After bending down in front of the symbol of Shiva the people return home with their plates and the food offerings. Now they can eat, but their food must not contain everyday preparations of cereals and curries. Mostly they eat boiled sweet potatoes and cucumber. Some of the lower castes, especially the barber, the washermen, the Vaddar and the Erkala, do not go to this Shiva shrine; but instead they go to a deserted shrine outside the village. Although this shrine has no *lingam*, they make their offerings here. On the other hand, untouchable Malas and Madigas do not go to any shrine, and make their offerings of food in the name of Shiva in some corner of their houses.

Most people consider it desirable to keep awake for the whole night following. None should go to bed until midnight at least. For this reason a programme of dramatic performances, or of singing devotional songs, is invariably arranged by a group of village youths.

Holi. Holi is the last major Hindu festival of the year. It is observed on the full-moon day in the month of Phalguna. Five days before the festival there is a sudden burst of activity among the village youths and boys, who start collecting wood and piling it up in a central place in the village. Stealing of fuel—especially wood and cow-dung cakes—is socially approved; and the young people show considerable ingenuity in this respect. By the Holi day they arrange a sufficiently large pile of this fuel, to be able to light a really big bonfire. As the prestige of the village youth depends on the size of the bonfire, they work hard to make it impressive.

In the evening at about 7 p.m. the Madigas beat their drums and go round the village collecting more fuel from the residents. It is all systematically arranged and the pile is made ready for burning at the auspicious moment, previously fixed. The carpenter makes a crude wooden image of Kamadeva (the god of love) and places it on the pyre. Between 9 p.m. and 10 p.m. the Madigas start beating their drums near the pyre. Women begin to come to the spot, bringing in their hands plates with burning earthen lamps and several preparations of food. On this day the Brahmin officiates for his own caste as well as for the Komtis; and the Kummari (potter) officiates for the rest of the community. In fact, the Kummari dominates the scene. When the Kummari women have brought their food offerings and placed them near the pyre, the headman of the potter's caste worships Kamadeva and offers small portions from these plates. The Brahmin does the same on behalf of the two twice-born castes of the Brahmins and the Komtis. The Kummari goes round taking little bits from the plates of all

107

the others and offers them to the god of love. Imitating the ritual of cremation, then, the Kummari goes round the pyre thrice sprinkling water, sets fire to it and breaks the earthen pot. Men make a funny imitation of the sounds made at the time of the funeral and the crowd bursts into loud laughter. People wait for an hour or so and go home with some ashes from the pyre. They must be careful, for the young men of the village are still active, and such objects as wooden bedsteads, fences, doors and logs of wood are eagerly sought by them and thrown into the burning pyre.

Next morning Madiga drum-beaters and village watchmen go from house to house and beg for money. People start playing *holi*. Until mid-day they throw dust, mud, cow-dung and earth at one another. Those standing in joking relationships with each other often engage in vigorous jest and banter. The singing of vulgar songs by men is permitted. At midday people bath and take their meal. Later in the afternoon they play *holi* again; but this time they only throw coloured powders and coloured water at each other.

New Eating. Twice every year, after each harvest, the 'New Eating' ceremony is arranged to initiate the eating of grain from the recently harvested crop. No particular day is fixed for it, and each family arranges it according to its own convenience. New paddy from the recently harvested crop is mixed with some old paddy, and is pounded and husked. If a family has no new paddy —and many non-agriculturists and agricultural labourers often do not—they borrow it from a neighbour. After being husked the rice is cooked and sweetened with jaggery. This is then offered to the gods and ancestor-spirits in the house, and later eaten by the members of the family. Prior to this ceremony, the eating of any grain from the new crop is forbidden by custom.

Muslim Festivals. Before coming to the common village festivals, it is necessary to describe briefly the festivals of the Muslims. With regard to religion and ritual the Muslim element in the village population has a separate identity of its own.

The Muslims observe seven important festivals. They are *Moharram*, *Meelad Sharif*, *Giarwin Sharif*, *Shabe Miraj*, *Shabe Barat*, *Ramzan* and *Id-uz-zuha*. These festivals follow the Muslim calendar, and unlike the Hindu festivals, which always occur in the same season, their time varies from year to year.

Moharram. On the tenth day in the month of Moharram, Imam Hussain, the grandson of Mohammed, was put to death in the plains of Karbala after being denied food and water for three days. Moharram is observed in honour of this martyr and his associates. On the Moharram day symbols of Imam Hussain and his family, known as *alums*, are taken out by the Muslims in a procession to a nearby river or tank. All along the route they beat their breasts and cry aloud 'O, son of Ali' or 'Hassan, Hussain' and wail over the martyr's death. *Tajia* or large paper models of his tomb are also taken out and immersed in water. In all Muslim households a sweet drink either of water and sugar, or of milk and sugar, is prepared and distributed among friends and relations. The giving of alms and charity on this day is believed to contribute greatly towards ensuring one's future.

Meelad Sharif. Unlike Moharram, which calls for mourning, Meelad Sharif is an occasion for rejoicing, as the Prophet Mohammed was born on the twelfth day of the month of Rabi-ul-Awwal. On the eleventh and twelfth days of this month people observe a fast. Muslim priests visit their homes, and passages from the Koran are read. Flowers and sweets are distributed in the name of Mohammed. The celebrations are continued for a month; although the festivities are at their peak on the two days mentioned above.

Giarwin Sharif. This is an important festival for the Sunni sect of the Muslims. It is observed in honour of Abdul Kader Geelani who belonged to Mohammed's generation, and was regarded as a very pious and holy figure. On the eleventh day of the month of Rabi-us-sani, the Muslims of Shamirpet fly the flag of Abdul Kader on their houses, and offer sweets, flowers and prayers in the name of their hero.

Shabe Miraj. On the twenty-sixth day of Rajjub, accompanied by an angel, Mohammed is believed to have visited the seven heavens and hell. Later it is said that he had an audience with Allah himself. To celebrate this event, this day is expected to be spent in meditation and prayer. If possible people keep awake for the whole night saying prayers and asking for Allah's blessings.

Shabe Barat. On the night of the fourteenth day of Shaban, Muslims offer sweets and bread in the name of their deceased kin. They visit their graves and offer flowers and prayers. It is believed that on this day the spirits of the dead come out to see their relations and to receive presents from them. Later all Muslims—men and women (if they are not in their menstrual period)—say their prayers and ask for God's blessing for their long life. Also they read the Koran. This night is important in that it is now that Allah determines the course of the lives of his followers for the coming year.

Ramzan. Ramzan is the most important month in the religious year of the Muslims. As far as possible, people try to fast for the whole month. They can have food before dawn and after dusk, but in between even a drop of water is not permitted. During these days one should devote as much time as possible to meditation and prayer. The twenty-sixth day of the month is specially important because it was on this day that 'Mohammed received the Koran from Allah'. People wear new clothes on this day, read the Koran and say their prayers. There is considerable enthusiasm in evidence as all Muslims—men, women and children—say their prayers and seek God's blessings. The month-long fasting ends on the day they see the new moon. The next day is spent in festivity and is known as 'Id-ul-fitr'. People breakfast early and wear their best—possibly new—clothes. The men go to the mosque for their Id prayers. After the prayers they go round to their friends' houses meeting and greeting them. On this day and on the two days following a sweet preparation consisting of vermicelli, milk and dates is made, and portions of it are sent to friends and relations. It is desirable that those who can afford it should distribute 2½ seers of grain per head to the poor and the needy.

Id-uz-zuha. This festival is celebrated on the tenth day of the month of Zilhij. People get up early in the morning and without breakfast go to the mosque for their prayers. When they return home they sacrifice goats in the name of God. The general rule is that one goat is sacrificed in the name of each member of the family; but if this is not possible financially, a goat each may be sacrificed for each adult member of the household. Of course, even this is too much for many of the poorer Muslims, who sacrifice just one goat on behalf of the whole family. The meat of the sacrificed animals is cooked and people have their breakfast. Then they go round to meet and greet their friends. Delicacies and meat dishes are prepared in fairly large quantities and distributed among friends and relations.

Village Festivals

In the foregoing pages we have briefly described the major family festivals of the Hindus and Muslims. Some of the Hindu festivals, particularly Dasara and Holi, are partly communal also, as at one stage the entire Hindu section of the village community participate in them. In the Dasara procession several Muslims also join in. Hindus do not spare their Muslim friends from the Holi colour-throwing. Similarly, Hindus co-operate in the Moharram procession of the Muslims. On the Id day Muslims meet all their friends—Muslim and Hindu alike. But there are some festivals which must be described as 'village festivals' as they do not occur in the regular religious calendar of the Hindus and Muslims; and are generally celebrated by the village community as a whole. The festivals of Pochamma, Batkamma and Maisamma are important celebrations in this category. Pochamma and Maisamma festivals are observed by the village as a whole. Batkamma festival is observed by the Hindu women of the village. The untouchable Mala and Madiga women who cannot join the groups of clean-caste women observe it separately. To these must be added the fair of Jalal Miyan which is sponsored by the Muslims but is largely attended by the Hindus also.

Pochamma Festival. The annual worship of Pochamma, the goddess of smallpox, is organized by the village community on a Thursday or Saturday in the month of Shravana. The actual day for the ceremony is fixed by the village elders in consultation with the Deshmukh and the Brahmin priest.

A day previous to the celebration the Madiga drum-beaters go round the village announcing the programme for the morrow and asking the people to get ready. The Kummaris clean the shrines of Pochamma, Mutyalamma and Mahakalamma. The Sakalis (washermen) whitewash them. Village youth construct small leaf sheds in front of the shrines. Wives of the Talaris (village menials) sweep and besmear with red earth the ground around these booths.

Early next day people start making preparations for the worship. It is necessary that every family prepares its *bonam* for the day. For this they cook rice in a new earthenware pot obtained from the potter; remove all soot from the exterior of the pot, apply vermilion and turmeric paste to it on all sides, and then close its mouth. This decorated pot containing rice is known as *bonam*.

Most people prepare it in their homes; but some prefer to do so near the shrine itself.

Early in the afternoon the Madigas go to their own Pochamma shrine, which is near to but quite separate from that of the other shrine belonging to the rest of the community, and offer their *bonams* to the goddess. They worship her, and sacrifice goats, sheep and fowls. Some are possessed by the goddess at this time. But they have to hurry back as their presence is required for the procession of the other castes. In the meantime the Kummari (potter) who officiates as the village priest for this ceremony goes round the village collecting from every house oil for burning lamps near the shrine, and rice for preparing the *bonam* on behalf of the whole village. The rice thus collected is cooked by the Kummari women in a huge pot near the shrine.

An hour before the scheduled time for worship, the Madigas start beating their drums at a central place in the village. People start collecting there with their *bonams*. Some carry these on their heads; others take them to the shrine in bullock carts. The Madiga drum-beaters walk at the head of the procession, followed at some distance by the Deshmukh and other respectable people and village elders, and then by the common people of the village. By the time they reach the shrine some people are possessed by the goddess. At the shrine, the Kummari first offers rice from the common village *bonam* to the goddess. After doing this he withdraws himself from the scene for a short while to enable the Brahmin and the Komti to make offerings from their *bonams*. Then the Kummari firmly establishes himself as the priest, and offers rice from the *bonams* of all other castes. In this, precedence is given to superior castes in a very rigid way. One after another, castes lower to each other in the traditional hierarchy are called upon to come forward to make their offerings. Within a caste itself, people occupying a superior status in respect of their position in the village organization, age and wealth are given precedence over the less favourably placed members of their group. This often creates difficulties, and is instrumental in causing tensions and enmities between different castes or between different families of the same caste. Alongside the offerings of rice; goats, sheep and fowls are sacrificed on behalf of the different families. The Golla shepherds present a specified number of goats and sheep every year to the community which are now sacrificed on behalf of the entire village. The head and the forelimbs of the sacrificed animal are left in front of the shrine; the rest of it, along with the *bonam*, is carried home by each family, and when all the sacrifices are over the people return home and feast on the rice and meat.

Muslims also participate in this festival. They do not believe in any Hindu gods, but are as afraid of the village gods and goddesses as the Hindus. However, they do not participate in the worship; sacrifices on their behalf are made by the barber or the washerman.

Batkamma Festival. The first nine days of the month of Ashvina are observed as days of festivity with singing and dancing and the worship of Gauri by the Hindu women of the village. Women from the two highest castes, i.e. Brahmin and Komti, do not participate in the dancing, although on the last day they too go out for the final worship with the rest of the village women. Similarly, women from 'respectable' families refuse to join in the dance; and, being untouchables, Mala and Madiga women cannot join the clean-caste women in their dance. Thus the two highest and the two lowest castes keep away from the major part of these celebrations, and so also do the women from urbanized and respectable families. The mythological background of the festival is not clearly understood by anyone: all they know is that during this period Gauri, the wife of Shiva, was piqued by her husband, and that it is to please her that they dance.

For the first seven days women mostly dance in small groups in their respective living-quarters and lanes. On the last two days women from different quarters of the village form small parties of twelve to thirty and dance in front of all the important houses; for this they get small presents of grain or money. In the evening at about 4 p.m. they arrange various kinds of flowers into beautiful designs on their plates and proceed in a procession towards the tank. At this time Brahmin and Komti women also join them. Near the tank these plates containing flowers are placed on the ground in the centre and the women dance around them. In this dance the Brahmin and Komti women do not participate. When the dance is over the flowers are immersed in water. Then a small portion of a sweet dish prepared with gram and jaggery is also put in the water and the women return home. This is done on the eighth and ninth days, which are the last days of the festival.

Maisamma Festival. Maisamma protects the village boundaries and ensures the fertility of the fields. An elaborate ceremony is performed in her honour whenever the crops are very good and demand an expression of special gratitude. This festival is not an annual feature in the life of the community and is celebrated only every three or five years.

The days for the celebration are fixed by the village elders after mutual consultation and agreement. The details are often finalized by the village council, which also decides the basis on which subscriptions will be raised from the different families in the village. When there are only a few days left for the festival, preparations for it are taken in hand under the supervision of some enthusiastic youths. For this festival several castes living in the village have to make their special contributions. For example, the Kummaris contribute the earthen pots and officiate as the priest; the Sakalis (washermen) whitewash the Maisamma shrine; the Mangalis (barbers), along with the Sakalis, sacrifice the goats, sheep and fowls; the Wadlas (carpenters) contribute the flag-posts; the Kammaris (blacksmiths) provide the iron fitting to these posts; the Sale (weavers) give cloth for the flags; the Darzi tailors the flag; the Gaondlas (toddy-tappers) provide the fermented palm-juice required for the worship; the Gollas (shepherds) have to contribute the goats and sheep for sacrifice on behalf of the entire village; and finally the Madigas play their musical instruments. The agriculturists provide the funds. Brahmins and Komtis, being vegetarians and averse to animal sacrifice, pay their share of the subscription, but otherwise keep away from the festival. The Muslims contribute towards its expenses and are present at the time of worship.

The festival lasts three days. On the first day an earthen pot is filled with fermented palm juice, marked with vermilion and turmeric, and carried in a procession to the Maisamma shrine to the accompaniment of Madiga drums and pipes. The Kummari officiating as the priest offers it to the goddess and distributes it later among the people present there. On the second day families of agriculturists, as well as some others, cook rice near the shrine and offer it to Maisamma. The third day is reserved for the final worship and for the making of sacrifices. People go in a procession to the shrine led by Madiga drum beaters. The Kummari burns incense, and sacrifices on behalf of the village the goats and sheep contributed by the Gollas. The animals are killed by the Sakali and the Mangali, but their heads and forelimbs are offered to the goddess by the Kummari. This is followed by sacrifices on behalf of families who, in fulfilment of a promise or in anticipation of a favour from the goddess, have brought a goat, sheep or fowl to be sacrificed. At this time some people become possessed by the goddess and go into a trance. Late in the evening the people return home and have a feast of rice, meat and other delicacies.

Urs of Jalal Miyan. Village Muslims have a tradition for holding semi-religious fairs in honour of holy persons who have had some association with their locality and who have given proof of their supernatural powers by doing some minor miracles. Every winter the Muslims of Shamirpet arrange a fair near the tomb of Jalal Miyan, a local Muslim divine. On the day of the fair a green cloth is spread on the tomb and green flags are hoisted near it. Shop-keepers from Shamirpet and nearby villages set up their shops on the open ground nearby. When people assemble there in the after-noon, incense is burnt near the tomb and flowers and food are offered to Jalal Miyan. The Mulla reads from the Muslim scrip-tures. If possible Muslim singers are invited from the city to sing religious songs. On this day also some persons are possessed. People having difficulties or some pressing problems seek remedies and solutions from those who are possessed by the spirit of Jalal Miyan. The fair sometimes includes a programme of country sports, acrobatic feats, singing by young men of the village, and even dramatic performances. Although it is primarily a Muslim fair, Hindus attend it in large numbers.

Analysis of this summary survey of the religious year in the com-munity reveals that the Hindus and the Muslims have two practically independent ritual systems, which have very few points of contact. Muslims participate in the common village ritual, but they do not actually perform any worship. However, most of them share with the Hindus the general belief-pattern associated with these cults. On a social basis, the Muslims join in the Dasara pro-cession of the Hindus; the latter join in the Muslims' Moharram procession. The two groups participate almost equally in Jalal Miyan's fair; but the Hindus do so not for a religious motive, but for the sake of the fun that they expect to find in the fair. A closer examination of the Hindu festivals and ceremonies reveals that a large number of all-India Hindu festivals are observed in the community; but a good many of these are restricted to the 'twice born' castes of the Brahmin and the Komti. Some of them are observed by a few other higher castes, or often only by a few 'respectable' families in these castes. Ceremonies and worship connected with these festivals are conducted by the Brahmin in castes occupying a level higher than that of the Sakali and the Mangali (excluding the Panch Bramha group). The Sakali and the Mangali invite the Brahmin if they can afford it, or else they manage with a caste priest. While the Brahmin and the Komti, of all the castes, are most interested in a majority of the festivals of this category, in the common village ritual they are passive and distant observers. In the two major festivals of the village, which involve considerable inter-caste co-operation, it is the Kummari who officiates as the priest and not the Brahmin. The bulk of Hindus celebrate relatively few of the all-India festivals with great enthusiasm, but it could be said that groups occupying higher rungs in the ladder of caste hierarchy are found to observe more of these festivals. In fact the higher the status of a caste the greater is the number of these that it observes; and thus we find the Komtis observing more of these festivals than any other Hindu caste, with the sole exception of the Brahmin who, being of a superior caste, observes a few festivals more than the Komti. The local village cults are still living and vital. In them the participation of the two highest castes is nominal; but that of the other castes complete. The Kapu group of agricultural castes occupying an intermediate position in the caste hierarchy participate in both sets of rituals with equal enthusiasm.

4. RITUAL OF THE LIFE CYCLE

The basic pattern of ceremonies connected with the major crises of life is the same in all sections of the Hindus in the village community; but in the minor details of the ritual there is considerable difference in the practices of different castes. More than this, even within a particular caste the rites and observances are not identical, for in some respects individual families have their own traditions. In the course of our field-work we found the cataloguing of these variant customs quite a stimulating, though somewhat tedious, task; but a full ethnographic record of them will be out of place here, and only a broad outline of the essentials will be presented, to illustrate their place in the socio-religious life of the Hindus. As the Muslims differ from the Hindus vitally in respect of their *rites de passage* their observances will be described separately.

Birth. On the birth of a child the mother, as well as other members of the family, is ritually impure. On the third or fifth day after the birth the *purudu* rites are performed which remove the ritual impurity of all members of the family except the mother. The mother continues to be ritually impure for twenty-one to thirty days. On the twenty-first day—in some castes on the thirtieth day—the name-giving ceremony of the child takes place. The mother is bathed. The child's head is shaved, and it is put in a cradle. If it is the first child, or the first son, relations from other villages are also invited to participate in the name-giving ceremony. Friends and neighbours from the village itself are always invited. Women sing songs suitable for the occasion. If an ancestor is believed to have taken re-birth the newborn is named after him; otherwise the elders, after mutual consultation or at the suggestion of an important and influential relation, decide upon a name for the child. The name is announced to the assembly of men and women present. Singing is continued for some time longer. The ceremony ends with a feast for relations and some very special friends.

The Brahmin may be consulted for his astrological predictions regarding the future of the child, and also regarding the implications of the position of the stars at the time of birth for the members of the family. On this occasion the Komtis, the Reddi agriculturists as well as other higher caste Hindus with urban contacts may also invite him. Women from the barber's caste act as midwives among all the clean castes; untouchables manage with experienced women from their respective castes. Services of four other castes are essential: the barber for shaving the child's head, the washerman for washing the linen and clothes before the twenty-first day ceremony, the potter for the supply of new pots for ritual purification, and Madigas for playing musical instruments. Payments for these services are prescribed by tradition; and are both in cash and kind.

Among the Muslims an expectant mother is sent for the birth of her first child to her parents; subsequent deliveries generally take place in her own home. During her confinement she is attended by a professional midwife. An amulet is often tied to the mother's waist to facilitate delivery. Within a few hours of its birth the child is bathed and clothed. His grandfather or an elderly relation says the prayers. A date is then dipped in honey and a drop or two of that honey is put into the mouth of the newborn child. Milk should not be given to the child before this has been done. On the sixth day the *chhatti* ceremony is performed. For this relations from both mother's and father's side are invited. They bring with them gifts for the child, comprising of sets of new clothes, dolls and playthings and possibly a silver spoon. The child is dressed in new clothes. On the seventh day its head is shaved, and the elders give it a name. Depending on the means of the family, feasts are given to friends and relations on the sixth and seventh days, The mother continues to be out of the normal round of life for forty days. On the fortieth day she is bathed. The midwife is given her remuneration on this day. Once again there is a feast, and presents may be given both to the child and to the mother.

Pre-puberty Rites. Among the Hindus, the Brahmin and the Komti perform the sacred thread ceremony for the boys before they attain puberty. At these rites the Brahmin priest officiates. The Panch Bramha group of artisan castes also perform this rite; but they do not invite the Brahmin. Their caste-priest conducts the ceremony.

In the Muslim community a boy must be circumcised any time between the age of two and ten. A few relations are invited for the occasion, the boy is garlanded and then the operation is performed. It is usual to give small presents to the boy at this time. Another pre-puberty rite is the *bismilla* ceremony done both for boys and girls. This initiates the child's religious instruction, for from now on it is taught the alphabet and is gradually enabled to read the Koran. In Shamirpet the *bismilla* ceremony is performed for all Muslim children, though relatively few of them learn to read the holy book.

Puberty Rites. Among the Hindus the girl's first menstruation is attended by elaborate ceremonies. She is secluded for five days, and at the end of this period is bathed and dressed in new clothes.

For three to ten days the household gods, as well as those at the family's favourite shrine, are worshipped. For the latter the girl is taken out with the village women in a procession, and the Madigas are summoned to play their musical instruments. With the exception of the Brahmin and the Komti, in all other castes the women from the neighbourhood assemble every afternoon for singing and dancing at the house of the girl for whom the ceremony is being performed. Among the Muslims, at the time of first menstruation the girl is secluded for seven to eleven days. At the end of this period she is given new clothes, which she wears after taking her bath.

Ear and nose boring of the girls is done before the age of puberty among both the Hindus and the Muslims. But this act has no religious rites attached to it.

Marriage. In the community people are as a rule married when they are adults; only in some cases are adolescents married. Child-marriage is rare. Out of 380 first marriages investigated by us, only 14 could be described as child-marriages.

Among the Hindus, negotiated marriages are common. People show an unmistakable preference for cross-cousin marriage when the subject is discussed with them; but out of the 340 Hindu marriages analysed by us, only 18% were cross-cousin marriages, the rest being negotiated marriages into unrelated families. Muslims permit both parallel and cross-cousin marriages, and indeed regard them as highly desirable. Our sample of Muslim marriages is not quite adequate, but out of 40 marriages fully investigated 19 were between cousins. Among the agriculturists, and to a lesser extent among others, it is necessary for the girl's parents to pay a dowry to the boy. This accounts for the relatively few marriages by service. When the parents of the boy are too poor even to arrange for the normal expenses of an average wedding—involving expenditure on the buying of clothes and ornaments for the bride and bridegroom, marriage feasts and other incidental expenses—the boy may serve with his prospective father-in-law for a stipulated period, at the end of which the latter marries him to his daughter at his own expense. Marriages by exchange may be arranged between two families to economize on the dowry; and further they may be celebrated at the same time so as to complete two weddings for the expense of one. Cases of run-away marriages occur at times, but they are regarded as breaches of the established rules of society and treated accordingly.

It is difficult to summarize the rites and observances involved in a Hindu marriage, for they differ greatly from caste to caste, and from family to family. Here only a very general outline can be given.

The wedding takes place in the bride's house, on an auspicious day fixed by the two parties on the advice of the Brahmin priest. The bridegroom's party, consisting of relations and friends, leave their village in good time to arrive in the bride's village at least a day before the actual date of the marriage. On arrival they are received with great ceremony by the bride's people, and are lodged in a house kept vacant and clean for their use. In the courtesies that are exchanged it is necessary to make some special effort to keep the bridegroom's mother and sisters pleased for any dissatisfaction to them is likely to lead to trouble which may hold up further rites. While the bridegroom's party try to settle down in their house, the bride's people finalize the arrangements for the first dinner. When everything is ready word is sent to the bridegroom's party. After the dinner nothing remains to be done on that day. The guests return to their temporary abode; the hosts get busy to make everything ready for the rites of the next day. When the next day arrives, the bride's mother and other female relations carry water and twigs to the groom's mother and other guests so that 'they may wash their mouths'. A little later breakfast is sent to them. The first major rite for the day is the worship of the bride's *kula-devata* or family god. In this both the bride and the bridegroom participate. The second major rite is known as *lagnam*, which must be performed at an auspicious hour determined by the Brahmin on the basis of his astrological calculations. The bride's party go in a procession to bring the guests to the marriage shed. At the appointed hour the *lagnam* is performed by chanting religious verses. The bridegroom ties a necklace of black beads round the bride's neck. This necklace symbolizes her married status, and she should not be without it unless she is widowed. He also puts rings on the second toes of her feet. Before the tying of *mangalsutra* (black beads) the two have to promise to stand by each other through all phases of life, for the mutual satisfaction of bodily, economic and spiritual needs. But the marriage is not yet complete. To put the seal of religious authority on it, the important rite of *seshahoman* must be performed. For this the bride and bridegroom are seated before a fire, sacred verses are read, and incense is burnt. This completes the marriage. Later the bride and bridegroom are seated facing each other for dinner. The ground around the wooden seats on which they sit is decorated with multi-coloured designs. While eating the two are encouraged to throw a few morsels into each other's plates. Several minor rites follow. In one the newly-married couple are asked to address each other by using personal names. The bride has to show great reluctance in doing this, for a wife generally does not utter the name of her husband. She is given a doll, symbolizing a child, and is asked to entrust it to the care of 'its father' on the pretext that she has to cook or to do other household work. The next day, after a few minor rituals, the girl is 'given away' to her husband and his parents. This is done to the accompaniment of heart-rending and pathetic songs. The father asks her to regard the home of her father-in-law henceforward as her own home; and never to do anything—in thought, word or deed—that might bring discredit to her parents. He then begs the girl's father-in-law to treat her well, to ignore her faults, failings and shortcomings, and to teach her the ways of their family. The girl goes away with her husband. In her new home she has to go through a series of rites, worship of the family god and feasting. After three to seven days she returns to her parents for a brief stay.

Among all the castes the general tone of marriage ritual suggests the influences of Sanskritic rites, but the Brahmin does not officiate at the marriages of all castes. He is invited by the Komti, the agricultural castes, the Kummari, the Golla, the Sale and the Gaondla. The barber and the washerman invite the Brahmin if they can afford it, otherwise they manage with their own caste-priest. The Panch Bramha group has its own priests. The other groups occupying lower positions in the caste hierarchy invite a specialist from their own caste to officiate at the ceremony. Naturally recitation of sacred verses and marriage formulae from the scriptures is confined to ceremonies conducted by the Brahmin; in the other castes, while the pattern followed is essentially the same, the Sanskrit chants are absent. Other occupational castes whose co-operation is required in the ceremony are: the barber, the potter, the Madiga and the carpenter. The barber assists the parties during negotiations, carries their messages, distributes invitations, offers his occupational services in matters of haircutting and shaving, and at the wedding itself, at the time of important rites during the night, holds a lighted torch. The potter supplies the large quantity of earthenware needed for the different rituals as well as for cooking. No marriage ceremony can be performed without the essential instrumental music played by the Madigas. The carpenter has to make the marriage-post, and other wooden fixtures as well, if they are required. The marriage rites require small payments to these occupational castes in the course of the ceremony itself. At the completion of the ceremony, depending on the means of the family, they are paid once again for their labours.

Divorce and widow re-marriage are allowed in all castes except the Brahmin and the Komti. Divorce or 'driving away the wife' is not very common. In the 380 marriages studied by us there were only 79 cases of desertion and divorce. In all such cases the elders, the village council and the caste council intervene and the parties involved in the dispute have to abide by their decisions. Brahmins do not conduct the re-marriage of widows. Polygyny is permitted among the Hindus; but it is rare. At the time of our investigation there were only seven polygynous Hindu homes in the village.

Among the Muslims the standard marriage ritual prescribed by Islam is adhered to with some regional and local variations. Marriage negotiations are initiated by the boy's people, and when they are successful a date for the *nikah* (rites of marriage) is fixed by them in consultation with a Muslim marriage priest. Four days before the actual wedding preliminary rites are started. The ceremony opens with the rite of *manjah* in which the womenfolk of the two sides grind turmeric in their respective homes, and playfully throw turmeric and coloured water on each other in their separate groups. On the second day the groom's people go to the bride's home with gifts for her. These gifts include jewellery, clothes and bangles. The bride is then garlanded by a responsible person from the groom's side; and a little later, with her mother's permission, *missi* (a thick black paste) is applied to her lips and teeth. This symbolizes the actual beginning of the wedding rites. On the third morning, the bride's people (with the exception of her mother) go to the groom's place. They take presents for the bridegroom, and he is garlanded by a younger sister or cousin of the bride. The girl and the boy are seated opposite each other, but are separated by a screen. The bride's sister or cousin asks the groom to extend his hand towards her so that she may apply *henna* (a perfumed paste) to his index finger. He refuses to do this unless she promises to be his slave. When he does give her his finger, she catches hold of it, and lets go of it only when he promises to be her slave. Later turmeric paste is applied to the bride and she is attired in her bridal clothes. At the appointed time the groom is brought on a horse or in a decorated carriage by his people in a procession. The bridegroom finds the main entrance closed. It is opened by the bride's brothers when small gifts are offered to them. The *kazi*, Muslim priest, solemnizes the marriage by reading the prescribed words of *nikah*. The signature of the bridegroom is obtained on a document which embodies all the terms of the marriage contract, including the *mehar* (alimony) which he will have to pay if he leaves his wife. While this is being done the bride remains inside. Her father and some responsible elders then go to her and say, 'You are being married to X, with a *mehar* fixed at Rs. —. Are you willing to be his wife?' Her consent is necessary; although she often indicates it not by saying 'yes' but by crying. The bridegroom's mother puts a necklace of black beads around the bride's neck, and a nose-ring in her nose. Ceremonies of fun and frolic follow. The two are seated on a decorated bed, but a screen is held between them, and they throw rice at each other. Then the screen is removed and a mirror is placed between the two. The groom is asked to read some passages from the Koran and to see the reflection of his wife's face in the mirror. Later the bride is given away ceremonially by her parents to the head of the bridegroom's family. The procession for going home is formed by the groom's party, and the newly-married couple are taken in a decorated carriage. More rites follow at the bridegroom's house, where the two have to wash each other's feet. During all these days feasting goes on, to which friends and relations are invited. On the final day an elaborate feast is given. Later, in a day or two, the bride is taken back to her parents' home. There the bridegroom's people are received with great courtesy and are given an impressive feast.

Islam permits polygyny, and a man can have up to four wives. In Shamirpet, however, there were only three polygynous Muslim homes in a total Muslim population of 340, at the time of our investigations. Their social system and usage permit divorce, and clauses pertaining to alimony are embodied in the written marriage contract. In actual practice, in all cases of desertion and 'running away' these conditions are not adhered to very strictly, and compensation when paid is substantially less than the figure mentioned in the contract. As pointed out earlier the marriage rites are conducted by the *kazi*, who is invited from the city for this purpose.

Death. Both Hindus and Muslims understand the physiological causes of death. It is generally attributed to natural causes, such as disease or old age; but in all cases where the circumstances or manner of death are unusual it is attributed to supernatural factors, such as wrath of gods and ancestor-spirits, witchcraft and black magic.

Among all the Hindu castes, the dead children are buried. The Brahmin and the Komti as a rule cremate their dead, except in cases of death from snake-bite and smallpox. Among the other higher castes both cremation and burial are practised. It is usual to cremate the aged as well as the rich and the influential. In the lower castes such as the Sakali, the Mangali and the Erkala, as well as among the untouchable Malas and Madigas, burial is more common. Soon after a death, word is sent round to relations and friends in the village and also in the neighbouring villages. The corpse is washed, clothed and tied on to a wooden or bamboo bier. It is covered with a new cloth, and decorated with flowers. If the family can afford it Madigas are called to play their musical instruments, which they do walking at the head of the procession. The bier is carried by four people on their shoulders. As they proceed slowly towards the graveyard or the cremation ground, people keep on repeating some solemn slogans, such as 'the name of God alone is true' or 'be truthful and your salvation will be assured'. When a person is to be cremated, his or her son, or in the absence of a son a younger brother or some other near kin, carries an earthen pot with fire in it. Midway between the house and the burial ground the bier is placed on the earth for a few minutes' 'rest', and then carried on. Before putting it on the funeral pyre or in the grave, the son, or a near relation of the deceased, goes round the pyre (or grave) three times sprinkling water all around it. The body is then put on the pyre with the bier, or is taken from it and put in the grave. A near kinsman sets fire to the pyre, or puts a few handfuls of earth in the grave. In the case of a burial all persons present at the spot take a hand in filling the grave. When the pyre is burnt half-way, or when the grave is filled up, the people return home, bathing on the way.

What happens to the soul of the dead? If the death is on an auspicious day and time, the soul goes straight to the Supreme Being; ordinarily it hovers round the house—mainly on the roof, above the main entrance—for eleven to thirteen days. This is the stereotype description; but further analysis reveals a rather diffused belief-pattern: (i) near the place of burial or cremation the person dwells in a ghost-like form; (ii) the soul goes to God, where according to the deeds of the deceased in his life-time it is sent to heaven or hell; (iii) it takes re-birth, often within a few days of the death—as a human being or in some other species; (iv) it can be called back through prescribed ritual to reside with the other ancestor-spirits in the house. Some of these explanations appear to be contradictory, but people believe in them all at once.

On the third day after death the first purificatory rites take place, involving the cleansing of the house, washing of all household linen and clothes, and the throwing away of all earthen pots used for cooking or for storing water. On the eleventh or thirteenth day further purificatory rites are performed which remove the ritual impurity of members of the household. On this day food and water are offered to the soul of the deceased, near relations have a hair-cut and bath (on the death of the father or mother all the hair on the head as well as moustache and beard must be shaved) and a feast is given. Among the higher castes a Brahmin belonging to one of the nearby villages comes and conducts the rites on this day; others follow their own caste customs. These higher castes collect the bones from the cremation ground and immerse them in a holy river—generally in the Godavari, which is the nearest to Shamirpet, but in exceptional cases in the Ganges, which is regarded as the holiest of all rivers by the Hindus all over India. As pointed out earlier, in the Petramasa fortnight water is offered to the ancestor-spirits; and during the first Petramasa after death the soul of the deceased is invited to 'come back' and is lodged with the spirits of the other ancestors in one corner of the house.

Abnormal deaths require a special treatment. A woman dying

in pregnancy, a young man dying without sexual satisfaction, or a person dying without having satisfied any of his deep cravings, will all experience difficulty in their rehabilitation in the supernatural world, and their souls will keep on returning to the world of the living periodically. These are the persons who often turn into ghosts, reside permanently in the village and create difficulties in the normal life of the community. To undo their evil special skills must be employed.

Muslim death customs differ from those of the Hindus. The toes of the corpse are tied together with a cord; and a small bundle of salt is placed on the stomach to prevent its swelling. Friends and relations gather together and make preparations for the funeral. A new cloth, to cover the body, is bought, and the communal wooden box used for carrying the dead to the graveyard is requisitioned. The corpse of a man is covered with three pieces of cloth; that of a woman with five pieces. Camphor powder is sprinkled on the forehead, eyes, palms and legs of the deceased. It is customary to sprinkle some perfume also. Relations and friends have a last look at the deceased, and then put the corpse in the wooden box. The box is lifted by four men, and carried to the mosque by the male relations and friends. As they go, people keep on repeating, 'There is no god except Allah'. Funeral prayers are said there, and the procession resumes its journey towards the graveyard. The corpse is put in the grave, passages from the Koran are read, and then the grave is filled up. All those who accompany the bier put some earth in the grave, reciting passages from the Koran. When this has been done, all step forty paces from the burial place, and return to it again saying prayers (*fatiha*) for the deceased and invoking the Almighty's blessings for him. For two days after the death 'there must be no fire in the hearth', and food for the bereaved family is sent by near relations. On the third day prayers are said in the mosque and, later, flowers are placed on the grave by the relations of the deceased. This is done on the tenth day also. On the fortieth day all those who have participated in the funeral assemble together. Prayers are said again, and some people go to lay flowers on the grave. This is followed by a dinner. On the occasion of the death anniversary, flowers are again laid on the grave, prayers said, and a dinner is given in memory of the deceased.

RITUAL STRUCTURE

5. RELIGION IN DISEASE AND DIFFICULTY

In the two preceding sections an attempt has been made to present the ritual cycle of the community covering firstly the festivals and ceremonies within a normal calendar year, and secondly, the rites and observances concerning the major crises of life. These cycles are rigidly observed, as their observance constitutes the *dharma* or the appropriate way of life, and leads to the prosperity and well-being of the family as well as to a desirable future for the individual after death. With the exception of these festivals, under normal conditions of life, there is very little spiritual or devotional activity in the community. But persistent difficulties, uncommon diseases, and frequent deaths turn the people's thoughts to supernatural factors; events are interpreted in terms of supernatural interferences, and are sought to be remedied by magico-religious procedures.

Most of the common diseases are interpreted as a 'fault in the physical system', and are treated with herbal medicines or modern drugs obtained from the dispensary. Common colds, headaches, fever, stomach-ache, scabies, gonorrhoea and syphilis are regarded as natural diseases, and an effort is made to cure them with medicines. But persistent headaches, intermittent fevers, continued stomach disorders, rickets and other wasting diseases among children, menstrual troubles, repeated abortions, etc., are attributed to supernatural forces. In all such cases medicinal cures as well as propitiation of the 'unseen powers' are attempted simultaneously. Similarly, such calamities as the failure of crops, total blindness, repeated failures in undertakings, deaths of children in quick succession and too many deaths in the family within a short time are taken to indicate 'misfortune' and 'the handiwork of malevolent supernatural forces'. Smallpox, cholera and plague are always attributed to the wrath of various goddesses. For these diseases worship is regarded as the only remedy; and no medicines are administered to the patients.

What are the major factors that cause these difficulties, distresses and deaths? In the village community they are attributed to one or more of the following:

(i) The wrath of ancestor-spirits.   (ii) Unfavourable stars.
(iii) Ghosts and spirits.   (iv) The wrath of gods.
(v) Black magic and witchcraft.

127

If ancestor-spirits are ignored and 'not given their due' they warn the family by causing some minor—but noticeable—trouble. It is for the members of the family to take this 'timely warning' and remove the cause of the ancestors' anger. Failure in this often leads to serious consequences and irreparable losses. Ill-luck and misfortunes persist all along the way of a person whose 'stars are unfavourable'. Hysteria, fits and 'possession by spirits' are the result of hostility of spirits and ghosts. The village goddesses are known for their violent temperament and retaliate quickly and severely, even for minor offences against them. The all-India gods are comparatively pacific; and punish people only for 'gross disrespect' shown towards them. Enmity may lead to the use of black magic or witchcraft, which may be the root cause of the trouble in many cases of persistent disease and ill-luck.

Most of the causes need the diagnosis of a specialist. Sometimes the ancestor-spirits convey their anger in dreams to some member of the family. Often the ghost possessing an individual reveals its identity through its victim. But in other cases a proper diagnosis is necessary. Why is the ancestor-spirit angry? What should be done to pacify it? How could the evil influence of unlucky stars be averted? Only the Brahmin or a local seer can answer these questions. For undoing the evil influence of spirits and ghosts the services of a competent specialist must be sought. Similarly, the hostile magician or witch must be matched by a more powerful magician.

The ancestor-spirits are not very difficult to please. When the cause of their anger is known, an apology followed by worship is often enough to appease them. Fasting, repentance and food offerings are generally enough to please the gods. Goddesses are more difficult, and require the sacrifice of a fowl or goat. Unfavourable stars require fasting, worship and certain ceremonies following the recommendations of the Brahmin. The giving of alms to the Brahmin and the poor generally follows these ceremonies. Several different techniques can be employed to keep ghosts and spirits in check, and for counteracting black magic and witchcraft. As far as possible, 'all the reasonable demands of a ghost should be fulfilled', but if it still persists in its mischief 'it should be tied down' and 'kept in captivity'. Against sorcery and witchcraft drastic steps are required. For action under both these categories, i.e. against ghosts, as well as against black magic and witchcraft, three techniques are employed: *mantram* (chants and spells), *yantram* (use of secret formulae and designs) and *chetla kriya* (counter black magic). Amateur practitioners succeed in some cases, but all difficult cases require the intervention of an established specialist. The techniques of these specialists are their closely guarded secrets.

In Shamirpet eleven people claim some knowledge of these techniques; although only three were recognized as having 'real and effective powers'. One person who claimed to be an expert in *chetla kriya*—powerful enough to use black magic as well as to counteract it—died, when this research was in progress.

Fourteen women had some suspicion of witchcraft against them, only two being regarded as established witches. A census of ghosts was difficult, but we listed more than forty of them. Four ghosts were particularly feared. The hillock to the north-west of the village was believed to be the abode of innumerable ghosts, but now it is inhabited by the ghost of a Reddi woman who died in pregnancy. She is known to have attacked several women and children. A Madiga woman who committed suicide by jumping in the well of their settlement also became a ghost. At first she went out of the village and troubled her daughter, but on being 'driven away' from there she is believed to have come back to Shamirpet. The dread of the village, however, is the ghost of a Reddi agriculturist who dwells in the eastern side of the village. Even tough young people are afraid to go 'to his place' at mid-day, dusk or late at night. A young Muslim who died without sex experience is alleged to have interfered with many young women. No effective checks have been improvised so far to keep these ghosts under control. Many others 'have been tamed'. They were the ghosts of persons from the following categories:

(a) Persons too much attached to sex, wealth and children.
(b) Persons dying without satisfying their sexual cravings.
(c) Pregnant women.
(d) Persons meeting an accidental death, by falling from a tree, drowning or by lightning.
(e) Persons committing suicide.
(f) Persons dying with an intense hatred for someone.
(g) Persons who have been murdered.

Serious difficulties created by supernatural agencies call for some of the measures enumerated above. For getting over minor difficulties, and for the fulfilment of comparatively simple wishes, recourse is taken to other methods. Fasting on a certain day in honour of a particular god or goddess for the satisfaction of a specific desire (or for overcoming a difficulty) is very common; and women take recourse to it quite often. Thus when T. was involved in a law suit, both he and his wife used to fast on Monday, and pleaded with their family god to get the court decision in their favour. Promising a food offering, sacrifice, or fasting for a specified period on a certain day, in return for the fulfilment of a wish is also resorted to. E. R.'s daughter was seriously ill and there was no hope of her life. E. R. went to the shrine of the goddess to whom her family was attached and said, 'Mother, we have always worshipped you. My daughter is on the point of death. I cannot bear to let her go before me. Save her and I will sacrifice two goats in your honour.' The girl recovered and E. R. did sacrifice the promised goats. S., a Komti woman, was worried because her daughter's husband was 'going astray'. She promised her family god: 'If you join what is breaking I shall fast on Mondays for three months and make offerings to you on all days of the fast.' The husband after a while, again started taking an interest in her daughter, and true to her word the mother kept her vow. When the wishes are not fulfilled people curse their luck, blame their own past actions, and reconcile themselves to the unfavourable attitude of the gods. 'All that we can do is to pray and worship. It is for the gods to hear or not to hear us. What else can we do? How can we have a quarrel with them?' would typify the average man's attitude in all cases where the powers of the supernatural world do not yield to their prayers and offerings.

The Muslims too have faith in ghosts and evil spirits. Their methods of dealing with them are similar to those of the Hindus. In addition they read passages from the Koran and invoke the assistance of their sages and seers. For overcoming minor ailments and difficulties they eagerly seek amulets from holy persons.

CHAPTER FIVE

The Web of Family Ties

IN the social structure of Indian village communities the family occupies by far the most important place. It derives its significance not merely from its economic functions and its dominant role as an agency of socialization and social control, but its ritual importance is also very great to the average Hindu.

Classical Hinduism has prescribed four stages of life: celibacy (*brahmacharya*), family life (*grahastha ashrama*), resignation (*vanaprastha*) and renunciation (*sanyasa*). In the first stage a person acquires concentration by controlling his instincts and impulses so that he may be able to dedicate himself to the pursuit of learning. This is the formative period of life, and in it a man is expected to equip himself for the proper discharge of his social responsibilities. In the second stage he enters life and begins to share his social obligations. Now he must marry and beget children. This is the creative period and covers a very considerable part of a man's life. The last two are the contemplative stages. As a preparation for the ultimate renunciation of worldly goods and worldly connections, he should first cultivate an attitude of detachment and devote himself to reflection. When this has been achieved, the time will have come for him to renounce formally all his possessions and relations. In contemporary rural India very few people can understand or explain the social philosophy that lies behind this system of *ashramas* or the 'stages of life', but its essence has reached them for countless generations through oral tradition and through the teachings of numerous saint-poets and has thus become ingrained in their thought-pattern and value-structure. Sex indulgence among children is socially disapproved in the Indian countryside. Marriage is universally regarded as natural and necessary. Only morons and cripples remain single. Though it is rare for people to renounce their home and property in old age, old men and women excessively attached to material goods come in for a good deal of criticism, and people often re-mark about them, 'Will they carry their wealth with them to the other world when they die?' It is at this time that their thoughts turn more to religion and to the destiny of their souls in the future life, and it is now that they generally undertake pilgrimages to holy places. In a sense the broad essentials of the philosophy of the *ashramas* can be said to permeate the life and thought of the Hindu villagers. The village Muslims share these social attitudes with their Hindu neighbours. With conversion to Islam they have changed their religious faith, but in the socio-cultural spheres of life they still continue to have more or less the same basic attitudes as the Hindus. In their family ethics and ideals the two groups demonstrate considerable similarity.

To the village people the necessity of both marriage and family is self-evident. It is necessary that the family line should be con-tinued. A male heir must be left. An unmarried person past the marriage age is an object of pity. A couple without a son are unhappy. Childlessness and inability to produce a male child on the part of a woman often lead to a polygynous household. Marriage is regarded as essential among all the castes and social groups in the village. In a community of 2,494 persons, demo-graphic survey reveals the presence of only two single persons—both women. One of these is a deaf-mute; the other has been a victim of epileptic fits from her childhood and has in addition the unenviable reputation of being a thief. For the clean-caste Hindus the continuity of the family line is necessary for a further reason. A male child must make a ceremonial offering of water to the spirits of his deceased parents and ancestors, without which their souls may not have peace. The untouchable castes as well as the semi-tribal groups also have this ritual in a modified form. The Mus-lims neither have this belief nor any attendant ritual, but they too share with the Hindus the sentiment against childlessness.

1. THE STRUCTURE OF THE FAMILY

The patrilineal and patrilocal elementary or joint family is the normal type of family unit met with in this part of rural India.

When a son-in-law settles with his wife's parents, we occasionally get examples of matrilocal residence. But this is rare and is largely confined to the cases of a few orphans and children of very poor parents who take recourse to the method of suitor service for securing a wife and then continue to live with their parents-in-law. The joint family is approved by social tradition. The following table illustrates an ideal joint family:

	Paternal Grandparents	
	Parents	
Brothers and their wives	Ego : Wife	Unmarried sisters
Nephews Nieces	Sons and their wives	Unmarried daughters
	Grandchildren	

It is indeed difficult to locate family units in which five generations live together under the same roof. In the villages of Andhradesa, particularly Telangana, it is impossible to find a family in which all nuclear families of three generations share a common house. Among the higher castes of the Hindus such large joint families are still met with in the small towns and cities, but they are not often seen in the villages. In actual practice joint families in this part of the country are much smaller units, and often they consist of parents and their married sons and their wives and children, or of brothers and their wives and children. While joint families are regarded as ideal, it is common for sons to separate from their parents within a few years of their marriage. As a result of this separation they start as an elementary family, which comprises at first only the husband and the wife. This elementary family gradually becomes larger as children are added to it. When sons grow up, get married and continue to live with their wives in their parental home the unit can once again be classed as a joint family. In this connection case-histories of one hundred and twenty families from the village were examined. In 34% of the cases sons had separated from their parents within two years of marriage. Thirty-six per cent separated between two and three years after marriage. Separation took place after three, but within five years of marriage in 28% cases. Only 22% of the sons were still found to be living with their parents five years after their marriage. As most marriages are between adults, effective married life begins almost immediately after the marriage ceremony, or at the most within six months. For the purposes of the above analysis, the year when their effective married life started has been regarded as the year of marriage.

Further analysis of the case-histories reveals an almost uniform pattern of development in a majority of cases. For a year or so after his marriage a son continues to live with his parents. His wife also lives with him. Domestic quarrels and dissensions develop within this period and compel him to start thinking about separation. In some cases this takes place in the course of the next year; in others it may take three to five years. Those who can hold together for five years generally continue to live under the same roof peacefully for a much longer period. Nevertheless, separation is known to have taken place in some cases even after ten to fifteen years of living together.

A young married man separating from his parents or brothers generally maintains close connections with their family or families. However, as the immediate cause for separation is often a quarrel or an acute difference of opinion, for some time the separating families continue to have strained relations. They may not even be on speaking terms. With the passage of time much of the bitterness of the dispute wears off and cordiality gradually returns to the different branches of the same main family. When the relations between the main family and the seceding family are once again cordial, they start taking interest in each other's affairs and problems. Ceremonies, feasts and festivals bring them all together. Rites connected with the major crises of life are great occasions for family reunions. Particularly in the event of death old quarrels and misunderstandings are generally forgotten and all near-relations assemble for the last rites. In the rituals that follow the presence of all the branches of the family is regarded as obligatory, and the absence of anyone at such an occasion is bound to be viewed very seriously. This would almost always lead to a permanent breach of relations between the absenting unit and the other units of the same family.

In this context it is necessary to point out that an equivalent of the term 'family' is used in the community to denote three different social units, each varying from the other slightly. It may mean: (1) the elementary family or the 'house', (2) the extended family unit, or (3) a still larger group comprising the near-kin on the paternal side. The composition of the family differs in different cases. In many cases it consists only of the husband and wife, their sons and unmarried daughters. In others one or both of the parents, unmarried brothers and unmarried sisters may also belong to this unit. Brothers and sons often establish their independent houses after marriage. In the same way, old parents may come to live with their son who had separated from them a decade or two earlier.

The *peddamanshi* or literally the 'big man' is the head of several family units which together constitute this extended family or allied families. In a still wider sense, family may include another category of near-kin who are one degree removed from the cluster of allied families.

In the diagram (overleaf) lines show the relatives who constitute the allied families, and dotted lines show the near-kin. Only unmarried girls belong to the family. On marriage they become members of their husband's family.

Each elementary family can be regarded as an independent unit of the extended family or the allied families. In everyday life it is practically free from the control of the other units of the allied families. Ordinarily these branches meet only on ceremonial and ritual occasions. Importance of the solidarity within the allied families is emphasized, and it is expected that any major decision will not be taken by any branch without consultation with the senior members of these allied families. Selling or buying land, starting litigation, obtaining large loans from a money-lender, leaving the village permanently for settling down in a different locality, and fixing the date and time for socio-religious ceremonies are among the subjects on which prior consultation with the senior members of the allied families is regarded as necessary. In any case the *peddamanshi* or head of these allied families should not be ignored. Often it is not difficult to get his permission and blessings; but people ignoring him inevitably come in for social censure. If the elders find the arrogance of the younger members too great they generally express their dissatisfaction and disapproval in their talk with the other people in the village. Their refusal to participate in a socio-religious ceremony of one of the branches of their family will cause a minor sensation in the village, and the comment of the society will generally be against the junior member who ignored the elders. If the affairs of any branch are in a

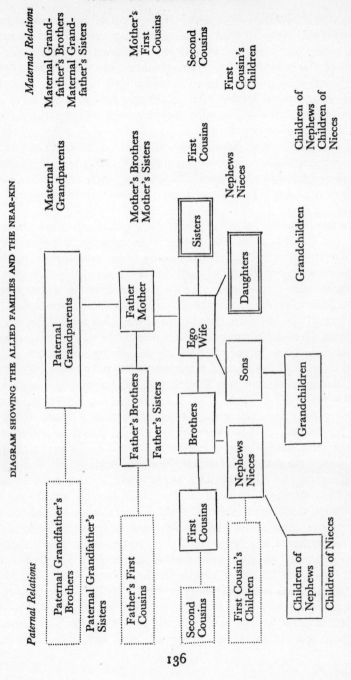

DIAGRAM SHOWING THE ALLIED FAMILIES AND THE NEAR-KIN

Paternal Relations

Maternal Relations

Paternal Grandfather's Brothers
Paternal Grandfather's Sisters

Maternal Grandfather's Brothers
Maternal Grandfather's Sisters

Paternal Grandparents

Maternal Grandparents

Mother's First Cousins

Father's First Cousins

Father's Brothers
Father's Sisters

Father
Mother

Mother's Brothers
Mother's Sisters

Second Cousins

First Cousins

First Cousins

Second Cousins

First Cousin's Children

Sisters

Ego
Wife

Daughters

Nephews
Nieces

First Cousin's Children

Brothers

Sons

Grandchildren

First Cousins

Nephews
Nieces

Grandchildren

Children of Nephews
Children of Nieces

Children of Nephews
Children of Nieces

bad way, the elders of the allied families are expected to intervene. Scandals or dishonourable behaviour in one unit are likely to spoil the name of all the allied families, and as such tradition enjoins elders to advise, warn and even admonish the erring members. A young man given to excessive drinking, gambling or any similar vice would often be admonished by the elders of this extended family. If he cannot keep his wife under control, or if the quarrels of the two become very frequent and too public, the neighbours would convey the information to the elders of the extended family and expect them to use their initiative in putting things right. In all such cases they will be within their customary rights if they intervene. They can demand that their advice is heard and followed.

Within the family unit the eldest male is generally regarded as the head. His wife or the next senior male is given the second place. A respectful son very often describes his old widowed mother as the 'head' of the family. However, in many cases the *de facto* head of the family may be a son under whose guidance and supervision the land is cultivated or the craft or profession of the family is practised. Parents dominate the scene in their youth and early middle age. With approaching old age they gradually recede to the background. Nominally they remain the heads of the family, but their sons are left more or less free to conduct the management of the family property and profession as they like. As long as the father remains the real head of the family, the internal management of the family remains the charge of the mother. Sons are expected to obey her and the daughters-in-law are expected to carry out her instructions. Any failure or reluctance on the part of a daughter-in-law to carry out the wishes of her mother-in-law leads to constant quarrels and complications, and in many cases to ultimate separation. Between sons and daughters, as a rule, preference is shown to the former, but if the sisters have considerable seniority in age, their younger brothers are expected to respect and obey them.

In the village community of Shamirpet, which has considerable variations of caste and class, and significant differences in education and urban contacts, it is only natural to expect great variations in the family ideals and ethics of the different groups. In the themes of their idealizations, the different sections of the population show striking similarities; but in their attitudes and reactions

to specific social situations the different levels present remarkable
contrasts.

For the purposes of such comparison, the population of the
village may be broadly classified into three levels:

(1) *Upper Level*: comprising the 'twice born' castes of Brahmins
and Komtis; rich Reddis and Muslims; and others who have
had urban contacts or education in the city.

(2) *Intermediate Level*: all ordinary agriculturists; clean occupational castes and Muslim tradesmen constitute this group,
which is by far the largest in the village.

(3) *Lower Level*: all the poorer sections of the population, such as
the untouchable Malas and Madigas, and semi-tribal
Vaddars and Erkalas, as well as poor Muslims, can be placed
in this category.

With their urban contacts and education, as well as considerations of 'respectability' befitting their class, the people on the
upper level set sufficiently high standards of behaviour. The stereotyped idealizations of the other two levels of population closely
resemble the ideal-patterns of the upper level.

All three levels regard solidarity, co-operation and understanding as the essential attributes of the family that may be
regarded as a model for the whole community. The ideal family
should work on the principle of 'one for all, and all for one.'
Different members of the family should function like an organized
team, and have mutual trust and understanding. Toleration, good-
will and a sense of give-and-take among its members are necessary
for the well-being and prosperity of the family. On the other hand,
dissensions, conflicts and lack of understanding lead a family to
its downfall.

There is unanimity in all three levels that the structure of the
family is founded on its recognition of four basic principles. These
are:

(1) Respect for age.
(2) Respect for position in the scale of kinship.
(3) Superiority of the male.
(4) Necessity of keeping certain family matters confined to the
responsible members of the family, or at the most, within
the family.

Further, in all three levels the importance of compromise as a tool for correct ordering of intra-family relations is emphasized. Mediation and reconciliation are regarded as the best methods of getting over family difficulties; timely partition of property and separation as the next best.

The people in the upper level not only believe in these ideals, but most of them consciously strive to achieve them in actual practice. A Brahmin will lose respect in the community if he gives up these noble ways and starts imitating the 'animal-like ways' of people on the lower levels. Prosperity of the Komti traders and money-lenders can be built up only when the whole family makes a concerted effort for it. A family of substantial agriculturists can further augment its land and improve its financial status by working hard as a team. This is equally applicable to both Hindu and Muslim agriculturists. People with urban contacts and education have also an urge to rise higher; and that necessitates solidarity, co-operation and understanding within the family. Great emphasis is laid here on correct behaviour towards different members of the family according to their age and kinship status. Disagreements must be expressed through permitted ways. Abuse and foul language should not be employed in referring to or addressing the elders. Any form of physical violence against them would be unthinkable and would cause great resentment in the other members of the family. Women on this level are generally kept confined to the home. Among the Muslims they observe strict *purdah*; among the Hindus for considerations of respectability it would be improper for them to go out to work. Thus they are largely confined to their houses. They have some ornamental value; nevertheless, in the entire social setting the comparative superiority of the male is latent. Family secrets on this level are always discussed in hushed tones, and all possible efforts are made to prevent them from leaking out. When husband and wife quarrel, the angry outburst must not be heard outside the home. If the husband beats the wife, her crying should not be loud enough to attract curious sympathizers into the house. The amours and intrigues of a member of the family, if they cannot be stopped, should at least be kept secret, and efforts should be made to prevent them from developing into open scandals. Mediation or arbitration by family elders is often effective for settling disputes within these families. If the misunderstandings and consequent difficulties seem to be beyond repair, property is gracefully partitioned, and separation granted to the members who want to secede from the family. This is sought to be done in an orderly way, and every possible effort is made to ensure that the differences within the family do not become the subject of local gossip.

When we consider the actual behaviour of the people on the intermediate level, we find that many of these ideals are very considerably diluted. The value of solidarity is understood, but the willingness to make concessions and personal sacrifices for the sake of the family is not sufficiently strong to make it really effective. Age is generally respected, but in angry outbursts abuse may be showered on parents and uncles. Unable to control his temper one may even spit at them, or throw dust at them (symbolizing their burial, and thus indirectly wishing their death), or strike them. It would probably be necessary to express some sort of an apology for this unbecoming behaviour later, but the unrepentant individual can repeat it when he is provoked again. This type of behaviour is confined to a few individuals, and is socially criticized but none the less tolerated. Here too the superiority of the male is insisted upon, but the woman also works and is not tied down to many of the shackles of respectability. She does not lose face if she is beaten by her husband semi-publicly; occasionally she hits him back. She expresses her anger or suffering by running back to her parental home. In many cases some effort is made to conceal family secrets, but when passions rise, a father and son, or two brothers, but more often a mother-in-law and daughter-in-law, will openly quarrel in the courtyard or the village lanes, and in the course of the hearty exchange of abuse these secrets may be broadcast by them at the top of their voices. Family differences are discussed privately and occasionally in public as well, but even when property is divided and separation is completed, mutual bickerings and exchange of harsh words continue for several months in most cases.

On the lower level the 'ideals' get diluted so much that it is difficult to find any traces of them in actual practice. Division of property and separation at this level are so frequent as to reduce the conception of family solidarity to practically a meaningless ideal. On ritual occasions, respect is shown to people on account of their age or kinship status, but in everyday life one can ignore these considerations with impunity. Although theoretically the woman is inferior, at this level she enjoys much more freedom. She can work for wages and has considerable freedom of movement. Sexual lapses on her part are more liberally viewed. If the husband beats her. she too can beat him. If the abuses of her husband are loud, hers can be louder still. She can leave her husband and take another with comparative ease, and without any social stigma. This would permanently lower the status of persons on the upper level, and would be commented upon very adversely in the intermediate class. The family secrets are announced to the outside world by the members of the family itself in their open-air quarrels. Compromises are often made through mediation and arbitration, but may be disregarded with comparative ease after a few days.

It is probably needless to say that the above three levels are not fixed, nor are they exclusive. Modern education and other modern means of communication—especially the cinema—often infuse a spirit of romantic individualism into the youth of the upper level, who, rather than working for family solidarity, often disintegrate it. Education, urban contacts, 'disgust with rustic ways', and desire for greater respectability according to accepted social standards in some cases set in motion efforts at vertical movement in families on the lower levels.

2. INTER-PERSONAL RELATIONS WITHIN THE FAMILY

HUSBAND AND WIFE

According to the traditional norms of the society a husband is expected to be an authoritarian figure whose will should always dominate the domestic scene. As the head of the household he should demand respect and obedience from his wife and children. The wife should regard him as her 'master' and should 'serve him faithfully'. It is the husband's responsibility to provide adequately for the support and maintenance of 'his dependants' and the wife's duty is to 'run the household frugally and efficiently'. In an ideal home 'all major decisions are taken by the husband in consultation with his wife and grown-up children', but the final say in all matters connected with the family is always with the husband. The husband should 'watch the activities and ways of his wife' as well as 'take care of the proper upbringing of his children'. The wife should 'serve her husband with loyalty and devotion'. The husband is 'superior'; the wife is his 'subordinate'. As a mark of the recognition of his superiority, the wife shows respect to her husband by touching his feet. She washes the husband's clothes, and eats the leavings in his plate. The husband cannot do likewise. When the wife errs, the husband reprimands her, and can abuse and beat her. However, a good wife is not expected to answer him back. Even when the husband is wrong she is supposed to bear her lot meekly and submissively. This cultural pattern is reflected in the lament of the wife over her husband's demise, when she wails, 'Where is my lord? Where is my master? Now who will support me? The shield that protected me is gone; now I am helpless.'

This, then, is the 'ideal'. Almost everyone in the village would verbalize the expected husband-wife relationship in similar words. But the reality appears to be very different; and a close study of the actual family records would reveal that these ideals are more or less a social fiction. The husband is, without doubt, superior, and has, in most families, the upper hand; but practically nowhere do we find him a completely dominant, authoritarian and patriarchal figure. Moreover, the quality of inter-personal relations between husband and wife change as they leave one stage of life and enter another.

It has been pointed out earlier that married life is started by a couple under the parental roof. During this stage, at least for the first few months, they are not supposed to show any special concern for each other. The man continues to work under the direction of his father or elder brother; the woman carries out the instructions of her mother-in-law. There is hardly any opportunity for them to meet and talk during the day, and when they do meet under the cover of darkness, possibly in a separate room, the proximity of the parents' room does not allow them the liberty of engaging in audible love-play or even of talking freely. Of necessity they have to speak in whispers. The cultural pattern demands that the wife must resist the initial advances of her husband for several nights. She often feigns complete ignorance regarding sexual matters and displays horror and disgust when the husband approaches her. After two or three weeks the wife becomes more co-operative. Now sex dominates their life for the several months that follow. There is casual conversation between the two, but in these first months household affairs are invariably not discussed by them. The husband generally speaks to her about the village affairs and his kinsfolk. He also tells her his experiences of the city.

The girl talks to him about her childhood friends in the village and about her relations. At this stage, even if she is troubled by her mother-in-law, she would not complain to her husband about her discomforts and difficulties at home. The stereotype norms that a girl unconsciously picks up from conversation between elderly women, or consciously learns as a result of direct instruction by her mother are: 'Unless the husband is completely under your influence, do not try to take him away from his mother. When your grip over him is firm, you can persuade him to do what you like. But any premature efforts on your part will only generate distrust about you in his heart.' Thus, she begins complaining to her husband about the bad treatment that she receives from her mother-in-law and the other women relations when she is sure that the relative strength of her influence over him is greater than theirs. The husband finds himself in a dilemma. He knows that a man who 'listens too much to his wife' is an object of social scorn and ridicule. Thus if he starts taking sides with his wife, the comment of the elders would generally be against him, and even the people of his own age-group would circulate funny, but often quite imaginary, stories about his submissiveness to his wife. On the other hand, he realizes that nearly everyone at some stage has to take sides, and that even his critics have had to do so, at some point in their lives. His position becomes really difficult when he is subjected to pressure simultaneously from two directions: when the mother complains about his wife and the wife complains about his mother. To begin with, most sons ignore these complaints and accusations, and refuse to take sides. In the next stage they side with, or at least pretend to side with, the mother. For the satisfaction of the mother the son would scold the wife once or twice. If the wife takes it ill, she would refuse to speak with him when they meet in the night. The husband has then to make some efforts to console her. Often he says to her that he did not intend any of his remarks to be taken seriously. Or he may even say that the mock-scolding was meant only to satisfy the old mother. The wife takes this opportunity to narrate more accounts of sufferings that she has to undergo in the house, on account of the troublesome mother-in-law and the other deceitful female relatives. In a joint family this continues, but in a great majority of cases after some years the husband and wife secede from the main family to set up an independent household of their own.

With the setting up of an independent houshold the nature of husband-wife relations undergoes a definite change. Now the two are free to run their own affairs. No doubt the husband has not now to work under anybody's supervision, but he also lacks the security provided by the joint family. Similarly, the wife has no longer to slave for her mother-in-law, but all the same she has to do the entire work connected with the running of the household. The husband is now the real head and has to work hard to provide for the maintenance of the family. The major share of the family's subsistence comes through his labour; in some cases the wife also assists him. In many families, a small part of the family's earnings may be contributed by the wife also. But the main task of the woman is to run the household and manage the domestic economy. As far as possible the house should be kept neat and tidy, children and cattle should be well looked after, and above all at fixed hours meals should be provided for the members of the family. Ordinarily a woman does not interfere with 'outside affairs', that is matters not directly connected with domestic management are believed to be the responsibility of the husband. Similarly, the husband is not expected to meddle too much in the actual running of the household. Nevertheless, major decisions connected with either of these spheres are arrived at after mutual consultation. Cases on record clearly show that in several instances a dominating wife effectively interferes in the management of 'outside affairs', and in time the husband learns not only to take her advice but to depend upon it. On the other hand, instances of the other type are not wanting, where a wife who is consistently negligent about her household duties is sharply rebuked by her husband and is made to carry out his detailed instructions regarding the actual management of domestic affairs. Care and education of the children are primarily the responsibility of the mother, but in this field the father is also expected to give some of his time and attention.

Both husband and wife watch each other's activities closely. Improvidence and spendthrift habits, excessive drinking and gambling, and extra-marital sex-intrigues to the neglect of the spouse on the part of the husband are critically watched and commented on by the wife. If mild hints do not prove effective, she takes recourse to taunts and threats. One of the most important and often-used weapons in the armoury of the wife is her threat of running away to her parental home. She often expresses her anger and discontent by neglecting the children and other household activities. If things still do not improve to her satisfaction, she begins to protest loudly, which often ends in open quarrels and altercations. On the other hand, among the men the stereotype that by nature woman is faithless is widely believed, and while they admit that there are some notable exceptions, they nevertheless emphasize the necessity of vigilance on the part of the husband and other responsible members of the family. The suspicion regarding a woman is directed particularly against two things: namely, possibility of a sexual liaison with a 'lover', and that of her stealthily giving money and grain to her relatives on the paternal side. If he suspects his wife, the husband makes suggestive hints and veiled threats. When subsequent events confirm his suspicion, he voices his protests loudly. Now he administers threats of dire consequences, and as a foretaste of what would come if she does not change her ways, he may even beat his wife. If things do not change for the better even with this, the subsequent developments may indeed be very complicated. However, much depends on the personality and disposition of the husband. Rather than allowing the affair to develop into an open scandal, some husbands overlook occasional lapses of their wives; others are so jealous that they cannot forget an incident of this type even when the wives mend their ways and keep on taunting them.

In a joint family, the daughter-in-law does not have any independence unless she becomes the mother of two or three children. Until then she should not be found even speaking to her husband. Efforts at endearment, smiling or even exchanging fond glançes would be enough to cause comment and would earn for the couple a reputation for being 'shameless'. The husband in such families often hears the complaints from both his mother and his wife, and leaves them to adjust their relations among themselves.

In the preceding section I have discussed the ethics and ideals of family organization on the three levels of village population. The authoritarian husband and the docile wife is the ideal of people on all three levels, but it is only on the upper level that we find them holding to the ideal in actual practice. Even there, the desire to maintain 'family prestige' and 'good name' forces the husband to overlook some of the faults and failings of the wife and to maintain silence about them. But if affairs cross the limits of decency, or the constant misbehaviour of the wife threatens to become the subject of public gossip, the wife receives very harsh treatment and may even be driven out of the house. If she once leaves the house, readmittance for her would be practically impossible among the people of the upper level. On the other two levels, while tempers are roused very quickly and are even expressed publicly in a violent way, the reconciliation is not difficult. Faults of the wife are often openly discussed among them, and she is ridiculed in the presence of others; but she is quite readily forgiven also, and if she does not go astray again, she soon regains her former position in the household.

The stereotyped attitudes of wives for husbands and of husbands for wives are common for the community—as a whole. 'A woman should not be trusted. You can never tell when and how she would slip out', say the men in a knowing manner. Others add, 'Much depends on the husband. He must control his wife properly. Once he relaxes his control, then she is practically gone for all times.' The women, on the other hand, regard all men as heartless. 'It is impossible to please a husband; to-day he likes a thing very much; to-morrow he will lose his temper over it.' 'The lot of a woman is difficult. Unlucky ones receive beatings every day; the lucky ones get them only periodically. But is there a woman whose husband never beats her?' In a philosophical vein they add, 'And why not? The man works and earns. If we do not please him he beats us. Of what use are our protests? If a bullock runs away from one owner, will not its second master yoke it to a plough and mercilessly goad it to move faster? If we leave one man and go to another, what guarantee is there that he will not treat us in the same way?'

The wife does not dominate the domestic scene, but if she is tactful she can manipulate things in such a way that her husband will rarely go against her wishes. Gradually she comes to occupy a key position within the household.

Finally two significant questions may be raised: what type of wives do most men want? and what type of husbands do most women want? While the ideals and likes and dislikes of individuals are bound to differ greatly on the basis of their personal equations, certain attributes are considered desirable by people from nearly all the different levels of the community. A wife should be, above all, of a pleasant disposition, and should endeavour to keep her husband pleased. She must be 'tactful' and should be able to 'dissuade the husband from going the wrong way' without causing offence to him. This tact would be a valuable asset to her in organizing her general relations with the other members of the family. 'Foolish wives grumble and cry, and go on slaving for the household; the intelligent one wins over everyone by her pleasantness.' Then the wife must be a good housekeeper and a tolerable cook. Her economic virtues would ultimately earn for her the key position in the family. She must spend the money entrusted to her care very judiciously. She should save enough to buy her ornaments; and should lay aside something to meet unforeseen expenses. The more she can save without the knowledge of her husband, the more she will be appreciated by the elderly women. In sex she should not be passive, but should not be violently active either. 'We don't want a woman to be like a log of wood in the bed; but the aggressive ones definitely repel us', the men often remark. The women also comment on oversexed women who are shameless enough to cross the limits of womanly decency. Husbands do not want their wives to be fussy. The womenfolk seem to be well aware of this. In the words of one of our informants, 'If we nag too much, our words lose their value and our husbands make it a habit not to listen to whatever we say.'

Women's 'ideal' of a husband is a man who 'works hard and earns enough' to feed and keep the family in good clothes. If he can buy ornaments for the wife, he will be all the more admired. He should 'take an interest in his wife and children', and look to their comfort and welfare. While the women take it for granted that no husband is ever completely faithful to his wife, they resent their semi-permanent or permanent affiliations to a woman outside. They protest if his amours prove too expensive to the family. No woman would like her husband to earn the epithet of being 'a woman's slave', but neither do they want him to be overstrict and temperamental. The suggestion that a husband could be meek and docile appeared rather ridiculous to most women; what they seemed to like best was a firm, but friendly husband. A man not given to any excesses and possessing personality-traits which mark him out in the community in some way would certainly be an object of pride for his wife.

PARENTS AND CHILDREN

In general the attitude of the children towards their parents should be one of respect and obedience. Very early in his life a child must learn to act on the traditional norms of showing respect to different categories of people on the basis of their age and kinship status. The parents are entitled to the highest respect from the children; the latter must show it by touching their feet on ceremonial occasions. Between the father and the mother, the former symbolizes authority to a greater degree, while the constant association of the latter develops ties of sympathetic understanding between her and the children. Both must be respected, but of the two the father is feared much more. The mother is generally responsible for the upbringing of the children, but vigilance is also expected of the father, who must provide the corrective when too much leniency on the part of the mother begins to spoil the children. Of course the mother is responsible for the daily care of the children. She baths, clothes and feeds them. She looks after them during their illnesses. While she is doing her normal household work, she is expected to keep an eye on the children, and to ensure that they are kept away from mischief. Until they are about five years old, the life of the children centres around the mother. It is to her that they look for protection and help. 'When he is in a playful mood, the father may fondle the child; but it is the mother who attends to his daily routine.' 'The father,' it is said, 'loves the smiling child, but it is the mother who has to pacify it when it starts crying.'

The nature of the parent-child relationship changes with the age and status of the children. The traditional themes of correct treatment during infancy and early childhood are very different from those of childhood and adolescence. Similarly, when the sons and daughters enter the phases of youth and subsequently of adulthood, the tone of the parent-child relationship undergoes a significant modification.

Traditional opinion regards a son as an asset; a daughter, a liability. While a son 'belongs' to his parents, a daughter is bound eventually to go to some other family. Care of a daughter is regarded as 'watering a neighbour's tree'; you take all the trouble with it but its fruit goes to someone else. In a large family having many sons, a girl is definitely desired and welcomed. A family having too many daughters and no sons is unhappy, for a son is both a psychological and a ritual necessity. Notwithstanding this preference for sons, in actual practice no discrimination is observed in the treatment of children on the grounds of their sex.

As a rule infants are treated with affection. Until a child is four or five years old, it is mainly a responsibility of the mother. The mother nurses it whenever it starts crying indicating its desire to be fed. The child sleeps with its mother in the night and is at liberty to suck whenever it likes. Feeding of the child is primarily the mother's duty. However, when it is six to eight months old, elder sisters, female relations and male members of the household may start sharing this task with her by occasionally giving solid food to the child. While other relations give some food to the child occasionally, its attachment to the mother does not diminish in any significant way, as it is breast-fed by her until it is four or five years old. In teaching the child regular habits of sphincter control, standing, walking and speaking the mother's share is very considerable.

On the whole, an infant is the cause of delight to the family, and it is often fondled and carried about by the elders. They all invariably make funny faces and peculiar noises to make the baby smile, fondle it in many different ways, and find great enjoyment in imitating its meaningless sounds.

The situation radically changes after the child reaches the age of five or six years. Now the parents must be strong and should start disciplining it. At this stage the child finds the father an authoritarian figure and begins to fear him. The liberty that he was allowed during his early childhood is increasingly curtailed. Now the accent is on good behaviour and regular habits. The child is more frequently spanked for being troublesome. Absorbed in the care of a younger baby, the mother may often have to leave the elder child to spend most of his time in his own way. During the day-time he mostly plays out of doors with other children of his age-group. As he grows older the discipline becomes more and more difficult. At first he was punished for being 'troublesome' or for 'crying without reason', but now he has to distinguish clearly between things to be done and things not to be done. The child must be very particular about the latter. These include mostly urinating and defecating inside the house, demanding food and money at odd times too often, beating younger brothers and sisters, stealing, lying and using foul language. As a general rule, the lighter punishments are administered by the mother, who deals with the minor faults and offences of her children. All serious offences and persistent defiance of the mother's authority are reported by her to the father. Very often the mother's threat that she would report the matter to the father is enough to set the recalcitrant children right. In point of fact, many mothers build up the father as a figure to be feared, and in some instances the children actually tremble when they are produced before him for disobedience and other improper conduct. The punishments inflicted by the father on his children are less frequent but more severe. But from the above it should not be surmised that the children's attitude towards the father is only that of fear, for that would obviously be wrong. Fear and respect there certainly are, but not without a definite feeling of confidence and friendship for him. While difficulties are more often referred to and help sought from the mother, the father is not unapproachable, and indeed many fathers teach their children new games, make them small playthings, occasionally take them out for sight-seeing, buy them sweets and other tit-bits, and on demand give them a little money too.

During later childhood and adolescence the girls draw themselves closer and closer to the mother and occupy themselves mainly with feminine pursuits. The boys continue to maintain close and intimate relations with the mother, but her authority over them gradually diminishes. They learn to coax and cajole her. They know her weaknesses and devise ingenious ways to tease her. She often threatens to bring matters to the notice of the father, but the boys know very well that in all probability the threat will not be carried out. But during this period the father watches the development of his sons with greater interest and when complaints are brought to him the punishment is often exemplary. Traditionally this is believed to be the period when 'boys go tough' and are difficult to manage, and it is during this phase that the father must exercise tact and firmness in keeping them under control. They must keep the right sort of company, and should not be allowed to spend all their time playing and planning mischief. Even if they go to the village school, they should give some time to their traditional caste occupations. By assisting their elders and seeing them at work they should be able to acquire the fundamentals of what in all likelihood is going to be their main vocation in life. Indirect education through folktales, parables and songs is now supplemented by direct and conscious instruction by the parents. The mother seeks to train her daughter to be a good wife; she would often say to her, 'The husband's home is very different from the home of your parents. Here you sit down and the meals are served to you by your mother; there even if you work to the point of breaking your limbs you will not have a word of appreciation. And if you do not work, your tormenting mother-in-law and sisters-in-law will not only abuse you, but will also remember your parents in the foulest language.' Through anecdotes and reminiscences, she creates a vivid picture in the daughter's mind of what she is likely to find when she leaves her first home to enter her second and real home. As the time for the girl's marriage approaches, she finds herself attached to the mother all the more. If the father disapproves of any of the ways of the girl seriously, rather than speak to her directly, he would bring the matter to the notice of her mother, through whom he would seek to influence the daughter. Of course on minor matters he can speak to her directly. Similarly, in the case of grown-up boys, when any action more serious than a mere warning, use of strong language or giving of a threat is called for it is the father and not the mother who is supposed to handle them.

When the children enter their youth and adulthood, there are further changes in the pattern of inter-personal relationships between the parents and children. By this time the girls are married off and leave the parental home to take their place as wives in the homes of their respective husbands. For three or four years they maintain a somewhat intimate and regular contact with their parental home, and their people too are interested in their adjustment and welfare in the new surroundings. Afterwards, however, the girl gets increasingly absorbed in the affairs of her own home, and the memories of childhood friends, as well as those of her parental home, gradually recede into the background. In later years, on ceremonial occasions she returns to her parental home more or less a stranger. Not that the parents are totally unconcerned about the welfare of their daughter, or that the girl has altogether forgotten them, but the distance that separates them (in time and space) gradually takes away much of the glow and warmth of the feelings which they have for one another. On the other hand, the boys also marry and their wives come home to live with them. They think that this ends their tutelage under their father and establishes them as independent members of the community. The parents do not necessarily share this view, and consequently in the period that follows there is considerable stress and need for understanding and accommodation on both sides. The son is divided between loyalty to his father and his new-found desire for independence on the one hand; his affection for the mother generated by close association from the day of birth and his attraction for the wife on the other. During this stage the parents cannot punish or chastise their sons; they can at best advise and warn. When repeated advice and warnings do not have the desired effect, methods of employing pressure or ridicule are resorted to. Pressure may be brought to bear on the son through village elders, other influential people and even through his friends. Stories about sons who forget their duties and responsibilities towards their parents because of their wives are legion. Socially it is bad form to be engrossed completely in the wife to the neglect of the parents; it is worse to deny them the respect and courtesy that is their due at the bidding of the wife. The traditional norms of respectful behaviour must be observed in dealing with parents. Intimate subjects, particularly those having a bearing on sex, should not be discussed in the presence of the parents. Opinion should not be proffered unless it is asked for. All forms of endearment must be avoided by the husband and wife in the presence of the elders. It is not very proper for a young father to fondle and kiss his child too often when his parents are present. Finally, parents should not be abused or beaten; as far as possible differences should be smoothed out by peaceful means. Nevertheless, when there are acute differences in the points of view of the parents and children, exchange of hot words and loud quarrels between them are not uncommon.

Tradition lays down fairly strict norms regarding the treatment of aged, dependent parents. A son failing in his duty of providing adequately for his old parents, and not caring sufficiently for their comforts, particularly during illness, invites strong social disapproval and comment. He is regarded as a bad example. Elders, well-wishers and friends are bound to remind him repeatedly about his obligations to his aged parents. At this stage the old people are expected not to interfere with the domestic management of the household, and as a price for this non-interference the sons and their wives are enjoined by tradition to forget all disputes and dissensions and 'give as much comfort to the old people in their last days' as they possibly can.

THE DAUGHTER-IN-LAW

The daughter-in-law, coming from a different family and often from a different village, finds herself in totally new surroundings in her husband's home. Now she enters the new phase of life about which she has heard so much since the beginning of her later childhood. She has now to encounter the mother-in-law for whom she has an unmistakable dread. She expects her to be wicked, cruel and heartless. She has learnt to regard her husband's sisters as cunning and deceitful, and the wives of his elder brothers as troublesome and scheming. She expects love and friendship from the husband, but has to bear in mind the oft-repeated dictum of the village women that 'all men are uncertain' and that 'they cannot be depended upon'. She expects sympathy and friendship from her husband's younger brothers and his younger sisters— from the latter only if they are not grown up and if they are not almost of her own age. With the exception of these she has either to respect or to avoid most other members of the family. She comes to her new home with considerable diffidence and fear. She knows that here all her acts will be closely watched and criticized, and she has been taught to believe that however well she may act, it will not be easy for her to please her new relations-in-law. She leaves her parental home with a sorrowful heart, and enters that of her husband full of misgivings and uncertainty.

Notwithstanding the mental picture that she has had, she finds the reception given to her quite cordial. In most homes an effort is made to create a 'good impression' on her. At least for a few weeks she has some novelty about her, and is therefore cared for and looked after very well. The mother-in-law and sisters-in-law do not spare her a critical eye, but their comments are invariably made when the bride is not within hearing distance. But this phase lasts only a few weeks, or at the most, two or three months. Later she must be initiated into the ways and traditions of the household and should be taught 'how to do things properly'. Each house has some peculiarities that are distinctly its own, and in order to adjust successfully into its pattern it is necessary for the bride to know and respect these. She must learn her own part in the domestic work, and do it to the satisfaction of the hypercritical female relations. If she wants to make an impression, she must relieve the mother-in-law and other elderly and important women in the house of a part of their work by undertaking to do it herself. A mother-in-law is bound to be pleased with her if she offers to massage her feet at night. 'Good mothers' often train their daughters to take recourse to these methods for making an initial good impression on the hard-to-please mother-in-law. However, in some cases a different pattern seems to be followed. Some mothers say to their daughters, 'The more submissive you are the more your mother-in-law will make you work hard. If by mistake you do her part of the work on one day, you will find that it will become a regular part of your duty from the next day. The best way is to avoid all work which is normally to be done by someone else.' This view too is not without some truth.

Gradually the enthusiasm for the bride cools off as she does not remain 'new' for a very long time. She is expected to pass the rest of her life in this house, and as such it is necessary for her to adapt herself to its ways. Her steps are watched; her contribution to the work of the household is critically evaluated, and comments are freely made to appraise her of the views of others regarding the quality and quantity of her work. The mother-in-law and the sisters-in-law keenly observe her talk and behaviour. Does she praise her parents and their home very much? If she does, the mother-in-law or one of the sisters-in-law will unearth some scandal about them. If she praises the fields belonging to her father, or even happens to mention the good food which she ate at home, her remarks would be noticed, and in return she would be taunted, either immediately, or at a suitable occasion later. Thus if she is tactless enough to say, 'I remember the rice in our house which had such a delicate flavour', in reply she would hear something like this: 'Yes, we know. In your parental house they served you platefuls of pearls and diamonds in place of rice; in this house you get only a handful of broken rice and paddy straw.' A casual remark from the daughter-in-law about her feeling tired, may be taken to mean that she is complaining about the hard work which she is made to do. The mother-in-law would retort, 'Yes, my flower, I know you are delicate. Why? In your parents' home you had dozens of servants and you did not have to move so much as a grain of rice, and here you work from dawn to midnight. They ought to have married you to a prince. Why did you come to a house as poor as this?' And so it goes on. The mother-in-law and her daughters, married or unmarried, form one clique. The daughters-in-law of necessity form another, but they are divided among themselves, and have rivalry, jealousy and suspicion for one another. The pattern of inter-personal relations emerging from it is very complicated. There is always considerable back-biting and telling of tales. Alliances are formed and broken periodically. A daughter-in-law working diligently to find some favour with the mother-in-law is envied by the other daughters-in-law, who never fail to find fault with her, and always manipulate things to place the blame for anything going wrong squarely on her. In a simple and casual utterance, very often, some hidden meaning is read: on the other hand, explosive remarks are couched in simple words and very innocently made. The intrigues and jealousies among the womenfolk in a joint family are the despair of men. 'If we listen even to a fraction of the goings-on in the family, we will lose our heads', say the men. Others add philosophically, 'God has made mothers-in-law to quarrel with the wives of their sons coming to their homes. We cannot help it. Men will not remain men if they cease quarrelling; we shall all become gods!'

This is indeed a very well-established social pattern. To a mother-in-law, none of the daughters-in-law is perfect, although she may have preference for one over and above the others. From the daughters-in-law's point of view, a mother-in-law would ever remain a mother-in-law: 'Good and bad scorpions, both have the sting; the difference is that the one uses it more often than the other.'

I have already pointed out that the wives of brothers living together occasionally unite against the mother-in-law, but they too have their mutual jealousies and disputes. Husband's sisters, when they are young, are often quite friendly towards their sisters-in-law, but as they grow up they 'get wings' and start indulging in back-biting against them.

The daughter-in-law must maintain sufficient distance from her husband's father and his elder brothers. Unless it is absolutely necessary they should not speak to one another, and when it cannot be helped they must communicate in the minimum of words. Familiarity or intimate talk between them is regarded as highly improper. On the other hand, with the husband's younger brothers the daughter-in-law has terms of privileged familiarity, and while they are not expected to cross certain limits, tradition permits them to indulge in joke and banter. Unmarried brothers-in-law provide sympathy and friendship to the harassed wife, but when they grow up they too are drawn to their wives, and the former ties of intimacy are gradually forgotten in the humdrum realities of life.

SIBLINGS

Social ideals demand that there should be solidarity between siblings, especially between brothers, and that they should 'love and help' one another. The older brothers and sisters, particularly the latter, must share the responsibility of looking after the younger ones with their mother. In actual practice up to the age of six or seven they are constant companions; later the sisters gradually become absorbed in feminine pursuits and are thus unable to participate as freely in the children's games as they did before, and the boys too develop greater interest in their respective play-groups. Thus, to begin with, the inter-personal relations between the siblings are closest in their early childhood, but later they develop on their own lines, and distance between the sexes increases gradually.

The older siblings can claim some 'authority' over the younger ones. When the mother is otherwise occupied or is ill, the older siblings have to look after and care for the younger brothers and sisters. Particularly the older sisters have to lend a helping hand to the mother, and very often children become so much attached to them that they come to regard them as substitutes for the mother. While siblings of more or less the same age-group have to 'help, support and defend' one another, in their dealings with the other village children, the older ones must keep an eye on the doings of their younger brothers and sisters and bring their faults to the notice of the parents. The older siblings can occasionally spank the younger ones under their charge, but they must not do it too often. In return for the limited authority which they enjoy, they have to make some concessions. When a younger sibling starts crying for something, it is expected that an older brother or sister should forgo his own share to appease him. 'He is younger; he does not understand it, but you are older and understand everything. Let him have the thing. After all, he is your brother', the parents often say when they want to persuade one of their older children to yield to an apparently 'unreasonable demand' of the younger. When there is a quarrel between the siblings, it is invariably the elder who is admonished. 'One can understand a young child being unreasonable, but being older you should know better', the parents would say. Younger children very often complain to the parents about the older siblings; the latter prefer to deal with them personally when the parents are away. However, if the parents are too partial to their pet child, the others conspire to put him in disfavour. Spying by the younger children, when it is discovered, is punished by the older siblings. They may boycott them, refuse to speak to them, may not allow them to partake of their share of good things to eat, and may tease them in various ingenious ways. They often have a silly nickname for such a child, or they may keep on referring to some oddity in him, and thus tease and cause offence to him constantly. When they are six or seven, brothers and sisters form different groups. Aware of the pattern of male dominance, the brothers begin to regard themselves as superior to the sisters. They dislike doing anything which is regarded as 'feminine work', and if compelled to do so do not fail to express their extreme distaste. They would prefer to do it only if unobserved by their playmates, for if one of them were to notice it the 'news' would soon spread and the other boys would have funny ditties and remarks ready when next they met him. At this stage they begin to assert their superiority over their sisters. The latter must not join them in boy's games. When they are discovered engaging in anything that is regarded as particularly masculine, they are told, 'Now go and mind the pots; there is plenty to do at home.' Family histories recorded for the purpose of this study do not reveal any permanent tender emotional ties between brothers and sisters. It has already been pointed out that a few years after her marriage a girl returns more or less as a stranger to her parental home. On the other hand, there is considerable attachment between the sisters before they are married, but in their case also it gradually wears off after marriage.

The brothers either continue to live in the same house, or, if they separate, they live in the same village. Migrations are comparatively few, and even when one of the brothers moves away he continues to maintain contact with the families of his brothers still resident in the village. Tradition emphasizes the necessity of solidarity between brothers, even if they live separately. They should stand by and support one another in the hour of need. Indeed, there are considerable misunderstandings and consequent quarrels between families, but they do co-operate and support one another when serious situations arise and call for such assistance. Those who fail to rise to the occasion and do not behave in the expected way are criticized by the community and may even be admonished publicly by the village elders. However, regarding the general tone of inter-personal relations between brothers it may be said that it is not characterized by deep sentiments and affection. Understanding is desirable, but it is believed to be rather difficult to attain. However, ties of kinship inevitably bring them close to each other on ritual occasions and in moments of distress.

OTHER RELATIVES WITHIN THE FAMILY

Brief mention may be made here of certain other categories of relatives who live together in the same house within the joint family.

Grandparents are believed to be indulgent. It is said that they 'always spoil the grandchildren'. It is remarkable that persons who have had a reputation for being very 'strict fathers' behave in an altogether different way with their grandchildren. They are lenient and friendly towards them, and indeed take a lot of interest in them. Amusing grandchildren and being in turn amused by them is one of the favourite pastimes of the grandparents. Most of the time they can be seen fondling them or carrying them about. When their parents are angry with them, young children often take shelter with their grandparents. Very few grandparents ever complain about the behaviour of the little ones, and they would rarely spank them.

An uncle must be treated like the father and an aunt like the mother. But in this relationship much depends on the age and personality of the uncle. If he is nearer in age to the children than to the father, he is regarded as a superior kind of elder brother, but if he is nearer to the father in respect of age, he is feared and respected by the children. Often the children develop their pattern of relationship with an uncle on the basis of his character and personality. 'Some uncles are friendly. They allow us considerable liberty and shield us when parents are angry. We like them and willingly do odd bits of work for them. But others are different. They always have a frown on their faces. At the slightest pretext they are annoyed. We do their work too, but very grudgingly. We make faces behind their backs.' The same applies to aunts. Cousins should be regarded as brothers and sisters, and in a joint family they are certainly treated as such. It naturally follows from this that one should treat one's nephews and nieces as one's own children. While this is found to be rather difficult in actual practice, any favouritism and partiality to one's own children to the exclusion of the brother's children is a fruitful cause of dissension within the family.

RELATIONS OUTSIDE THE FAMILY

Affinal relatives do not maintain close contacts. They meet only on ceremonial and ritual occasions and in such meetings follow the mode of correct behaviour prescribed by tradition. A man will show respect and touch the feet of both his father-in-law and mother-in-law, but his relations with them would always be of a formal nature and would rarely be characterized by intimacy or emotional attachment. Similarly, between the respective parents-in-law of a husband and wife, the relations are rather formal. When they do meet on ceremonial occasions or visit one another, they try to be polite and consciously avoid controversial issues which may cause unpleasantness. If the father of a girl is compelled to intervene on behalf of his daughter who finds life rather difficult in her husband's home, he will exercise considerable tact and refer to the matter in a roundabout way. Amicable settlement is preferred, and all possible efforts are made to avoid a show-down.

Outside the family circle the relations between a person and his or her mother's brother are of special significance. As cross-cousin marriages are preferred in the community, a boy expects to get his wife from his maternal uncle's home, and a girl feels that she may have to go there as a daughter-in-law. With the younger brothers and sisters of his wife a man would have joking relations, and would frequently exercise the privilege of familiarity permitted to him by custom. Other relatives such as maternal grandfather and maternal grandmother are so distant, and contacts with them so rare, that there are no traditional norms regarding them.

However, in dealing with such relatives who are outside the family circle, one must observe the prescribed etiquette. They must be invited on all ceremonial occasions, and when they arrive they must be 'received well'. At the ceremony itself they should be given a place of honour befitting their age and relationship status. The relationship entitles them to hospitality, and according to the 'resources and capacity' of the family they should be well looked after when they are staying as guests. It is customary to cook special dishes in honour of such guests, and the choicest share of what is prepared is invariably given to them. Due attention should be given to their comforts for the entire period of their stay as guests in the house.

Among Muslims, besides cross-cousin marriage, marriage between parallel cousins is permitted and indeed encouraged. As a consequence of this the pattern of inter-personal relations between the children of two brothers is somewhat different from that described for the whole community. Cousins of opposite sexes spend their childhood together with each other playing and behaving as brother and sister. At the age of eight or nine an effort is made to segregate them, but this segregation is neither strict nor complete, and they continue to meet, and if they like they can find opportunities to talk with each other. But when formal negotiations for marriage are opened, it is expected that the girl will start observing *purdah* and start veiling herself. From this time onwards the cousins should not have any direct contact. If the cousins are not to be married, they can continue as before. The correct mode of behaviour for them would be to regard each other as brother and sister.

CHAPTER SIX

The Levels of Living

I. STATUS DIFFERENTIATION IN THE COMMUNITY

Six major factors contribute towards status differentiation in the village community of Shamirpet. They are:

  i. Religion and caste.
  ii. Landownership.
  iii. Wealth.
  iv. Position in government service and village organization.
  v. Age.
  vi. Distinctive personality traits.

Religion divides the community into two distinct groups: the Hindus and Muslims, standing out in marked contrast to each other. Hinduism is the older and longer established religion, and the majority of people in the village are Hindus. The Muslim group is largely composed of local converts, drawn from a number of castes—high and low. The Hindus naturally have a feeling of superiority regarding their religious faith and its antiquity, and do not view with favour the indiscriminate mixing of different castes in the Muslim community. But until 1948 they could not express these feelings openly as the Muslims had the backing of the State administration. The State was under Muslim rule, and being of the 'ruling race' the village Muslims were naturally in an advantageous position. They claimed superiority over the Hindus, and tried to dominate the village scene. While practical considerations forced the Hindus to remain silent, the Muslims aggressively denounced them as heathens. It had its reaction: after the Police Action, when Hyderabad was no longer a feudal

161

Muslim State, the Hindus had their revenge by pouring scorn openly on Muslim religion and society. It was now the turn of the Muslims to observe silence, and tolerate humiliation and insults. At the time of our investigations, however, most of these passions had subsided, and no significant tensions were observed. As groups both Hindus and Muslims regard themselves as superior in point of religion. From the socio-economic point of view the Muslims can be regarded as an exclusive caste whose social standing is roughly equal to that of the agricultural castes.

Caste as a factor of social differentiation is more significant. It has been pointed out that in its structure, the caste system has definitely a hierarchical character. Between the highest and the lowest castes, there are several intermediate levels. The social status of a person is largely determined by his caste. The mere fact of birth in a particular caste gives a good initial start to some and puts obstacles in the way of others. In a subsequent chapter I propose to examine some of the stereotypes current in the village community regarding the qualities and characteristics of different castes; but notwithstanding these the relative position of the different castes in the village community is determined by the traditional scale.

Religion and caste are more or less fixed and permanent factors. While change of faith is possible, and under certain circumstances a person can even descend from one of the higher castes to the lowest, such changes are very rare. At any rate no one takes recourse to them to bring about a change in his social status. The only case of change of faith recorded by us in the village is that of the present headmaster of the school who was a Brahmin to begin with, but later embraced Islam. No case of change of caste came to our notice.

In a predominantly agricultural society it is natural to expect that possession of land and cattle would contribute greatly to an individual's social status. Birth into a family of landowners ensures that a person will grow up to be a respected member of the village community. Acquisition of land would very materially affect the social position even of a person of humble birth, and if he does not behave tactlessly it would greatly enhance his prestige. An untouchable Mala peasant is now counted among the influential cultivators of the village and is given a place of honour in its counsels. He is still an untouchable and would continue to remain one, but in village matters his voice is now more effective. He insists on being regarded as low and humble, never offers his opinion unless it is specifically sought, and never fails to behave correctly towards the superior castes. Through this he earns the respect and admiration of the whole community. Again, two Madiga cultivators, belonging to the lowest untouchable caste who are now well-off and own land, are never forced to do free menial work like the other poorer members of their caste.

What is true of land ownership, is true also of the possession of other forms of wealth. Different kinds of houses denote different social status. The rich and the well-to-do people live in substantially built bhawanti-type houses. The average families have pen-kutillu-type houses; while the poorer people live in gudse huts. Along with the house go the other household possessions. Shining brassware, items of furniture, and other similar objects add to the prestige of a family. The significance of gold and silver ornaments possessed by women is also very great in this respect. In the families on the upper level there is keen rivalry among the women to acquire more and more ornaments of precious metals, so that their 'worth' in the estimate of the community may rise. Clothing, food and the type of work done by its members largely go with the financial resources of the family. In determining the social status of a family due consideration should be given to these factors also.

In recent years government service has come to be looked upon as important and desirable. It ensures a fixed and steady income, and permits the possibility of close contact with higher officials. Because of the feudal and authoritarian tradition in the administration of the State, even the minor district officials are viewed with· awe and respect by the village-folk; and as such the minor village officials and menials who, having contact with them, can possibly influence them gain in prestige among their neighbours. Persons holding very small menial posts may not win the respect of the village community in general, but within their own income—and caste group—their prestige is noticeably enhanced. Those who hold office in the internal administrative set-up of the village, that is to say the village headman, the Ganadi and the members of the village council, enjoy very considerable prestige and influence by virtue of their office.

Age is still another important factor of status differentiation. As a general rule the aged and elderly people should be respected: they have 'the authority of grey hair' and wide experience of the vicissitudes of life. The younger members must consult the elders of the extended family in all important matters, and should give due regard to their suggestions and advice. Even where the obligations which emerge from kinship ties do not dictate this respectful behaviour, it is considered polite for young people to show regard to the elders. Intimate social relations, even outside one's family and caste, find expression in the adoption of kinship terminology and one must address the people of another family as 'grandfather', 'uncle' or 'brother' according to their respective ages. Deliberate disregard or disrespect to village elders is adversely commented upon in the society.

Finally, distinctive personality traits and possession of uncommon or difficult skills also adds to the prestige of an individual and consequently alters his status in society. Ability to talk persuasively and impressively is regarded as a definite asset. An individual's success or failure in inter-personal relations, as well as his advancement in society in general, would depend to a considerable extent on this factor. Sense of humour is an allied personality trait which is greatly admired. One who can make others laugh is regarded as highly desirable company. Special knowledge and skills contribute substantially towards enhancing an individual's prestige. Two persons belonging to the Sale caste have risen in social esteem because of their local reputation as village doctors practising the indigenous system of medicine, although the traditional status of their caste is not very high. C. R., an untouchable Madiga, enjoys some social prestige because he composes songs in the folk style. B., a barber, too has a similar reputation for being a local composer.

Four other factors should also be taken into account at this stage. They are sex, education, urban contacts and political affiliations. Of these, considerations regarding the first are ingrained in the social pattern; the other three have a comparatively recent origin. In general man is regarded as superior to woman. In the internal organization of the village all offices are held by men, and with the exception of a few families which have no adult male members, it is a man who is regarded as the head of the family. However, the status of a woman is governed largely by the other factors, particularly her caste, landownership and wealth, age, distinctive personality traits, and relationship to persons holding a government or village office. But within the same caste, income-group and age-group, the position of a woman will definitely be inferior to that of a man.

Education is now regarded as important, because it provides 'the key to' the understanding of the 'wide world' and equips one better to assert one's rights and claim one's due from officials and the cunning townspeople. It is easier for educated people to get government jobs. It is generally believed that they can contact and influence government officers much better than their illiterate counterparts in the village. However, most of the 'educated' people in the village had just four years of schooling in village schools. No one has so far had any higher education. At the time of our investigations four boys from the village were studying in secondary schools in the city, and they are the first people in the village to learn the English language. Economic benefits and gain in social prestige derived through modern education have made it a mark of respectability, and it is expected that in the near future a larger number of village boys will attend secondary schools in Secundrabad and Hyderabad.

Although there is considerable prejudice and scepticism among the village people regarding city ways and other urban traits of culture, in general it may be said that the village-folk acknowledge the importance and superiority of the townspeople. Those who have urban contacts seek to distinguish themselves from the ordinary village folk in their dress, manner of speech, food and recreations. Imitation of urban ways in the last decade and a half has come to be recognized as a distinguishing feature of respectable elements of the village population.

Introduction of democratic government in Hyderabad after the Police Action, has brought about a sudden burst of activity by a multitude of political parties in the rural areas of the State. Politics and elections appear to the people to be a sort of game, and they have not yet realized their deeper and wider implications. Affiliation with political parties provides an outlet to those who are ambitious and seek recognition of their importance.

Social status conferred on an individual by the caste system must be classified as 'ascribed status'. It is still a vital factor of status differentiation in the community, but the other factors leave sufficient scope for an individual to work his way towards the achievement of a new and higher status. While the social framework of caste is rigid and does not easily admit any variation in one's position in the traditional scale of social respectability, by taking recourse to the other factors a man can still improve his position and gain social prestige. In general it could be said that under the impact of modern socio-economic trends in the criteria for status differentiation there has been a swing from an ascribed status system to an achieved status system. However, the grip of the traditional system is still firm, and people from lower castes or others with humble origins must behave with considerable tact and discretion if they seek to enhance their influence and importance in the community. If such people acquire land, wealth, official position or some special skill by their own efforts, they can gain social prestige if they avoid ostentation and exhibitionism and insist on not transgressing the limits imposed on them by tradition. If such a man behaves with becoming modesty, people would say, 'Look, even wealth has not turned his head. He has not forgotten his low birth and traditional status. He is a good man. Such people always succeed in life.' On the contrary, display of self-importance and lack of courtesy on his part would lead to adverse comment. People would say, 'If a person of humble origin grows rich, his head is turned. Look at this man! Until the other day his father was a bricklayer. With a few hundred rupees in his pocket he behaves as if he owns the village.'

Birth, wealth and special personal qualities are marks of distinction, but they do not fall to the lot of the average man. The common villager regards self-sufficiency and stability as a mark of respectability. Here is a generalized picture of such a person in the words of one of our informants belonging to an average family of Reddi agriculturists: 'He is not rich, but he lives well and eats well. Quarrels are not heard in his home and there are no scandals about them. He lends to no one, but neither does he borrow from anyone. He is a contented man.' In the words of a Muslim cultivator, 'If you get enough to eat twice, if not thrice every day, if your wife and children have sufficient cloth to cover their bodies, and if you have a small house, a pair of bullocks and some fields of your own, there is nothing else that you should desire.' To quote one more informant, a Madiga untouchable: 'How many people can be rich? It is no blessing to worry half your life in order to amass wealth, and spend the rest of it worrying about its safety. The cultivator need not be rich. It is enough if he has not to lower himself before others begging for their favours.'

2. STANDARD OF LIVING: FOUR LEVELS

In Shamirpet four levels denoting different standards of living are vaguely recognized by the villagers. They are:

i. Rich.   iii. Average.
ii. Well-to-do.   iv. Poor.

It is difficult to lay down any precise rules to classify the different families living in the village into these levels on the basis of their standards of living. As these distinctions are based primarily on the differences in earning, it may be generally said that families with an income of Rs. 200 per month or more would be regarded as 'rich', those earning between Rs. 100 and 200 as 'well-to-do', those earning Rs. 45 to 100 as 'average' and those earning less than Rs. 45 as 'poor'. The average family unit in these calculations consists of five—three adults and two children.

According to this test which reflects the consensus of opinion in the village, our socio-economic survey of the community would indicate the following classification of the village population:

Rich   4%   Average   34%
Well-to-do   22%   Poor   40%

The following table indicates average percentage of consumer expenditure on different items, based on the family budgets of three consecutive years of a total sample of one hundred and twenty families representing the four levels of living:

ITEMS AND PERCENTAGE OF EXPENDITURE

Level	1 Food (including fats and spices)	2 Clothing (including ornaments)	3 Feasts and ceremonies	4 Repairs and maintenance of the house	5 Luxuries (including tobacco and liquor)	6 Miscellaneous (entertainments, medicine, etc.)
	%	%	%	%	%	%
Rich	34	15	18	11	12	10
Well-to-do	40	14	18	10	12	6
Average	48	12	12	8	15	5
Poor	56	10	11	5	15	3

From the above it is clear that on each successive lower level the percentage of expenditure on food—that is, on cereals, meat, vegetables, salt, spices and fats—increases steadily. The 'rich' and the 'well-to-do' spend more on clothes and ornaments: on the lower levels expenditure on these items is proportionately less. Similarly expenditure on feasts and ceremonies is proportionately higher in the two upper levels and lower in the poorer sections. Maintenance and repairs of the house and all immovable property other than agricultural land, cattle and implements necessitate a higher percentage of expenditure on each higher level successively. This is accounted for by the fact that on the lower levels people do most of this work themselves, and do not hire any labour. It appears rather paradoxical that the 'average' and 'poor' people spend proportionately more on 'luxuries', but this can be explained by the fact that tobacco and liquor are included under this head and most people in the village are addicted to the habits of smoking and drinking. Finally, under the head 'miscellaneous' —which includes expenditure on entertainments, recreation, medicine and other unforeseen domestic expenses—the 'poor' spend the least, and on each higher level the expenditure is greater.

The visible manifestations of a family's standard of living are: type of dwelling and household possessions, clothing and ornaments, nature of work done by the members of the family and diet. Brief reference has already been made to the different types of dwellings and their average possessions. In a general way it can be said that a house and its belongings indicate the owner's standard of living. Gold and silver ornaments as well as expensive clothes are regarded as marks of superior economic status. Brahmins, Komtis, rich Reddis and well-to-do Muslims are expected 'to wear clothes befitting their status'. Persons belonging to lower castes, particularly untouchables, are criticized for imitating the dress-styles of the higher castes, and even when they acquire wealth they are expected to continue the traditional style of clothing suitable for their humble social status.

In the next two sections we shall examine the division of labour and differences in diet on the four levels of living in the community.

3. WORK: DIVISION OF LABOUR

Division of labour in the community is governed by a variety of factors. Important among them are: caste, sex, age and social status.

Caste is an important and rigid determinant of division of labour. Under this system several occupations have been preserved as caste monopolies, while some are 'open' and may be adopted by persons belonging to all castes. This system of division of labour by occupation has been examined at some length in Chapter III.

The factors of sex, age and social status govern the division of labour in nearly all types of work in the community. First, 'masculine' and 'feminine' pursuits are clearly distinguished: a woman doing man's work is laughed at; a man undertaking any specifically feminine tasks provides a favourite theme for popular gossip. Household work, agricultural activities, traditional craft or occupation of the family, and socio-religious rites and ceremonies are all marked by division of work on the basis of sex.

The age factor is equally important, but not so rigid. Six basic age divisions are recognized in the society: (i) 'Infant' from birth to weaning. (ii) 'Child' from weaning to about twelve. (iii) 'Grown-up boys or girls' from twelve until marriage or even a year or two later. (iv) 'Grown-up people' from twenty to about thirty-eight. (v) Middle-aged from about thirty-eight to fifty. (vi) 'Aged', over fifty. Each of these age divisions carries with it a more or less recognized status which determines the nature and quantity of work to be done by the individual in question. Only in the lower strata of the community we find the 'child' burdened with a regular share in domestic and occupational tasks. The children in the families on upper levels may occasionally do odd bits of work, but no responsibility is thrust on them. As they grow up, girls have to take an increasing interest in domestic tasks. 'Grown-up boys and girls' must seriously start 'learning to do things', and are gradually entrusted with some responsibility. However, it is on the 'grown-up people' that the main responsibility of 'doing all the work' and running the affairs of the household rests. The 'middle-aged' people continue to do a part of the practical work; but their time is more occupied by planning, direction and supervision. Depending on their age and personality, the 'aged' continue to supervise and direct the work of the younger members. As they grow older they content themselves merely by giving suggestions and eventually retire from active work or its planning, and devote their time mostly to their grandchildren.

Considerations of general social status also determine the nature of work to be done by an individual. For example, a man of recognized social status will not draw water from a public well, where he could be seen doing so by others. Womenfolk from such households will not be seen collecting cow-dung from the streets, nor will they do any work in the fields.

With these preliminary observations we can proceed to describe at greater length the actual division of labour in the community. The following table will illustrate the traditional division of work between men and women:

Activity	Man's work	Woman's work
(1) Domestic work (daily routine and maintenance of the house)	Occasional repairs to the house	Sweeping the house every day, and keeping its surroundings clean. Throwing away the rubbish. Sprinkling water in the courtyard and in front of the main entrance. Assisting husband in repairs to the house
	Cooking during the illness or menstrual impurity of the wife (when no other woman is available). Scrubbing the utensils during wife's serious illness	Fetching water from the well. Cooking. Serving food to menfolk and children. Scrubbing the utensils. Husking paddy. Grinding grains
	Occasionally washing his own clothes	Washing her own, as well as children's and husband's clothes
	Occasionally making beds	Making beds
	May look after children	Looking after children
	Chopping firewood and bringing it home	Collecting fuel in the nearby jungle
	Killing and cutting up goats and sheep	Preparation and storage of pickles, preserves and dried vegetables
	Marketing	Marketing, especially purchase of provisions
	Climbing trees for fruit	Collecting vegetables, picking gourds and okras from the backyard garden
	Erecting and repairing the cattle-shed	Feeding the cattle. Keeping the shed clean

Activity	Man's work	Woman's work
(2) Agriculture	Cutting shrubs. Repairing bunds of the paddy fields. Digging earth	Helping men in disposal of shrubs and in repairing the bunds
	Ploughing	— — —
	Sowing	May help in sowing
	Weeding	Weeding
	Harvesting	Harvesting
	Carrying the crops home	Carrying the crops home
(3) Festivals and ceremonies	Decorating the house if necessary	Cleaning the house
	Arranging feasts. Distributing food at feasts. Cooking if necessary	Cooking for feasts
	Actual worship, making sacrifice and offering food	Making initial preparation for worship, sacrifice, offering of food, etc.
		Singing
(4) Birth, marriage and death	(i) Birth. Waiting outside for running errands	Attending to the expectant mother. Assisting at the time of actual delivery. Taking care of the newborn. Disposing of the after-birth. Care of the mother
	(ii) Marriage. Negotiations and settlement regarding marriage	Women consulted at all stages: final settlement generally with their approval
	Making provision of food and money	Making initial preparation for the ceremony. Buying cloth and ornaments
	Arrangements for feasts	Cooking and looking after 'internal' arrangements
		Singing
	(iii) Death. Carrying the corpse. Digging the grave or preparing the pyre	Preparing the corpse for cremation or burial. Wailing. Throwing away the earthen pots

Activity	Man's work	Woman's work
(5) Village administration and politics	All village offices, as well as minor government offices held by men. Village council composed entirely of men	May appear before the village council only as witnesses
	Intrigue and factionalism	Generally instigate the menfolk indirectly. Quarrels among women often lead to complications in the inter-relations of men

In the above table no reference has been made to the division of labour between men and women in the practice of their caste occupations and crafts. In this sphere the role of the sexes has been defined by the traditions of the individual castes. Some typical examples will suffice. Among the Brahmins, only men perform priestly functions; women have no share in this task. Komti women may manage their shop at home, but they do not go round, as do their menfolk, setting up their shops at all the weekly markets in the neighbouring villages. Among the potters, both men and women can work at the wheel. Similarly, the caste traditions of the weavers permit both men and women to work together without making any sharp distinction between masculine and feminine spheres of activity. The same is true of the washerman's caste. Among the other occupational castes, however, the respective fields of men and women are well defined. Only men among the Golla take out their flocks and herds for grazing. Among the Gaondlas, again, only men go round the village collecting juice from the palm trees. Their womenfolk, however, assist them in fermenting it, storing it in the shop, and also in selling it. Hair-cutting and shaving are done only by males in the barber's caste. The traditional rules of the Panch Bramha group of village artisans enjoin that the principal roles in the occupations would be those of men, whilst women have only minor and secondary functions connected with them. Thus the smiths dealing in gold and silver, iron, and bell-metal, do not allow the women to work at the forge, for their caste tradition specifically lays down that this task should be done only by men. In another section belonging to the same group, the women are prohibited from handling the principal carpenter's tools. Lower down in the social scale, among the Erkalas, the men occupy themselves with hunting and trapping, while women weave mats and seek some additional income by fortune-telling. Among the Madigas males deal with dead animals; women come into the picture only when the meat has to be carried home and cooked. Both men and women may work at curing hides. Shoe-making and other leather-work is mainly done by men. On ritual and ceremonial occasions, musical instruments are played only by Madiga men.

Earlier it has been pointed out that men avoid tasks which are generally known as 'feminine'; and women in their turn are expected not to undertake pursuits which are traditionally regarded as 'masculine'. It is true that during the illness or absence of his wife, a man has to perform some of her domestic duties, but that is obviously a compromise with necessity. Any man taking undue interest in feminine tasks soon earns the unenviable epithet of 'half-woman', and is exposed to the ridicule of the community. Asking a man to do some feminine work would be almost tantamount to questioning his masculinity. 'Put bangles on your wrist, husk the paddy and cook the meals', is a remark often used in reproach to admonish those who lack manly qualities and courage. A woman going out of her way to do anything which is regarded as 'man's work' is noticed and adversely commented upon by the society. It is unthinkable that a woman can handle the plough. It should be pointed out here that sometimes a woman deliberately undertakes to do masculine work to 'bring home' to the husband the realization that he is not fulfilling his manly obligations and thus to awaken him to his proper responsibilities. Middle-aged women and widows can do some men's work without social censure.

Reference has been made to the six basic age divisions recognized in the community. Among the 'rich' and the 'well-to-do' families children do very little; but among the 'average' and the 'poor' they have to help the parents. Grazing the cattle, assisting parents in their work in the fields during the busy season, looking after younger siblings, and running errands are regarded as children's work. The girls have to help their mother in the kitchen. As they grow up their share in work gradually increases. Boys take more interest in 'outdoor' work, whilst girls are absorbed in the domestic routine. During this stage of life the 'grown-up boys and girls' even of rich and well-to-do families have to apply themselves to work. The major responsibility rests on the adults and the middle-aged people, and here the social status of the persons concerned will determine the type of work to be done by them.

This brings us to social status as a determinant in the division of work in the community. The rich and influential people will not do anything which is regarded as humble or is otherwise classed as menial work. The men on this level generally 'plan and supervise', but the hard manual labour is done by hired labourers. They go to their fields, but only stand in a corner and instruct the servants. They will never be seen taking their plough and the bullocks to the field, or even participating in ploughing or sowing. The popular conception regarding women at this level is 'they sit in their homes loaded with gold and silver, whiling away their time chewing betel leaves and areca nuts.' However, even in these homes, women are never idle, for they have to do the cooking and look after the children. But considerations of respectability prevent them from doing several things which their counterparts in the lower strata of society regard as their normal day-to-day work. They can never be seen going to their fields, carrying head-loads, drawing water from public wells, or washing clothes in public places. In fact they do not have to do any work outside their homes and are not expected to earn for the upkeep of the family. The rich Muslim women observe *purdah*, i.e. they never go out of their house without a veil, and considerations of respectability demand that their sphere of activity should strictly be confined to their houses. The situation is materially different in the case of the 'well-to-do' families, but no generalizations can be made regarding this level as a unit, as the social ideals and standards of different castes differ very widely. In general, however, it may be said that the Brahmin and the Komti, being higher castes and respected people in the village, more or less follow the ideals of the rich and refrain from doing heavy manual labour as well as from all other work traditionally regarded as inferior. This is true also of the Muslims on this level who, because of their urban conceptions of middle-class respectability, think it below their dignity to do any inferior work publicly. The women from the above three groups seek to emulate the examples of the women in rich families. But in the other well-to-do families belonging to the agricultural and occupational castes notions of respectability relating to work are different. Among them also, labourers are hired for heavy manual labour, such as carrying loads; but menfolk do not object to ploughing their own fields, nor avoid out-of-door work. Of course, the women mainly look after the management of their household affairs and are never expected to earn for the family's support.

The conditions on the two lower levels are more or less similar to one another. Unlike the two upper levels, the menfolk from these groups can be compelled to do government work on a nominal payment. They do most of their work with the assistance provided by the members of the family itself. Even when labourers are engaged by the 'average' people, members of the family continue to work side by side with hired men and women. On both these levels women have comparatively greater freedom. They work out of doors, assist the menfolk in their agricultural activities and crafts, and go out for marketing. Women from 'average' families work mostly in their own homes and in family fields, but during the busy agricultural season they can work for wages as well. This is not regarded as derogatory in any sense. In the poor families, on the other hand, women have to work very hard for, besides doing their quota of work in the running of the home and assisting the husband in agriculture and caste occupation, they have to accept occasional work for wages. Among some of the lower castes, women are expected to work and earn for the upkeep of the family.

4. DIET

The standard of living of a family is judged very often from the quality and quantity of its food. In describing the status and standard of a family, people generally say 'they eat well', 'they live somehow, eating the little that they can grow' or 'they live like animals, eating even wild leaves, flowers and roots'. However, the basic diet of the people consists of rice, millets, lentils, meat and fish. The difference in standards of living is judged by the quantity and kind of rice eaten, the frequency of meat intake in the diet and by the use of spices, fats and oils, jaggery and sugar in the food. Green and powdered red chillies are used by all classes of people in considerable quantities. Vegetables are grown in the backyards during the rainy season, and eaten when ready. When

this supply is exhausted, very few vegetables are bought for everyday home consumption. Tender leaves of the tamarind tree are
curried and pickled, and are popular with all sections of the community. The poorer people collect wild leafy vegetables; those
who are better off buy brinjals, okra and unripe bananas. Tea
and coffee are regarded as fashionable, and are regularly used by
the rich people as well as those who are educated and who have
had some urban contacts. With the exception of the Brahmin and
the Komti all castes permit the drinking of fermented palm-juice
by men; in most of the lower castes women are also not denied its
use. Some Muslims claim never to touch it as its use is not permitted by their religion; others drink it openly. A limited quantity
of other liquor imported from the city is also consumed in the
village.

Among the Hindus, the Brahmin and the Komti are vegetarians; and the eating of all kinds of meat, fish and eggs is forbidden to them. All the Hindu castes abstain from beef; although
the Madiga untouchables are allowed to eat the carrion of cattle
which they are expected to dispose of. The Muslims eat beef, but
refuse pork. With the exception of the Erkalas and the Madigas,
no other Hindu caste eats the domestic pig; wild pigs, of course,
are regarded as a delicacy by all meat-eaters except the Muslims.

Milk and *ghee* (clarified butter) are greatly valued, but are difficult to get, and indeed very few people can claim to have them as
a part of their everyday diet.

Very little fruit is eaten in the village. When in season, mangoes,
guavas and *jamun* (*Eugenia jambolana*) are eaten by the people,
more commonly by the children. The only fruit-bearing trees
grown by them in their backyards are lime and drum-stick trees.
Few people buy any fruit in the markets and shops of the city.
Coconuts and bananas are bought for ceremonial occasions, and
occasionally large varieties of mangoes too are bought from the
shops.

Those who can afford eat three times, others eat only twice daily.
According to the seasons there are variations in the type of food
and also in the time when the principal meals are eaten. The
following menus will illustrate the kind of food eaten by families
at different economic levels:

LEVELS OF LIVING

First Meal

Paratha (thin cakes of unleavened bread made of wheat flour, fried in
    edible fat).
Meat or vegetable or lentil curry.
Hot. pickles.
Tea.

or

Khichri (rice and lentils cooked together with spices).
Meat or vegetable or lentil curry.
Hot pickles.
Tea.

Second Meal

Rice.
Meat or vegetable or lentil or fish curry.
Pickles.

Third Meal

Same as second, with a possible variation in the curry.

AVERAGE FAMILIES

First Meal

Millet gruel.
Chilly powder and salt.
Pickles.

or

Millet bread.
Curried bringals, leafy vegetables or drum-sticks.
Pickles.

or

Rice gruel.
Chilly powder and salt.

Second Meal

Rice.
Meat or vegetable or lentil or fish curry.
Pickles.

Third Meal

Same as second.

In those families which do not eat three meals regularly, rice
left over from the previous evening may be eaten early in the

morning; and a combination of any two menus given above may be adopted for the two principal meals.

POOR FAMILIES

First Meal

Millet gruel.
Chilly powder and salt.

or

Rice left-over from previous evening.
Chilly powder and salt or pickles.

Second Meal

Rice.
Boiled vegetables or lentils (with salt and chillies) or meat curry.

or

Millet bread.
Boiled vegetables or lentils (with salt and chillies) or meat curry.

or

Rice.
Chilly powder and salt.
Pickles.

Third Meal

Rice.
Meat or vegetable or lentil or fish curry.

In the making of curries the rich people use considerable quantities of oil or other fats, and their choice of spices too is more varied. In the average households the curries are not so rich. Finally in the poorer sections they are more or less boiled vegetables and lentils with the addition of salt and chilly powder. It may be added that sweets do not form a regular part of the diet of the people in the community. They are prepared on ceremonial occasions, and may be prepared now and then in the comparatively richer homes. As fish and meat are very expensive, the average and poor families have to depend for most of the time on watery lentil curries or cheap vegetables.

The ethnographic record of the diet appeared to be so appalling that we organized a comprehensive nutritional survey of the community in conjunction with our research project. This work was planned and carried out under the supervision of a nutritional expert from the Medical Faculty of the Osmania University. A random sample of families covering all levels of living in the community was selected, and, following the universal weighing-method, every item of the diet was weighed correctly to an ounce in these families. The International Scale of Family Coefficients was used to calculate the number of consumption units in each family, and data was carefully analysed for working out the mean intake of diet per consumption unit and the intake of calories, proximate principles, minerals and vitamins. Simultaneously, a medical examination of all members of the families selected for the survey was also undertaken; in the course of which along with height and weight measurements a general clinical examination with special reference to abnormalities of hair, eyes, skin, lips, gums, tongue, and the peripheral nervous system was done. While a detailed summary of the above survey would be inappropriate in a sociological study, some of its main conclusions will not be out of place here:

(i) The picture of nutrition emerging from the survey gives room to believe that there is mild sub-nutrition in the 'rich' and 'well-to-do' families and mild malnutrition in the 'average' and 'poor' families.

(ii) There is a sub-clinical deficiency of thiamine, riboflavin and Vitamin A. Phrynoderma of the skin, cheilosis, multiple fissuring of the tongue, gingivitis, and xerosis of the conjunctivae are fairly common in the community; their incidence being greater on the lower strata. The use of un-milled, slightly home-pounded rice explains the lack of any gross Vitamin B^1 deficiency. It may partly be explained also by the consumption of fermented palm-juice in nearly all sections of the community.

(iii) The protein intake is slightly inadequate. This is more apparent in the families classed as average and poor. In the lower income brackets the intake of fats is also insufficient.

(iv) With the exception of venereal diseases and malaria which are evenly distributed in all levels of the society, the incidence of other diseases—particularly deficiency diseases—is much higher in the lower income groups.

As a rule menfolk eat first, women follow. Children are served as soon as the meals are cooked. Among men, it is expected that the elders as well as others occupying a higher position in the scale of kinship should be served first and younger members of the family should wait for their turn. But during the busy season, or on all other occasions when exigencies of work demand it, the younger people can sit down to eat with the elders, and can even precede them. However, it is regarded as bad form for women to take their meals before the menfolk have eaten. In all the higher castes this would indeed be viewed very seriously, and a woman found to be indulging in anything like this would be ridiculed by the other family members. On the lowest strata of the society, occasional exceptions to this rule can be observed. There too it is regarded as impolite, but is nevertheless tolerated.

CHAPTER SEVEN

Living Together

1. INTER-PERSONAL RELATIONS

THE people of Shamirpet, like the other peasants of Andhra, exercise considerable reserve in their initial dealings with outsiders. The first impression that one gets regarding their attitude is one of extreme constriction, suspiciousness and guarded behaviour. When this initial reserve is broken down, they reveal themselves in a totally different light—as emotional, communicative, and at times even boisterous. Nearly all of them have great curiosity, and are easily attracted by anything that is even slightly uncommon or unusual. Opinions are freely expressed, and all public gatherings—big or small—are rather noisy. Middle-aged and elderly people generally have a grim expression, and it is considered a mark of respectability in women if they walk with their eyes downcast. But unobtrusiveness is not regarded as a virtue, and the people freely make comments and counter-comments on all subjects with which they may or may not have any concern. There is a great tradition for argument, which can easily drift into becoming a noisy quarrel or altercation. Tempers rise easily, and abuse may be showered volubly by both sides; but differences are patched up as easily, and it is not uncommon to see two people walking together as great friends although on the previous day they may have quarrelled bitterly on some trifling issue. In their inter-personal relations the people are hypercritical and very sensitive. This leads to a perpetual attitude of fault finding. As the people do not easily let go an opportunity of commenting on and criticizing their neighbours, their relations are never very smooth and certain. However, on occasions which demand a display of good-neighbourliness and generosity people come forward very readily to help those who need it. It is common to suspect others' motives; and not unusual to be always on the alert to read hidden meanings into the seemingly innocent utterances of others. Analysis of their life-histories shows that the people are not given to introspection. They are always on the defensive; but their inter-personal relations are not characterized by detachment. In their thoughts, likes and dislikes they are quite open, and all persons having even casual contacts have a fair acquaintance with one anothers' ideas and attitudes

It is not uncommon for people to analyse and describe the personality-traits of other inhabitants of the village as well as of outsiders coming into the settlement. Positive qualities, having obvious approval, find expression in such epithets as: 'good person', 'hard-working', 'honest', 'respectable', 'well-behaved', 'intelligent', 'generous' or 'large-hearted' and 'faithful'. Epithets describing negative traits which do not meet with social approval are many and varied, and among others include: 'bad person', 'lazy', 'dishonest', 'shameless', 'mannerless', 'foolish', 'miserly', 'small-hearted', 'unfaithful', 'good-for-nothing', 'liar', 'all talk but no deeds', 'ill-tempered', etc. Analysis of such traits is firmly established in the culture-pattern, and occupies an important place in the conversation of the people when they meet in small groups. Although conformity to social norms is idealized and emphasized, when there is a breach of traditional ways the person responsible likes to confess it in confidence to someone else. Long conversations and the mutual sharing of secrets are quite frequent. However, when friendships break up the sanctity of earlier secrets is not protected by any code of honour. Within limits originality and innovation are admired; but excess and ostentation soon lead to social censure and ridicule.

Subjects coming under the critical eye of society are: (i) breaches of traditional norms, (ii) display and exhibitionism, (iii) sexuality, (iv) efforts to rise in the power hierarchy, (v) conspicuous success, and (vi) originality and 'too many new ideas'. Carrying tales and 'whispering about the doings in others' houses' go on in the community on a wide scale. It is criticized by the aggrieved persons and their sympathizers, but no one regards it as inherently bad. 'Incidents' or breaches of established norms are discussed in small conversational groups at first, and the more important ones among them gradually filter through and reach the responsible village elders. Few such breaches escape the attention of society, although in many of them no action may be called for by the caste or village elders. Display and ostentation are severely criticized in the community. Individuals inviting social censure for this fault are frequently nicknamed and mimicked. The behaviour of persons who have just come into wealth or a position of authority is subjected to a particularly critical scrutiny. Sexuality, in all its different aspects, provides another popular theme for gossip. Although bragging about unusual potency and sexual adventures is very common, in general the community watches and comments upon all abnormalities, particularly excessive indulgence and lack of adequate sex vigour. The comments of the group in this sphere too are merciless. Those who are on the higher rungs of the ladder of power hierarchy jealously watch their own position, and anyone casting a covetous eye on a position of influence at once becomes the target of the criticism of several pressure groups in the community. People attaining conspicuous success are invariably the subject of malicious criticism. Their actions and speech are closely watched, and later commented upon. Opportunities for taunting them are eagerly sought, and indirect references to their humble origin are frequently made. Finally, persons having too many novel and original ideas also invite the criticism of society. While people are unsparing in their comments, they are very much reserved in their praise.

Anger is freely expressed. Loud shouting, use of foul language, and occasional physical violence are the principal channels for the expression of aggressiveness. Sentiments of love and friendship too are publicly expressed; the only exception in this case being the suppression of all sentiments suggesting sexual intimacy.

Concepts of 'manliness' and 'defending the honour' play a significant part in governing inter-personal relations within the community. It is not manly to beat anyone who is too young, too aged, weak or infirm. On the contrary, a fight between equals is always considered fair; although it may necessitate action on the part of village elders. Notions of personal and family prestige differ in different castes, as well as at different income levels. Any challenge to personal prestige or family honour is bound to arouse a violent reaction.

Truth and straightforwardness are acclaimed as social ideals; but intelligent and ingenious ways of deception too receive unmistakable appreciation, Cowardice and treachery are condemned, but people still indulge in malicious gossip and back-biting. Mutual suspicion characterizes the general nature of inter-personal relations. Two families on the road to prosperity are likely to be jealous of each other; but adversity almost never fails to bring them nearer and closer. Exercising little control over their emotions, people get excited very quickly; anger and friendship are both aroused in them with equal ease.

A study of inter-group relations will give us a better idea of the nature and quality of the attitudes that largely govern inter-personal relations in the community. For this we shall first examine the inter-caste attitudes embodied in stereotypes, and later analyse similar attitudes and opinions covering two sets of rival groups—educated and uneducated, and those with urban contacts and those without them.

INTER-CASTE ATTITUDES: SOME STEREOTYPES

Inter-caste attitudes find expression in several stereotypes which are a part of the thought patterns of the people, and find expression both in jest and banter as well as in quarrels and outbursts of anger. Among others, the following stereotypes and related anecdotes were noted in Shamirpet.

The Brahmin is 'pious from outside, but not so at heart'. He is 'tricky and calculating'. 'He instigates people, but always keeps himself in the background.'

The Komti is 'a born coward, but a shrewd business man'. 'When he says anything on oath, take it that he is telling a deliberate falsehood.' 'He spares no ingenuity to save even a counterfeit coin.' 'Gods do not penalize a Komti for telling lies, he is born to do that.' The anecdotes concerning the miserliness of the Komtis are indeed many and varied. 'If a fly falls in butter-milk, rich people will throw the butter-milk away, the poor will throw away the fly and drink the butter-milk. But the Komti squeezes out the butter-milk before throwing the fly away.' 'If a relation comes to the house of a Komti and the time of the evening meal approaches, he will think, "If this guest goes home, I shall be able to save one meal." The guest on the other hand thinks, "If I stay here a little while more, one meal will be saved at home." And a battle of wits goes on to save just one meal.' The stories of their cowardice are also many. 'A Komti is a warrior in words, but a rat in deeds.' 'If you strike him once he will say, "Strike me a second time and I will see." If you strike him a second time, he will say, "Strike me a third time and I shall show you what it means to beat me." You go on beating him, and all that he will do is to repeat his threats without having the courage to hit back even once.'

Of the Kapu, or agricultural castes, general public opinion seems to be good. 'They are a hard-working people, faithfully attached to the soil.' 'The Kapus are the *annadata*, literally producers of agricultural wealth. If they do not cultivate the land and produce grain, what shall we eat?' Social comment is generally unfavourable on the rich Reddi landlords who make excessive demands on the tenants.

The Kummari's place in common village talk is not very enviable. 'Living in the world of his earthen pots, he knows little of the world outside.' 'Because he works continuously at the wheel, no strength is left in his loins. No wonder, he cannot satisfy his wife.'

More than anyone else, the Golla is the butt of many cruel jokes. He is criticized for his simplicity, for his dirtiness and for his awkward gestures and rustic manner of speech. His shocking cowardice too is often commented upon. 'He tends sheep. He is no better than one of his flock.' 'The Golla is a model of cleanliness. Look at his body, it is covered with lice all over.' 'See, how a Golla talks! If you hear him from a distance you will think that he is quarrelling with someone; but no, he is discussing with his wife what to cook for the evening meal.' In animated discussion the Gollas are certainly given to much gesticulation. 'Others also gesticulate but the mannerisms of the Gollas are remarkably different.' 'In sheer cowardice only a Sale will excel him.' 'Bluff him, threaten him and a Golla will readily agree to what you say. He is too thick-headed to understand you otherwise.' 'You can never know what a Golla will do. Give him a sweet-smelling flower and he will put it in his anus.'

In the village community the Sale caste symbolizes cowardice. If anyone is afraid of going out in the dark or runs away from a fight, people remark, 'Are you the son of a Sale? That alone can explain your remarkable bravery.' This is one of the most widely prevalent and generally accepted stereotypes. Many a Sale would also accept it, and using different words would say, 'We mind our work and do not get mixed up in local affairs. What use is it fighting like animals?' Others generally say, 'If you strike a Komti with a stick, he will hit you back with his tongue. He has at least a store of filthy abuse which he uses as a weapon of defence. But the Sale is too timid to do even this. All that he can do is to run into his house and hide himself.'

The Gaondla, 'when he is poor, carries empty pots of palm-juice from every house; but when he amasses wealth, his head turns. Then he learns to speak the language of the urban people.'

The Sakali is 'after all a washerman. One who washes the dirty clothes of the rest of the community cannot himself remain clean.' Women belonging to this caste have a reputation for their great capacity for drinking. 'They do not require much persuasion for granting sexual favours to people outside the caste; and the devils —Sakali women—are such adepts in sexual technique that anyone falling into their clutches once remains their slave for ever.'

There are several witty stories about the status of the Mangali (barber). 'No doubt his general status is low, but he always has the advantage of the company of rich and influential men. Do you not sit with him while he is cutting your hair and giving you a shave? Even rich agriculturists have to allow him to sit near them as if he were their equal in status.' 'It is true that his status is not very high. But who does not bow to him? While cutting a king's hair the barber orders "Bend a little towards me", and the king unquestioningly obeys him. Who else can catch hold of your hair, pull your ears or slap you on the cheek? Ask a barber to cut your hair and shave you, and you will have the answer.' 'The agriculturists always have to worry about their crops—in some years they grow well, in others they do not. But there is no uncertainty about the crops harvested by a barber—the beards of his clients grow with an unfailing regularity.'

The castes in the Panch Bramha group are not regarded as particularly auspicious. 'While starting on a journey if you happen to see a person belonging to one of these groups, you should take it as a sign of ill-luck. It indicates a possible failure of your mission.'

'The Mala and the Madiga will be rude if you are gentle with them, and will be gentle if you are rude to them.' 'Kick him first and then ask him to do a thing, a Madiga will never refuse. Ask him to do something in soft words and he will have a thousand excuses ready.'

Although Shamirpet has maintained, even in the worst years of communal tension, a fairly honourable record of communal harmony and the relations between the Hindu and the Muslim sections of the village population have been cordial in every sense, the two communities have some generalized notions about the inherent qualities and attributes of each other. The Hindus will say, 'The untouchables are impure, but Muslims are poisonous. If you touch a Madiga you may have to sever only the finger with which you touched him, but if you touch a Muslim you will have to cut off the arm itself.' 'The Muslims are good only in two things —they eat and copulate like beasts. Who else except a Muslim would ever think of going to bed with his uncle's daughter, who is next only to his real sister.' The Muslims are regarded as showy and ostentatious. 'A Muslim will eat stale rice inside his house, but when coming out he will apply some clarified butter to his lips. Then he will belch loudly and say, "How much fried rice and meat have I eaten to-day".' With regard to conversion to Islam the Hindus often say, 'A Hindu untouchable of yesterday becomes a Muslim to-day; and to-morrow he will start proclaiming that his forefathers lived in Arabia!' The Muslims, having for generations prided themselves as the ruling race of Hyderabad, tend to look down upon the Hindus, and make fun of their numerous gods and superstitious beliefs. On the whole the Muslims regard the other community as 'cowardly and mean'. But the recent changes in the political fortunes of the State, resulting in the end of Muslim rule, have had a sobering effect on the Muslims, and now they do not take the offensive against their Hindu neighbours, as some of them very commonly did in the period preceding the Police Action of 1948.

I have pointed out earlier that most of these stereotypes find expression in jest and banter, and occasionally in outbursts of anger. While each caste seeks to proclaim and prove its own superiority in some respect it invariably holds some generalized notions, such as those described above, about the inherent qualities of the other castes. It is believed that there can be individual exceptions to the rule, but regarding the castes themselves these stereotypes are valid. However, very few of these notions influence the general tone of life in the community. Inter-group tension between Hindus and Muslims, engendered partly by political controversies in the Hyderabad State, threatened disharmony and possible breach of peace in the village in the period preceding and following the intervention of the Government of India. The recognition of the *fait accompli* in the State by the Muslims and the change in their approach and attitude towards the Hindus soon established cordial relations between the two communities. At the time of our investigations the Brahmin/non-Brahmin controversy, which was governing the political alignments of people within the State to a considerable extent, had its echoes in Shamirpet also. In the Telangana area, in general, it was taking the shape of an open conflict of interest between Brahmins and Reddis. In Shamirpet the individual relations between the Brahmin household and the Reddi residents of the community were very cordial; but in the discussion of general political and social questions there was a persistent anti-Brahmin feeling. Casteism was a force of no mean significance in the first general elections under the Republican Constitution, and manifested itself in such slogans as 'Reddis must solidly stand together', 'Irrespective of party considerations Reddis must vote for a Reddi candidate', or 'Non-Brahmins must unite to strike a blow to Brahmin domination'. As the interaction between the different castes in the wider political field is still in its initial stages, the pattern of group alignments has not emerged very clearly. A third factor may also be mentioned here. Under the influence of the social and political propaganda of the Scheduled Caste Federation, the untouchable castes have started voicing their grievances and protests against their position in the caste hierarchy. So far these protests have been mild and verbal only. Perceiving the economic advantages of the traditional system, the untouchables have not yet seriously challenged the assumptions that underlie the structure of the community. However, the abolition of untouchability by law, the granting of equal shares to them in all public utility services, and protests against the traditional system by the more vocal and assertive untouchables have aroused some tension with regard to them in the higher castes. 'Times are changing. The untouchables were admitted to schools first, then they started travelling with us in the same railway trains and buses; and now they want to draw water from our wells and eat with us in public eating-houses. The government is indulging them; and for vote-getting the political parties are spoiling them. If things go on like this, in the future these low castes will want to marry our daughters and sisters,' remarked a Reddi agriculturist. Those standing nearby nodded their assent. The above remark is illustrative of the general attitude of 'responsible' persons in the higher castes.

EDUCATED VERSUS UNEDUCATED

Adverse comments are frequently heard from the educated and uneducated people against each other. The uneducated especially have some stereotypes regarding the educated; and the latter often express derogatory opinions about the illiterate members of the community.

Remarks echoing the following opinions and sentiments are commonly heard from the uneducated people: 'What use is education to us? After four years at the school all that our children learn is to hold a pen in their hands. What we really want them to learn is the holding of the plough firmly.' 'By learning to read a couple of books at the school the youngsters begin to think that they have in their skulls all the knowledge and learning in the world. They scoff at their parents, belittle the experience of the elders, and seem to think no end of themselves. Realities of life soon teach them a lesson. Sooner or later they repent and fall at the feet of the elders.' 'Everyone says, "Send your children to school; uneducated people are like animals; education makes them human beings." But what do we get out of education? Boys learn to read and write, but they forget the traditional ways. They do not want to cultivate the family land, and are ashamed of their traditional profession. They all want jobs in the city. If things go on like this what will be the future of the community?' 'The educated people excel each other in tall talk and boasting. They will drink, gamble and intrigue. There is nothing else that they can do.' 'What service do the educated people render to the community? They instigate simple illiterate people to quarrel, and later exploit the situation to their own advantage.' 'We village people are simple. Education makes us crooked.' In substance the average attitude boils down to this: education shakes a person's belief in the traditional ways and creates in turn new desires and ambitions; these factors operating simultaneously make the educated persons misfits in the community.

On the other hand, the educated people think: 'The illiterate

villagers are simple, superstitious and stupid. They believe anyone.
Conditions in the village will never improve so long as they dominate the scene.' 'Without education a man is like a beast.' 'As
you goad a bullock, you can goad an uneducated villager.' 'Why
do petty government officers harass us so much? Only because we
are illiterate.'

It may be pointed out here that so far the educated section
consists only of people who have attended primary or secondary
village schools for four to six years. The number of these people
does not exceed eighty, and from among them also many have
virtually relapsed into illiteracy. With the exception of some
government officials who are not a permanent part of the village
population, none has so far had the advantage of modern scientific
education in one of the better schools of the city, although at the
time of our investigations some half a dozen boys from the village
were attending higher schools. It is interesting to note that persons having education in rural vernacular schools have the same
fear, suspicion and general sentiments regarding those who have
modern or 'English education', as the illiterate section of the
population has about those who have a background of village
education. Notwithstanding the popular prejudice against education of both types, its economic advantages as well as prestige
value are now generally recognized. With the gradual improvement in the standards and practices of the schools more parents
are now anxious to enrol their children there. Fears still persist,
however, and people urge that, besides imparting literacy, the
school should also equip them better for earning their livelihood.

URBAN VERSUS RURAL

The general pattern of comment regarding urban and urbanized people is the same as that of the comment of the uneducated
about the educated. In the context of urbanization, or even in
that of the adoption of some urban traits, supplementary opinions
are often added. 'We villagers are simple-hearted; but the town
people are crafty, calculating and self-centred.' 'When the relations from the city come to stay with us we receive them well,
and give them the choicest share in everything. But when we
happen to go to them they have difficulty even in recognizing
us. And they treat us as if we were an unwelcome burden on them.'
'Never trust a town-dweller, for he never distinguishes between

truth and untruth. He is sweet when he wants us to do something for him; and coarse when the work is over.' 'The ways of city people are strange. They will go to bed even with their cousins and aunts.' 'The villager who has lived in the city for some years learns all the ways of the townspeople. He may be an insignificant menial in the city, but when he returns to the village he behaves like a big lord.'

The people with urban contacts, on the other hand, regard the village-folk as rustic and crude; and consider themselves more forward and civilized. They have an unmistakable tendency to look down upon 'these simple and uncomprehending people', make fun of their ways and occasionally exploit them by exerting undue pressure. 'These people are timid and foolish. They are afraid of anyone who can make some show of authority, and yield very easily to the pressure of officials', said a village youth when he was asked to give his opinion about his fellow villagers, who had not had the benefit of contacts with city ways.

Those who have some urban contacts are gradually coming to the fore in village leadership. They are often criticized and commented upon, but nevertheless their opinions are valued and in general the community looks to them for guidance in all situations 'where it has to face the outside world'.

2. CHILDHOOD, YOUTH AND OLD AGE

This section is devoted to a brief study of the three most significant stages of life—childhood, youth and old age. While family, kin-group and caste are important units of social structure which influence the course of an individual's life-cycle, from the point of view of socialization and social control the significance of the village as a unit cannot be minimized. Apart from the family and the caste, people spend most of their time in their respective age-groups, and through this process of growing-up together, common play and participation in youth activity the people tend to have a common value—orientation and certain common basic attitudes towards life.

For the first two or three months of a child's life the mother remains almost in sole charge of it. A young mother is invariably instructed in the technique of mothercraft by an elderly female relative, but at this stage it is her responsibility to look after the needs of the child. Attention given to the infant during these months is fairly constant. Even in the poorer families the mother does not go out to work, leaving the child alone at home, during these months; although her domestic duties may require partial abandonment of the child in the busy hours of morning and evening. In the families on the upper economic levels of the community the infant is well looked after indeed; its crying is looked upon as a sign of distress and everything is done to pacify it. In the matter of breast feeding no definite schedule is followed: the child is fed whenever 'it is hungry and asks for food, by crying' or when 'the mother's breasts become heavy'. At night the infant sleeps with the mother, generally with a nipple in its mouth and is allowed to suck whenever it desires. Toilet training at this stage is completely neglected, and soiling of clothes does not arouse any disgust. It is taken in a matter-of-fact way, and the wet clothes are changed whenever they are noticed by the mother or any other female relative. When the child starts crying the usual way to pacify it is for the mother to offer it her breast. If this is not possible at the moment, or if it fails to achieve the desired objective, other methods may be tried. The mother, a female relation or a sibling may take up the child, mildly pat it continuously on the back and hum a lullaby to send it to sleep. It may be put in a cradle attached to a swing and rocked slowly. Another method very commonly employed by anyone who happens to be near the crying child is to distract it by making funny noises or by engaging in a one-way conversation with it. Recourse may also be taken to a gentle massage of its genitals by the mother or one of its siblings.

After this stage of early infancy, during the pre-walking stage, the pattern of treatment accorded to the child is somewhat different. About three months after birth the mother is called upon to take her full share of household and economic duties, and consequently she can no longer give her undivided attention to the child. Other women members of the household, particularly older sisters, now come increasingly to share this responsibility. When the child is a little older and 'it is easy to handle it' menfolk also begin to look after it now and then. At this stage it does not receive the constant attention which it received during the earlier stage, and the frequency and duration of periods of partial abandonment also increase. Feeding continues to be irregular. At four or five months some soft foods are gradually introduced. When the child shows signs of digesting these well, siblings and other members of the family begin giving bits of food to pacify the baby when it starts crying. During this stage people love to handle the child, and there is very considerable fondling and play. No effort is made to establish sphincter control in the child at this point. Every possible help is given to the child to learn to stand and walk. While people take great delight in imitating the sounds made by the child, efforts are also made to teach him to talk. Words for grandfather, grandmother, father, mother, uncles and aunts, brothers and sisters are generally the first to be taught. In a state of mental agitation and worry the mother may occasionally spank the child; but this is definitely disapproved and when detected the mother is always reproached by the elders for doing so.

With some modifications this continues even during the early childhood, up to the age of about three. When the child learns to walk it is carried about less by the elders. Now and then it may be left to play by itself in the backyard or in the lane in front of the house. Help in its learning processes continues to be given, and elders indulge in considerable fondling of the child. Weaning is not attempted unless necessitated by the mother's pregnancy or by the 'drying up of her breasts'. Attempts at toilet training are made at this stage. When the child wakes up in the morning the mother seats it on the hollow made by joining her feet and keeps on making a hissing sound which is believed to induce a child to ease itself. Now and then the child is taken to a corner, the cloth covering its genital organs is removed, and the hissing sound is made to make it urinate. If the child wets or soils its clothes at this stage the mother or a sibling will say, 'Chhi, you are dirty'. But this is done with a smile and there is hardly any reproach in the remark.

When boys are seen manipulating their organs the elders smile and playfully remove their hands from them. Boys invariably start doing so again, and are not admonished. This amuses rather than irritates the older members of the family. While the sex experience of the children is confined wholly to their manipulation of genital organs, their sex knowledge is considerably wider. Sharing the same room with their parents, they have frequent opportunities of watching them engaged in the coital act. Even at the age of three the vocabulary of several children includes the words for penis, vagina and copulation.

193

Sponging children with warm water is now often replaced by two or three cold baths per week; the frequency being more among the Brahmins and Komtis and less among the Muslims and the untouchables. The elders practise considerable deception in their dealings with the children. Efforts at disciplining them tend to be rather erratic; and extremes of affection and strictures are by no means uncommon. Jealousies between siblings may be induced by members of the family who take delight in watching the irritation, anger and aggressiveness of little children. Tantrums during this stage are frequent. The methods commonly employed to pacify the child are: distracting it by making funny noises, rocking it in a cradle, offering it food or milk, scolding it loudly, threatening it, and finally boxing its ears and spanking it.

Later childhood begins at about five and continues until the advent of adolescence. At this stage the children form their own play-groups; spending several hours of the day in their respective age-groups. Now they are free to play in the streets and the open ground outside the village. Maternal attention is now considerably reduced; the elders keep an eye on them, but apart from this they have considerable freedom. As they grow older solicitation of affectionate responses through handling, play and fondling gradually diminishes. Toilet training becomes strict, and the child is expected to have full control over defecation and urination. Cleanliness is insisted upon, and any failure on his part in this respect arouses anger in the elders. The erring child is ridiculed, chastised and punished. Now they must wear clothes and begin to learn to hide their genitals. If the elders find their organs exposed they point to them and ask, '*Arre*, what is that? Why are you exhibiting that little thing?' Children often develop a sense of shame at this stage, blush at such remarks, hide their organs and run away from the elders. Discipline becomes more rigorous and physical punishment is more frequent. Rewards for good behaviour include praise, partiality and favoured treatment on the part of the parents, larger share of food and small gifts of money. Punishments, on the other hand, include rebukes and threats, ridicule, threats to report the matter to the father, spanking and occasionally denial of food or playing things or even locking up in a solitary room. Considerable dishonesty is practised by elders in their dealings with children, which is often detected by the latter and angers them all the more. The play-groups cut across the boundaries of family and caste and include boys and girls from different castes. This necessitates the giving of instruction to them by the elders, who explain the hierarchy of the caste system and indicate clearly the groups among whom participation in eating on a basis of equality is permitted. Rules of inter-dining and untouchability are enforced at the age of six or seven; although until the age of adolescence their breaches are not very strictly punished. At the age of six or seven boys and girls come to have their separate play-groups, although their occasional playing together is not prohibited. Sex knowledge and sex experience of the children widens considerably, partly through secretly watching and imitating the elders, partly through oral instruction by older members of the play-group. Masturbation is now stealthily practised. Elders do not take an indulgent view if they find grown-up boys manipulating and rubbing their penes. Ridicule and threats are often employed to cure the habit. The threats commonly given are: 'If you persist in this habit your organ will not grow'; or that 'It will become crooked and you will be useless.' Threats of exposure cause great shame among the boys. Nevertheless, knowledge acquired from older and more experienced members of the age-group indicates that 'the penis grows larger by the practice of masturbation', 'maturity is arrived at earlier' and 'boys not doing it are not tough—they are half-girls', and consequently boys continue to masturbate secretly. A small group of boys may occasionally have a session of joint masturbation. Mutual masturbation is known, though it is less frequent. Similarly, little boys lie down together and imitate the coital act, although this does not involve actual anal penetration. Homosexuality is said to be confined to young people and boys with urban contacts; but we have reason to believe that it is practised on a limited scale by others also. However, it is confined only to pre-adolescent and adolescent groups. A boy persuades a smaller boy to lie down with him, and just rubs his organ at his anus—only in very rare cases is any anal penetration effected. A popular game with the boys is to make a female figure in dust and play at copulation. In the three instances observed by us the imitation was perfect, and resembled normal coitus in all its essentials. Boys and girls play at marriage, which in a few cases culminates in the act of 'sleeping together'. In most cases this is just lying together and no more; in a few it reaches the point of rubbing genital organs. Girls masturbate either by pressing and releasing their clitoris with their fingers or by rubbing their thighs. Obscenity and talk about sex are disapproved by the elders, but the boys regard it as a mark of toughness and as an indication of their grown-up status, and as such indulge in it fairly regularly. Their vocabulary of abuse includes all the major sexual words, and they can often be heard abusing each other in terms such as: 'Copulate with your mother', 'Cohabit with your sister', 'My penis!'—or the rather curious 'Your mother's penis'.

Most children's games involve competition in the use of skills and stamina. The children are divided into several groups and factions, and these often come into conflict on account of intense jealousies and rivalries. Elaborate group *mores* and codes of ethics govern their inter-relations during states of friendship, neutrality and enmity. Toughness in boys is the admired quality; weakness, refined ways, spying and complaining coming in for criticism and ridicule. Running away from fright, crying and treachery to the group are remembered long after the quarrels and restoration of peace between conflicting factions. Outside the play-group the growing children have to lend a helping hand to their parents. Grown-up girls assist their mothers at their domestic tasks and take partial charge of their younger siblings, while boys do odd jobs for the father and other older male relatives. It is now time that they should take their first steps in preparing for adult life.

Adolescence brings about a significant change in the life of both boys and girls. By this age girls are expected to become proficient in all the major domestic tasks. Negotiations for their marriage are invariably started at this age. They grow up faster than the boys. While boys of a comparable age are still regarded as 'grown-up children who do not understand', girls come to be looked upon more or less as fully-grown women. Now they must be careful about their dress; particularly their breasts should never be exposed. They should 'not run about the village like boys', nor should they talk or laugh so loudly as to attract notice. Mothers advise them to be cautious in their behaviour, for this is the age when young people start giving attention to them. Young people have a special fascination for adolescent girls 'whose youth is just beginning to blossom'. Young men succeeding in fondling 'the unripe, half-developed breasts' of a girl and in having intercourse with one 'whose pubic hair is just beginning to grow' easily win the admiration of their age-group. For the girls it is a rather difficult period, as they have to find a middle way between the dictates of their romantic impulses and the fear of the social censure that comes to all wayward girls. Adolescent boys divide their time more or less equally between 'learning to do things' with their parents and being with their playmates. Childish games in the dust are now replaced by more vigorous country sport. Within the age-group itself thoughts and efforts in the domain of sex come to occupy a very important place. Masturbation is now regarded as 'unmanly' and gradually given up. Lying with other boys is also looked down upon. Efforts are made to attract younger girls for first experimentation in heterosexual love. Far more than these actual experiments, fantasies occupy an important place in their thoughts and conversation. Imaginary affairs with a woman believed to be of easy virtue—or with a completely fictitious character from a distant village—are vividly and elaborately described. Growth of the pubic hair and genital organs is closely watched and compared. In this way they slowly reach their youth when talks for their marriage are opened. On marriage they acquire a new social status.

After marriage the young men and women have to give considerable attention to their economic pursuits and crafts, and as such they have relatively little time left for group activity. Yet, their leisure and time are generally spent in the company of persons belonging more or less to the same age-group, who constitute 'a set of friends'. Important activities of these groups include loafing, playing card games, gossip and conversation. They may even go to the city together; and always act in unison when planning mischief. Confidences are exchanged within these groups; and people often narrate to each other their recent exploits. One of the favourite themes is boasting regarding success in sexual adventures. Success—real or imaginary—with an adolescent girl is vividly described within this narrow circle. Graphic and vivid details are always added to make the account more colourful. 'It was her very first experience. Oh, there was so much blood. I did not know whether to pacify her or to concentrate on the act', one would say. This would start a chain in which all others would narrate their parallel experiences—many of which would be slightly modified editions of often-told tales. The *motif* of a girl being frightened by the largeness of a man's organ also keeps on repeating itself. Some young men introduce a note of slight sadism when they talk of their 'forcing-in' acts against unwilling partners. General comments about the goings on in the village are an important item in the activities of these groups. The latest scandals are discussed and spread to the rest of the community in one or other of these groups. Women are classified into sexual categories, such as 'the easy' type, 'invite you and later say "no"' type, 'the wrestler' type and 'the hollow'. Code words are employed to describe different persons. Peculiarities and weaknesses of men are also noted and commented upon. Domestic duties do not leave much leisure to young married women. Consequently they cannot plan any group activity. But they too can exchange views, and discuss the latest affairs and developments while they wait near the well for their turn to draw water or when they go out for washing the clothes and bathing.

Middle-aged people have their own groups. These are informal conversational gatherings; but their membership and attendance is nearly fixed. Groups of men and women meet separately; although two or three women in the village are privileged and have access to some of the men's groups. The village has twelve to fourteen men's groups, out of which three are politically and socially influential and important. In practically each quarter of the village there are one or two groups of elderly women. While the membership of the men's groups remains fairly stationary, that of the women's groups changes very often, varying according to recent quarrels or patching up of past differences. Most of the men's groups are formed round some central, politically influential figure. Gossip and politics appear to be their most important functions. Day to day developments in the village are discussed, and often the line to be taken in the central village council is worked out here long before the council's session. All these groups consist of two kinds of members—'regulars', whose loyalty and affiliation are not in doubt; and 'occasionals', whose affiliations are shaky, but who turn up periodically out of curiosity or with a definite purpose. These groups play a significant part in managing the affairs of the village, for their comments circulating in the village by word of mouth set the pace and direction for further action by the community in most matters. It should be added here that these groups comprise mostly the middle-aged people. While some ambitious young men seek to attend them, the aged generally

stay at home. The middle-aged people have in effect the controlling hand in village affairs; the truly aged retire into insignificance
and fade away. Some people cannot become reconciled to such
retirement, having enjoyed authority and influence during their
active days. They find adjustment difficult, and a life of dependence rather trying. But most people accept their position with
good grace, leave active management of the home and family
occupations to their sons and consequently find that their adjustment is much less difficult and inconvenient.

3. CO-OPERATION AND CONFLICT

Within the village community there is an appreciable degree of
inter-caste and inter-family co-operation. Earlier it has been
pointed out that the social system enjoins co-operation between
a number of castes in the fields of economics and ritual. Several
aspects of community life depend for their smooth running on
this traditional system of mutual give and take. Apart from these
conventional ties which are a constituent part of the social structure, several relationships involving voluntary co-operation can
be observed. The simplest type of such voluntary co-operation
found between neighbours or between friendly families is the
system of 'accommodating' each other in time of need. Borrowing
little sums of money or small quantities of grain, cooking for a
friend during her menstrual impurity or confinement, and looking
after children during the short absence of the mother may be cited
as examples of this type of co-operation. House building and
annual roof repairs also call for the help of friendly neighbours
among the peasants of average and poor economic status. Careful
mental note is made of all such favours received, so that they may
be returned at the appropriate time. Refusing help and returning
favours inadequately are looked upon as gestures of unfriendliness
or as marks of 'a small heart'. Emergency aid is rushed to friend
and foe alike. In cases of serious illness, fire or other accidents it is
necessary to help a fellow villager; and in all such cases aid is
rarely refused. Socio-religious ceremonies, particularly marriage,
and those connected with death, are also important occasions that
demand co-operation and help from neighbours and fellow
villagers. The burden of the household in which the ceremony is
to be performed is considerably lightened because of the help

given by friends and neighbours. The average and poor peasants extend this co-operation to the sphere of economic activities also, particularly during weeding and harvesting their families help each other in the speedy completion of the work. Among the occupational castes, families of a specific caste-group are expected to accommodate each other during time of illness, difficulty or temporary incapacity, by lending manual or monetary assistance to them for continuing their vocational craft. Fairs and ceremonies organized by the village reveal the co-operative spirit in the community. On some such occasions, one faction or other may refuse co-operation—sometimes it may even cause obstructions and create difficulties, but on the whole it can be said that organizers have the enthusiastic support of the bulk of the community and dissidents tend to lose the sympathy of wavering camp followers. In inter-village quarrels as well as on all such occasions that demand vindicating the honour of the village, the residents of the settlement often act with spirited unison. Behind most forms of voluntary co-operation there are no social sanctions; but the general attitude of society regards them as desirable and necessary. In the words of an informant, 'Who can say that he will not require help from anyone at any time? Money can buy many things. Power too can get many things done. But there are several situations in which neither money nor power helps. When you require sympathy and help your neighbours come forward.' To quote another informant, 'To-day you are well; to-morrow you may be very seriously ill and it may not be possible for you to get a doctor. What saves your life? A cheap herbal concoction suggested by your neighbour! One can never know how and when one is going to need the help of another.' Finally to quote a third informant, 'To-day I need your help; to-morrow you may want it from me. Why do we live in a village? Why do we not live in the wilderness? Only because we cannot do without human sympathy and occasional help.' Rendering help at the time of need is of value in itself. It partially relieves the distress of the person receiving help; and gives a psychological satisfaction to the person giving it, who incidentally also gains some social prestige through it.

But I do not want this picture of co-operation to be too idyllic, for conflicts and tensions in the community are also numerous. The analysis of the quality of inter-personal relations in the community, earlier in this chapter, suggests that an extrovert and sensitive people who cannot conceal their approval or disapproval and who do not suppress their immediate reactions cannot have a very peaceful and quiet life. Indeed most of the tensions are short-lived, but quarrels and conflicts are numerous and frequent. As the community is partially autonomous in several spheres of life, it is necessary for it to have an effective mechanism for the control of these conflicts.

Shamirpet, however, is only partially autonomous, for it is a part of a wider social system. The extent of caste organization is regional, and covers a very large number of villages. In several spheres of life it is the caste rather than the village that has the upper hand in controlling the behaviour of its constituents. Details of ritual connected with the life-cycle, and observance of the *mores* and norms of the caste fall in this category. Further the village is but a small unit in the national political structure of a sub-continent. Its laws are made by the State Legislature and the Union Parliament; and the law-enforcing arm of the State extends to it as effectively as it does to the rest of the country. This brings the State police and magistracy on the scene. All important breaches of law go to the civil and criminal courts. What remains of the autonomy of the village appears quite insignificant, but in actual practice relatively few cases go to caste councils, fewer to courts of law, and left to itself to control the inter-group and inter-personal relations of its members the machinery responsible for social control and justice within the village finds itself burdened with considerable work.

How is this mechanism set in motion? How does it work? Presently I shall give a few illustrative cases which will reveal the process in certain typical situations. At this stage it is necessary to point out that all cases of conflict do not go to the village council. In many cases the parties to the dispute boisterously quarrel over the issue and there the matter ends. For a few days they probably will not be on speaking terms, leave each other out of social functions and ceremonies, and continue to indulge in mutual recriminations and behind-the-back slander; but in course of time normal relations will be resumed. In other cases mediation or arbitration of the elders may be sought or may be volunteered by the elders themselves. When influential village elders notice disorderly or unbecoming behaviour on the part of someone repeatedly they intervene, and seek to set things right by the pressure of their personality. They ridicule, admonish and threaten the wrongdoer, and leave it at that. This intervention is often effective and succeeds in achieving the desired result. Disputes may be specially referred to influential and impartial elders, and thus a settlement is sought without the necessity of having to appear before the village council. When these efforts fail, or when the seriousness of the offence or dispute warrants it, it is taken to the headman or to one of the elders with a specific request that it be decided by the village council. On the other hand, elders may take cognizance of a serious matter and may themselves bring it to the notice of the village council. Of course all cases of murder, serious theft, and grievous bodily injury, as well as of default in payment of substantial loans are taken to the criminal and civil courts. Abduction and adultery can be referred to law courts; but generally they are taken either to the village council or to the caste council. Misconduct with a married or unmarried woman, running away with a married woman, default in fulfilling the terms and conditions of a marriage contract may similarly be referred to either or both the caste council and the village council. Of the two, whichever happens to be more powerful and effective attracts most of these marginal cases to itself. Personal disputes, minor property and land disputes, sex offences and conflicts arising out of breach of contract generally come up for hearing and decision before the village council.

The composition of the village council has been described earlier. When cases come up for hearing before it, the proceedings are carried on with considerable dignity. Available evidence and eye-witnesses are examined. The motive for the offence, and the situation in which it was committed—particularly its immediate cause, as well as presence or absence of provocation—are also taken into account. Outwardly an attitude of objectivity and impartiality is maintained by everyone; although in reality the rival factions within the council try to tip the scale their own way so that the evidence may later be construed in such a way that it may prove advantageous to the client to whom they have already promised their support. At the time of actual decision the parties to the dispute have to withdraw, allowing the council freedom to discuss and analyse the issues involved. Divergent and often contrary opinions may be expressed by the rival factions at this stage.

But when the decision is announced, it is done so in a manner that indicates unanimity among the members. Besides attempting arbitration and mediation, the village council also administers punishment when a person's guilt is proved. The nature of punishment itself differs in different categories of cases, also on the basis of persons involved in the dispute. It ranges from a simple warning to a complete social boycott; the intermediate stages being stern admonition, firm demand for apology, compensation to the aggrieved, and fining.

Absence of internal unity within the council has undermined its authority considerably. The fact that some of its members allow and encourage their protégés to defy—fully or partially—its decisions, contributes further to its growing weakness. Dissatisfied with its judgement one can always take the case to a regular court of law where the decision of the council may be reversed.

With these preliminary observations we can now proceed to examine a few illustrative cases which represent typical situations met with in the life of the community:

(1) V. R. R. and his brother B. live together. Their parents are dead, and being minor B. lives with his elder brother. V. R. R. has had elementary education. Being married into a respectable lower middle-class family in the city, and himself with some experience of urban life, V. R. R. regards himself as the leader of a band of city-influenced youth. As most of his time is spent in loafing, planning mischief, gambling, drinking and instigating people to quarrel, he cannot devote much time to the land, and consequently the financial position of the family is not satisfactory. V. R. R. adds to his income by extorting money from the villagers by offering his advice, help and support— often for unjust causes— but this money is spent almost wholly on himself. B. is now an adolescent, and is fast approaching a marriageable age. Noticing his elder brother's indifference towards him, B. approached some of the elders of his caste. His main complaints were: (a) V. R. R. does not spend his (B.'s) share of the land and its produce on him. (b) Nothing is being saved for his marriage. One day V. R. R. lost his temper over some trifling issue and scolded his younger brother. B. ran to E. D. R.—an influential man in the village, and the hereditary leader of his caste. Fearing that B. might be beaten by his elder brother, E. D. R. accompanied him to his house and asked V. R. R. to come out of the house and listen to

him. Partly because of anger, and partly under the intoxication
of his power and influence as the leader of a youth gang, he curtly
remarked to E. D. R., 'Have you nothing else to do? What brings
you here? Is it because of jealousy that you cannot see our welfare
and prosperity and you are instigating my brother to separate
from me?' This was too much even for the sedate, cool and level-
headed E. D. R., who enjoys great reputation in the village for
his sobriety. He lost his temper and said, 'You bastard, you seem
to have developed great notions about yourself. After spending a
few months in the city—and with the support of that band of
rascals—you think that you can defy the authority of village elders.
I shall show you what it means to be impertinent to me.' V. R. R.
was still defiant, but less impolite. E. D. R. said, 'If you have the
cheek to answer me back I shall make life impossible for you in
the village. You have a long tongue, but if you wag it against us
we shall pull it.' At this stage V. P. R.—a rival of E. D. R., who
had also been approached by B. on an earlier occasion—entered
the scene. But now he was on the side of E. D. R. and joined him
in scolding the unrepentant V. R. R. Within a short time a small
crowd gathered at the spot. Some other elders persuaded V. R. R.
to apologize to the elders whom he had offended. This he did
rather reluctantly. E. D. R., V. P. R. and the other elders
assembled there decided that V. R. R. should give more attention
to his agriculture, save at least two hundred rupees every year for
the expenses of his younger brother's wedding; and after his
marriage at the end of three years give him his share of land and
cattle. V. R. R. agreed to do this and the crowd dispersed.

(2) E. R. is a middle-aged woman, and is counted among the
colourful personalities of the village. In her day she was regarded
as a local beauty and was known for a degree of laxity in morals.
Now she has a sort of romantic attachment with C. M.—a local
Muslim small-trader. Her husband is meek and docile; and her
children ignore this affair. This particular case refers to her
quarrel with her son Y., who not only abused her but added to
the gravity of the offence by striking her in public. Outwardly
the quarrel appeared to be an ordinary, everyday affair; but careful investigation revealed to us that the roots of the trouble lay
somewhere else. The fact of the matter was that E. R. had got
her son Y. married to a rather young and immature girl who
happened to be her friend's daughter. Y. at this time was a grown-

up man; but his child bride was unable to take her place as his wife for some three years more. To keep her son away from eloping with a young woman, E. R. not only tolerated but encouraged—some people say she actually brought it about—Y.'s liaison with a woman of the same caste living in the neighbourhood. For three or four years everything went on well and the relations between the mother and child were most cordial. Trouble started when Y.'s wife came to live with them. E. R. had expected that her son's amours with the other woman would end shortly. In this she was wrong. The young wife failed to win the affection of her husband, who remained deeply attached to his former mistress. E. R. could not tolerate this. She tried different methods to dissuade her son, and with every failure her relations with him were more embittered. Quarrels between them became frequent. Tired of the incessant flow of criticism and bitter remarks from her, one day Y. struck her—with fists first and later with a stick. He also perhaps pulled her hair. All this happened so suddenly, and E. R.'s husband was at the time so overcome that he found himself helpless and could not intervene in the matter. Infuriated by this E. R. ran into the street and started wailing and cursing loudly. Very soon this attracted a large crowd. Her husband tried to pacify her, but E. R. would not let him come near her. She said to him, 'You claim to be a man! Do you? You could see your son beating me in your very presence and did not lift even your little finger. For me you are dead. Go, go away—for me you are dead. Did you hear that?' Saying this she started breaking her glass bangles. This was quite serious for a Hindu woman breaks her bangles only when she is widowed. The crowd tried to pacify her. Sympathizers made efforts to find out what the matter was. For over an hour E. R. continued cursing her son and husband, spitting 'at their name' and throwing dust, signifying their burial. Then she gave a detailed and rather exaggerated account of the happenings of that evening. Three elders who were present at the spot immediately summoned the son and asked him to touch the feet of his mother and apologize to her. This he did readily, although with a sullen face. But E. R. reacted with another spurt of abuse and foul language. After a while people took them home. The gravity of the matter demanded its consideration by the full village council. Once again the son had to apologize to the mother, and in addition had to pay a small fine for his unbecoming behaviour.

(3) This case is illustrative of some of the internal goings on in the village, and of some of the typical reactions manifested by the people.

K. was an average peasant. He had a son who lived separately in the village on account of his bad relations with his father. K.'s landholdings were modest in size, but some of his fields were quite first class. He was getting old and could not cultivate all the land by himself. Some of his relations came forward to help him, but he rejected their help. At this stage B. N.—an untouchable but influential cultivator—was ingratiating himself with K., and claimed to be his friend and well-wisher. It is said that B. N. persuaded a very influential figure in the village to lend him his helping hand in the pursuit of something which he had in mind. (It is rumoured that the influential figure agreed to lend his support in consideration of a substantial monetary gift.) After a few days it was known that K. had sold his best fields to B. N. Although the documents showed that B. N. had paid a reasonable price, it was generally believed that the amount which had actually changed hands was very small. K. had not consulted any of his relations about this deal. As if to add insult to injury, the old man had chosen an untouchable for this favour in utter disregard to the claims of his kinsfolk, and after the deal K.'s relations with them broke down completely. He went out to another village to visit some other relations, fell seriously ill and returned to Shamirpet in a very precarious condition. Everyone realized that it was his end, but his relations did not do anything for him. B. N. arranged for him to stay in a room of the village rest-house, and arranged with a shopkeeper and a young man of clean caste for the supply of rations and for the cooking of his meals. In a few days K. died.

His relations did not show any inclination to touch his corpse. When the headman sent word to them, they said 'We are not his relations. Did he ever remember us during his lifetime so that we may remember him now? He has his untouchable son who will inherit his property. Let him perform the last rites for him.' Hearing this, B. N. said, 'I am an untouchable. I cannot perform the rites. But I shall pay for them, and see that they are done in some style.' He sent for a band from the city, advanced money for necessary preparations, and with the support of the headman secured the co-operation of four clean caste unmarried youths to carry the bier. The relations took it as a challenge. They changed their attitude. One of their spokesmen said, 'The deceased was our seed; and not an untouchable. We may not have riches, but we shall perform his last rites.' They sent for another band, and the last rites were performed in a memorable style. K.'s son felt offended and kept himself away from the ceremonies.

(4) Robust and sturdy C. R. has several remarkable traits. Because of his personality and a rather impressive way of speaking he has considerable influence over his community and is looked upon as its leader. He is an untouchable. Some of his acts now and then disgrace his family, and bring about a temporary eclipse of his reputation. Several times he was accused of petty thefts, and once or twice fined by the village council. But when he stole a blanket and some brassware from his employer, and ran away with the wife of a neighbour, the matter was viewed very seriously. People from the village had seen him at a nearby railway station with all the three stolen things—blanket, brassware and the neighbour's wife. The theft was reported to the village council; and after some preliminary consideration the local caste group referred the elopement also to it. In the meantime news was received that C. R. was working in a sugar factory, but was anxious to return to the village. The village council came to the decision that C. R. should compensate his employer to the full value of the articles stolen, return the woman to her husband with a certain sum of money by way of compensation, and pay a fine to the council for the two offences. C. R. returned to the village, accepted the verdict of the council, but asked for a reduction in the amount of the fine. This request was granted.

(5) R. was a widow, and after the death of her husband had returned to Shamirpet to live with her mother. She was still young. In a few days she became the mistress of M. who belonged to her caste. They never lived openly as man and wife, but their relationship was well known. M. bought several expensive presents for her, and these included a silver necklace and bracelets. After about three years R. fell in love with an outsider who agreed to take her as his wife. M. did not object to this arrangement, but he insisted on having his presents back. R. was not prepared to part with them. One day when she was passing along the street in front of M.'s house, he ran towards her and started snatching the ornaments by force. R. shouted for help and people rushing to the spot separated them. The matter was reported to the headman,

who convened the full council. Opinion in this case was divided, but the final verdict was that since M. had enjoyed sexual favour from the woman for three years he had no right to demand the return of the ornaments. R. married her new lover and went away to live in his village. M. was greatly dissatisfied with the decision, but there was nothing that he could do about it.

(6) D. worked in Bombay and when he returned to the village brought back with him his savings—estimated at four hundred rupees or so. He spent the money lavishly on drink and gambling. In less than a year he had squandered all his savings. Now he started ill-treating his wife. One day when the wife's father had come to take her home for a short stay, he asked her for eight annas to buy some drinks. She said that she had no money, and he beat her mercilessly. The noise attracted people to their house, and the woman's father reported the matter to the headman. The headman called some other members of the village council, and then summoned the husband and wife. He asked the wife, 'Why did you not give him the money?' The wife said, 'I did not have any with me.' She repeatedly asserted that she had no money. Thereupon her belongings were searched. This revealed that she had seven rupees. She tried to convince the council that this was her personal savings from her own earnings from the making of country cigarettes. But the Deshmukh said, 'Why did you lie before the *panchayat*? Why did you say that you had no money?' Encouraged by this turn of events in his favour the husband accused her of stealing three hundred rupees and asked her to leave him. She went away with her father to his village.

(7) L. and P. both belong to the caste of potters. Their houses stand facing each other. A tamarind tree standing midway between the two houses is a bone of contention, and over this tree there were several pitched quarrels between their families. Who has the right to its fruit? Who should sweep up the dried leaves when they fall? Who should enclose the tree within his own enclosure? Mediation of elders did not succeed in finding a satisfactory solution to the problem. The matter was reported to the village council; but there too no decision could be reached as both sides had their own supporters in nearly equal strength. Efforts at bringing about a compromise were mostly fruitless, or else agreements between the rivals were short-lived. The village council considered it time and again, but in the meantime the matter was

reported to a government officer. For four years the matter lingered on, and the tree continued to disturb the peace of that particular living-quarter. Ultimately, at the suggestion of the government officer, the decision was given that the tree should be cut down; its wood be sold and the proceeds distributed equally between the two parties. To effect this a time-limit of a month was prescribed, after which the council was to have the liberty to dispose of the tree and thus to deprive the disputants of the proceeds.

(8) I. and S. are brothers. After their father's death they continued to live together and cultivate their land jointly for two years. Then they had some family difficulties, and had to seek the mediation of village elders. Three influential persons acceptable to both the brothers worked out the details of partition. The family land was divided into two equal parts, but one of these parts was inferior to the other. Equal division of good and inferior land between the two would have meant fragmentation of some of the tiny fields with loss to both; and so it was decided that the one who accepted the inferior land would get all the plough cattle, and the one who got the superior land would have no share in the cattle left by the father. Both the brothers were to contribute two hundred rupees each for three years for the wedding of their sister. I. chose the superior land and S. agreed to have the inferior land with the cattle. For a time the arrangement worked well. The land was still in the name of I. in the government records, because he was the elder of the two. At the time of the partition there was a tacit understanding that they would contribute equally towards the payment of land revenue. But S. had a feeling that his share should be less on account of the fact that his land was inferior. He was instigated by some people to pursue the matter further. I. would perhaps have agreed to an amicable settlement had his brother approached him; but he was annoyed to notice that he sought outside help and unjustly maligned him. Intervention of the elders failed to bring about a compromise. The village council could not come to a decision quickly, as both brothers had powerful factions supporting them. Ultimately its verdict was against S., but his advisers suggested that rather than yield to this decision he should take the matter to a civil court. At the time of our investigations the issue was still undecided and no settlement was in sight.

These examples could easily be multiplied. Failure in implementing the terms of an agreement or contract, inability to pay off small debts, serious sexual intrigues, domestic quarrels assuming serious proportions, etc., keep on coming before the village council again and again. It is very rarely that it has to take the final step of ordering the social boycott of an individual. Caste *panchayats*, on the other hand, take recourse to this weapon very often when breaches of caste convention are brought to their notice. Eating with a lower caste, sex intrigue outside the caste, failure in observing injunctions attached to the status of ritual impurity, and inability to perform any major ritual are all punished by ostracism. This involves denial of social equality to the ostracized family. No one will share food or drink with it. No member of such a family will be invited to attend a socio-religious ceremony, nor will anyone accept his invitation. Its status of social equality will be restored when it performs the necessary rituals for the expiation of its offence.

Our investigations did not reveal the existence of any serious inter-group tensions and conflicts in the community. Just before and after the Police Action there was some Hindu-Muslim tension: in the first phase Muslims terrorized the Hindus; in the second the Hindus looted property from one Muslim house and terrorized the other Muslims generally and their ringleaders particularly. Between different castes or living-quarters of the village, within living memory, there were only two major disputes. Their details are not remembered, but it is claimed that the tension was short-lived and cordiality was established very soon between the warring sections.

The corporate unity of the village finds its fullest expression when the inhabitants come into conflict with outsiders. The village of Aliyabad shares with Shamirpet the water from the tank for the purposes of irrigation. The ratio of water supplied to Shamirpet and Aliyabad has been fixed at 5:2. Over this there are always some difficulties. One night the floodgates were opened, and the water that should have irrigated Shamirpet fields was diverted to Aliyabad fields. Next morning an organized team from Shamirpet attacked Aliyabad. There were three different theories regarding what had happened the previous night. Aliyabad people said that the guards of the floodgates had asked them to take the water under the impression that it was their turn. The guards said that being threatened with violence they allowed the Aliyabad men to divert the water to their area.

Perhaps the fact of the matter was that Aliyabad men had obtained the favour by bribing the guards; but their excessive greed in not allowing any water into Shamirpet fields had exposed their game. Prompt official intervention checked ugly developments; and later the issue was resolved at inter-village level. But in the dispute itself the two villages had forgotten their internal differences and dissensions and each of them had acted as one body. Another instance of such concerted action and village unity is provided by the conflict between the residents of Shamirpet and eight army men from the nearby cantonment. These eight people came to the village in two army trucks and started loading their vehicles with firewood cut and stored by a resident of the village. Obviously the army men intended to take it away without payment. The owner of the house tried to check them, and in the process he was badly beaten up. In the meantime the news had reached the other village people, who came rushing to the spot armed with sticks. They did what they thought proper at the time to avenge the honour of the village. Outnumbered by the villagers, the army men returned to their camp, threatening to bring their company to destroy the entire village. Police intervened and the trouble was not allowed to develop further.

In a society resting on rigid division of the population into castes separated by strict rules governing touching, eating and drinking, sex relations and matrimony, and social distance prescribed by tradition it is essential that people realize certain limitations and accept certain conditions. Caste consciousness develops quite early in one's life and these limitations and conditions are absorbed long before maturity by all through conversation groups, play-groups and general social experience. So far there has been no attack on the general premises on which the society rests, and therefore no serious inter-group or inter-caste conflicts have arisen. The lower castes have accepted their inferior status, and while they have made efforts to improve their lot they have not openly revolted against it. In their turn the higher castes have also shown considerable adaptability, and recognizing the general social trend they have readjusted their attitudes and curbed some of the earlier excesses and injustices. They may still object to being touched by a low caste man, but they will not protest against his wearing superior clothing befitting only the upper castes.

CHAPTER EIGHT

The Changing Scene

THERE is a tendency among some Western writers to regard the rural societies of the East, particularly of India, as almost static and unchanging. For over a century 'the timeless and changeless Indian village' has been the ideal of the romanticist. However, a micro-sociological study of a village like Shamirpet, which was insulated in feudal surroundings and was thus kept almost unaffected by the currents of social, economic and political changes that were sweeping the countryside in British India, shows certain unmistakable trends in the direction of cultural and institutional variation.

To analyse the changing scene in the village a brief recapitulation of its history is necessary.

According to government records there was at first a small hamlet on the site on which the present comparatively large village of Shamirpet is situated. Nearly two hundred and eighty years ago the ruler of Hyderabad State decided to get a large tank constructed near this hamlet. When the construction was started the population of the village increased considerably by the influx of labourers from the neighbouring villages who built temporary shelters for themselves mid-way between the place of work and the existing settlement. As the work progressed, some of these people started building permanent huts for themselves. With the completion of the tank the village acquired excellent irrigation facilities. This finally induced most of the families working at the construction of the tank to settle down permanently in the village. In addition to these people, there was also a fresh wave of immigrants. This included the Reddis and Muslims who were attracted by the irrigation facilities now available in the village. They bought land for cultivation, built substantial houses, and thus became a part of the permanent population of the village. With the extension of agriculture a number of artisan and occupational castes were drawn into the village population. These castes are a necessary adjunct to the traditional system of agriculture in rural India, and the growing number of agriculturists in the village had already created a demand for them. Thus the population of the once-small hamlet of Shahpur gradually increased and consequently its status among the neighbouring villages was also enhanced. It has been pointed out that at this time it was re-named as Shamirpet to commemorate the engineer who had planned and supervised the construction of the tank. One of the ancestors of the present headman, who had successfully undertaken a contract for the carting of materials required in the construction of the tank, was duly rewarded by the ruler of the State with a substantial grant of land. He invested most of his earnings from the contract in buying more land. Thus he became the biggest landowner in the village. He was also appointed as the Mali Patel, a village official responsible for assisting the State officials in the collection of land revenue. At this time he was granted a *sanad*, a document appointing him as the headman of the village. In the context of these continued changes the internal organization of the village kept on modifying itself. Finally, when the population of this comparatively large village had become stable it reorganized its *panchayat* (village council). It now consisted of the Deshmukh (headman) who was its presiding officer, the three Ganadi (organizers of village ritual) and all the Kulam-pedda (heads of the different castes living in the village).

In the later history of the village there are two significant turning points. The first of these directly affected the village. The second affected Hyderabad State as a whole and brought in its wake certain currents which had significant repercussions on the countryside.

To begin with, about one hundred and fifty years ago the Nizam of Hyderabad granted Shamirpet, along with several other villages, as a *jagir* or feudal estate to one of his nobles. In the villages granted to him the feudal landlord replaced the normal district administration of the State. Shamirpet was selected as the headquarters of the estate, and as a direct consequence of this decision several substantial houses were built in the village to accommodate its offices and officials. Forty years ago an ambitious Nawab built a row of modern-looking houses for his various offices. These were built in stone, had plastered and white-washed walls, and also had tiled roofs. Obviously they were in keeping with the urban styles of that time, commonly met with in the small towns having subdivisional administrative offices. One by one a school, a police station, a dispensary and a post office were added to the village.

In the race for modernization and introduction of Western technology feudal Hyderabad was much behind British India. Apparently very little happened in the rural areas of the State during the first one hundred and twenty-five years of British rule in India. Modern roads, buses and railways came in here much later than in the rest of the country outside the domains of native princes. In the later phases of this period the State maintained an impressive array of 'nation-building', 'welfare' and technical departments, but their activities in the rural areas were limited. However, these were very crucial years in the life of the village as a variety of complex socio-economic factors were influencing the fabric of the rural community. Urban contacts and modern education were acquired by a small section of the village population. Administrative contacts with State officers and law courts increased in this period. Owing to its nearness to the capital city Shamirpet received a somewhat favoured treatment at the hands of the nation-building and technical departments whose touring officials and propagandists visited this village more often than the other remote and distant villages.

The last fifty years of British rule in India witnessed the gradual emergence of a strong national movement for the liberation of the country from foreign political domination, and under the leadership of Mahatma Gandhi the Indian National Congress took the message of non-violent non-co-operation and passive resistance to the masses in the different parts of the country. This had a profound influence on the rural areas in several parts of the land, and led to some modification in the ways and outlook of the people. In Hyderabad there was no such mass movement, but what was happening in the rest of the country was not without significance for the people of this State. Later, inspired by the Indian example, there was some agitation for political reform and self-government in the State. This too had some influence on the village.

The major influences that were at work during the Jagir period, especially in the last five or six decades, are illustrated in the following diagram:

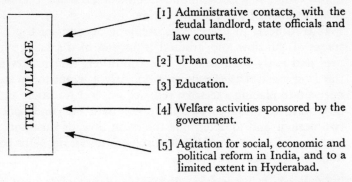

[1] Administrative contacts, with the feudal landlord, state officials and law courts.

[2] Urban contacts.

[3] Education.

[4] Welfare activities sponsored by the government.

[5] Agitation for social, economic and political reform in India, and to a limited extent in Hyderabad.

The year 1948 witnessed many vital changes in the Hyderabad State. As an outcome of successful intervention of India, Hyderabad became an integral part of the Indian Union. This paved the way for several radical reforms in the State. The Nizam himself became a constitutional ruler. With the abolition of Jagirs the feudal system within the State came to an end. Rural development and welfare activities were intensified. Finally, democratic institutions were introduced and in 1951 the people went to the polls for the first time to elect their representatives, for the State Legislature and the Union Parliament.

The Police Action was the second turning point in the life-history of the village, as it inaugurated the operation of a new set of influences in the life of the community. These influences were:

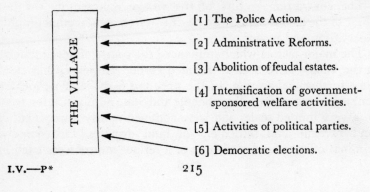

[1] The Police Action.

[2] Administrative Reforms.

[3] Abolition of feudal estates.

[4] Intensification of government-sponsored welfare activities.

[5] Activities of political parties.

[6] Democratic elections.

In some respects the factors of social change operating at these two stages and the resultant trends are complementary, while in others they stand out in marked contrast. It will be useful first to analyse the changes that came about in the life and ways of the people in the last fifty years of the feudal period, and then to follow it up by an examination of some of the more recent changes brought about by the Police Action.

It is difficult to present a systematic account of the different stages of the slow and gradual transition of the village from its pre- and early-Jagir days to the conditions that it presented in the later part of the feudal period. Any attempt to do so would necessitate placing excessive reliance on oral tradition about the near past. In order to be able to compare the conditions in the two periods and to determine the main lines of variation, reconstruction of a picture of the first stage is necessary. This could be done on the basis of:

(*a*) Factual information regarding comparable, but remote villages of the region, which because of their comparative isolation and lack of urban contacts present to-day, in a broad sense, conditions that Shamirpet would have presented in the pre- and early-Jagir period. Cautious and limited use of this method of translating space into time is useful in providing us with a starting point.

(*b*) Oral traditions and memories of the people, in so far as they do not concern themes pertaining to family glory and personal pride, or those involving subjective idealization.

(*c*) Fragmentary evidence from documentary and historical sources reflecting conditions of life and living in that period. Police, revenue and other semi-legal records obtainable have been used in this connection.

The contrasting picture of the village representing the last phase of the feudal period can be drawn from actual ethnographic observation and record.

The major factors which influenced the course of developments in the village have been mentioned earlier. However, they need some further elaboration. In the pre- and early-Jagir period the contacts between the village people and State administration were on a very limited scale, and were confined mostly to payment of land revenue and settlement of land disputes. Occasionally, criminal offences and civil suits of a serious nature were tried in the law courts in the city. Now and then State officials visited the village on tour. In the second half of the Jagir period these administrative contacts increased very considerably. At the same time the urban contacts of a section of the village population also grew gradually. These included visiting relations and friends in the city, receiving relations and friends from the city, occasional excursions for shopping in the large city stores and markets as well as for sight-seeing, temporary stay of a short or long duration for work in the city, and finally being in everyday touch with officials resident in the village, who were regarded as an urban element in the village population. Increased contacts with the towns and cities were greatly facilitated by the construction of the metalled road joining Hyderabad with the district headquarters of Karimnagar in the interior of the State. This road touches Shamirpet. With the introduction of bicycles and buses frequent and regular contacts with the urban areas were made possible. The progress of education has been rather slow. In the early-Jagir days only a few children belonging to the higher castes, and also to the upper level families, received any schooling. Even this was confined to a bare acquaintance with three R's. With the opening of a school in the village education was placed within the reach of a much larger section and even some untouchable children started attending the school. Some ambitious parents sent their children to the higher schools in the city where they could learn English. Books, periodicals and newspapers which occasionally found their way into the village conveyed to the people 'strange truths regarding the wide world through the medium of the printed word'. The State administration initiated some of its welfare and nation-building activities in the countryside. Agriculture, Veterinary and Animal Husbandry, Medical and Public Health, and Co-operation and Rural Development departments of the State started functioning in the rural areas. Their representatives and propagandists brought some new ideas and techniques to the village. The villagers saw their demonstrations, heard their talks, and were at times even coaxed into doing things in the new ways. This was indeed novel to them. In the earlier period government had only collected land revenue, heard some of their disputes, tried cases arising out of breaches of law, and occasionally forced them to provide practically free labour and 'presents' for touring government officials, but had never interfered with their agricultural practices or with their methods of cattle keeping. Compulsory vaccination and inoculation were introduced. The village people did not clearly understand the implications of the political movements that were developing in the city. The Muslims, thinking that they belonged to the 'ruling race', supported the Nizam and later the communalist Muslim party. The educated and city-influenced Hindus had sympathy with the Arya Samaj (a Hindu revivalist and reformist body), and the State Congress (a democratic political party affiliated to the Indian National Congress and dedicated to the ideal of self-government and democracy within the State), but could not express their sympathies openly. At least outwardly the landed Hindu peasantry maintained a loyalist attitude towards the established authority. These were the major influences that operated in the community. Nearly all of them had a slow and uncertain start, but gradually their intensity and effectiveness increased. As an outcome of their operation, at the close of the Jagir period, we get a picture of the village which is very different from the one that it would have presented in the pre- or early-Jagir period.

What then are the main lines of variation? In what spheres of community life are the changes most pronounced? As we find them most pronounced in material culture and technology, it would be appropriate to begin our analysis of change with this aspect of life. These changes have resulted in the acquisition of new habits and styles, of new tools and technological processes, and of a new outlook on things in general.

In the dress and ornaments of the village people there has been very noticeable change. The old-style peasant dress is now giving way to new-style clothes cut and stitched in imitation of the urban style. While it is still common to see an Indian lower garment—Hindu *dhoti* or Muslim *pyjama*—Western-style shirts with collars have mostly replaced the native upper garments. In the former times only the village headman, rich Reddis and Muslims, and the high-caste Brahmins and Komtis wore 'respectable' and semi-urban clothing, and that too only when they were to receive an important visitor or while going to the city. With the exception of this small minority, all others wore the traditional peasant dress. Spinning was done on the hand-wheel at home and cloth was woven by village weavers. Now the situation has changed. At present hardly any spinning is being done by the people, and the village weaver

218

buys his yarn from the shops in the city. The clothing to-day can
be classified into three main types: the average peasant dress, the
old-style respectable dress, and the new-style clothing. In all the
three types of clothes mill-made cloth is extensively used. For shirts
and vests practically everyone uses mill-made cloth. The same is
true of materials used for the bodices and blouses of women.
Before the Second World War mill-made women's *saris* were
capturing the village markets, and were making the position
rather difficult for the village weaver who was unable to withstand
this competition. However, due to acute war-time shortages,
particularly of *saris*, there was a switch back to the locally woven
material. In the three styles of clothing enumerated above, those
adopting the new are imitating the current urban styles. In these
two different trends can be observed: Indian clothing and semi-
Indian clothing. Most people in this group are young men. During
the Muslim régime they had taken to *pyjama* (thin white trousers)
and *sherwani* (long, buttoned-up-to-the-neck coats) which were
then extremely popular. The *kurta*—long loose tunic popularized
by the Congress in the civil disobedience days—became a mark of
patriotism and is currently the accepted respectable dress with
young men. It can be worn with both *dhoti* and *pyjama*. Shirts
with collars, shorts and European-style jackets were also used by
this section. Knitted vests too became very popular. Items of
clothing introduced more recently are trousers and bush-jackets.
These are confined mostly to people who have served in the
Hyderabad Army or who have had some small jobs in the city.
In the old-style respectable dress not much change is in evidence.
During the Muslim régime the clothing of the respectable people
had acquired a definite court touch, and a long coat and lambskin
cap became the dress of the respectable city-going village people.
With the decline of Muslim rule in Hyderabad this cap was dis-
carded by the Hindus as it symbolized their subordination to the
Muslims. It has been replaced by an ordinary black cap, and the
traditional long coat is still in use. The average peasants' and
workers' dress has not changed much, but it is now made of mill-
cloth. Many of the agriculturists and artisans, and indeed some
poorer people, buy shirts with collars, and coats, to wear on special
occasions. Among women brightly coloured and gaudily printed
clothes have become popular. City manufactured trinkets are
eagerly bought by them. Bangles, which every Hindu woman whose

husband is alive must wear, were formerly made by one of the local castes from indigenous materials. Now factory-made glass bangles have captured the market almost completely. Children's dresses are now generally of Western style. Frocks, rompers, shirts and shorts are bought for them from the local market or from the shops in the city. Among other items of everyday wear Western-style shoes with laces are now being used alongside country shoes and sandals.

To the list of articles of daily requirement there have been several significant additions. Aluminium and 'German silver' utensils became very popular with the poorer sections of the population on account of their low prices. Glasses, as well as china cups and saucers, could be seen in several homes. Besides the public buildings five private homes now possess wall or alarm clocks. Kerosene lanterns can be seen in several homes, and there are five kerosene pressure lamps in the village. Some old people use reading glasses, and more then half a dozen young men from the village have bought sun glasses. Several people in the village use safety razors and torches. Cheap fountain-pens are also very fashionable.

In the food habits of the people there has not been much change. Sweets and other dainty eatables are bought from the shops in the city or from the bazaar. Five small stores in the village sell, among other things, lozenges, fruit-drops and biscuits made in Hyderabad. Tea and coffee are also very popular. Even those who do not drink these beverages regularly at home, occasionally have them in the village shop ostentatiously known as the 'hotel'. Aerated waters enjoy an amazing popularity as they are believed to provide relief from many stomach disorders. The cigarette factories at Hyderabad have been producing and popularizing cheap brands of cigarettes, which have been progressively replacing the country cigarettes in which tobacco is rolled in dried leaves. Along with fermented palm-juice, some people now drink other liquors supplied by distilleries in Hyderabad.

Side by side with the traditional recreations of gossip, loafing and playing indigenous games, several new varieties of entertainments are now available to the village people. The village has three gramophones. In the tea shop there is a crystal radio. Some young men in the village play volley-ball. Many people patronize the circus and cinema in the city.

Changes in tools and technical processes are also important. Barbers, carpenters, blacksmiths and goldsmiths are now using factory-made tools and instruments. The village tailor has a sewing machine. It is significant that there has been no mentionable change in agricultural tools. In farming methods, however, some changes have taken place. Improved seeds are being used by many cultivators. The value of green manure is realized by an increasing number of agriculturists. Oil cakes, castor, ammonium sulphate, and a special concoction of chemical fertilizers known as 'paddy mixture' are now being used. More attention is given to growing vegetables. A greater percentage of cultivators is now growing 'cash crops'.

Communications too have now improved. Many persons take advantage of the bus service. There are six private bicycles in the village. A shop-keeper has four more which can be hired. The headman of the village has recently bought a 1928 model Ford. The traditional bullock carts are still largely used for transportation of goods, and also for travel.

The opening of a small dispensary in the village, and the availability of excellent facilities of modern medical treatment in the city have considerably changed the attitude of the people towards diseases and their treatment. Although people still believe that smallpox and cholera are the result of the wrath of two goddesses and annually organize ceremonies in their honour on behalf of the village, the old fear of vaccination and inoculation has now practically disappeared. People no longer run away from the village on the appearance of the vaccinator, nor do they offer him bribes or threats for being spared the cruelty of vaccination. Divination, protective magic, chants and spells are all still employed to ward off disease and difficulty, but at the same time increasing use is being made of modern medicine. Age-old prescriptions of indigenous herbs are generally used for fevers and other common ailments. But when the disease takes a serious turn the patient may even be removed to a hospital in the city. Injections which were greatly feared a few decades ago are now eagerly sought as they are believed to give quick and sure relief from all ailments. Some people keep a limited stock of some of the popular and cheap patent medicines. Medicines for virility and strength prominently advertised in newspapers are obtained by post.

The social structure of the community is basically the same,

221

although with every administrative or political change in the village there were several organizational changes. The primary unit in this structure is either the elementary family (maintaining close contacts with allied families) or it is a large joint family. The head of each family is known as the 'big man'. The next unit is the caste; or in the case of the Muslims, the group sharing a common religion. Each of these groups has a hereditary caste headman who represents it in the village council. Finally, this council consists of these headmen of the different castes, three Ganadi and the headman of the village who is its presiding officer. The following tables show the significant lines of variation in social organization, with special reference to family, caste and village council:

I—FAMILY

Then	*Now*
(1) Insistence on family solidarity and cohesion.	(1) Growth of individualism.
(2) Greater attachment to the soil and settlement.	(2) Migrations more frequent.
(3) Intra-family relations governed by regard for age and kinship status.	(3) Less regard for these traditional principles.

II—CASTE

Then	*Now*
(1) Occupational specialization on the basis of caste.	(1) Caste no longer the final and only determinant of occupation.
(2) Prohibition on inter-dining with some equal castes and all lower castes.	(2) Rules of inter-dining less rigid.
(3) Hierarchy and permanent distance between different castes.	(3) Mild protest against social hierarchy: some modification in actual practice.

III—VILLAGE COUNCIL

Then	*Now*
(1) Constituted on hereditary principles.	(1) Also admits people with 'achieved status'.
(2) Little outside intervention.	(2) Considerable outside pressure.
(3) Decisions generally accepted.	(3) Defiance or avoidance possible.

In the organization of the family the changed conditions and changing attitudes of the people have brought about some significant variations. It is difficult to present it statistically, but it could generally be said that in recent years the cohesion of the family has suffered on account of the growth of the spirit of individualism. Thereby family solidarity has been adversely affected. The people no longer have the same attachment for the soil of their settlement, and consequently mobility has increased. Among the younger people, especially among those who have had some education or urban contacts, the desire to go to the city is manifesting itself on an increasing scale. In making records of the biographies and general attitudes of the people, the contrast in the attitudes of the two steps of people emerged clearly. While the elderly and the middle-aged, mostly illiterate, complained about the inconveniences of village life, they still regarded it as the only way of life possible for *them*. On the other hand, the younger people seemed to idealize the city and its numerous attractions, and made no effort to conceal their contempt for the rustic ways of the village-folk. This change in attitudes and preferences has on the one hand encouraged migration to cities of young people who take up the small jobs there; and on the other it has generated disharmony and dissensions within the family causing considerable dislocation in the established principles according to which priorities and concessions went with age and kinship status. Service in the army, and city restaurants and the influence of the cinema tend to accentuate all this, but so far the number of young men with these tendencies is not more than 10% or 15% of the total in their age-group.

The caste system in the community presents only slight variations in some directions. As before, caste still retains its endogamous character. Similarly, caste continues to be a part of, and is sanctioned by, the traditional religion. However, its occupational character has undergone some change. People are now taking to new occupations. A goldsmith has opened a tea shop. Washermen and similar other castes are accepting menial jobs in the city. These are not their traditional occupations. Besides Muslims some non-Komti Hindus have set up general shops in the village; in the traditional system only Komtis could do so. Thus people are either giving up their traditional occupations, or they are taking to occupations which by tradition belong to some other castes.

223

Prohibitions on inter-dining are still there; but they have been greatly relaxed. As a general rule people observe them within the village, but ignore them when they eat in the shops or restaurants in the city. The caste system is still characterized by its traditional hierarchy, but some ineffective verbal protests can now be heard against it. Among the castes on the lower level of the agriculturist group there has been some effort made at rising in the social scale by the adoption of surnames and caste appellations traditionally belonging to the higher groups. Although it has been legally abolished by the Constitution of the Republic of India, untouchability is still practised within the village. However, untouchable children can now attend the village school. Clean castes and unclean castes both ride in the same buses. No objection is taken if untouchables now dress like respectable people of the higher castes. As the colonies of the two untouchable castes are quite separate from the main village settlement and have their own wells, there has so far been no problem of their being able to draw water from the well used by the higher castes. Untouchables certainly resent their degraded status, but they are careful not to voice their protests too loudly or too publicly for they are conscious of the advantages of silence in view of their dependent position in the economic structure of the community.

Traditionally the membership of the village council is hereditary and should be inherited by the eldest male child on the death of the father. In the case of the inheritance of the office of village headman this principle has been strictly observed. Two Ganadis inherited their office from their fathers, but an additional post of Ganadi has been created in recent years to accommodate a young man who had considerable influence over his age-group and who was creating problems in the village. From among the heads of the different castes resident within the village, eight are at present-ineffective, titular members, and are represented in its deliberations by some other more vocal and assertive members of the caste. Seven other rich and influential persons are also invited to participate in the proceedings. It is said that before the Jagir period there was very little outside pressure on the village council. In the Jagir period the estate officials tried to influence it indirectly. At present government officials residing within the village discreetly pull the strings and exert pressure on the council to secure favourable decisions in certain cases in which for some reason they happen to be interested. In former times, as a general rule, the decisions of the village council were accepted unconditionally. Even to-day none can defy them openly, but often the cases are taken to superior law courts and factionalism within the council is exploited to get its decisions altered or modified.

In the traditional economic structure of the community the following characteristics were important:

(i) Occupation was determined by the caste of the individual.

(ii) Mobility was limited and people had great attachment to the settlement.

(iii) Different castes were integrated into the overall pattern of village economy on the basis of their functional specialization. For their co-operative labour payment was made in kind at the time of harvesting.

(iv) There was barter of occupational services between the various artisan and occupational castes.

It has already been pointed out that in the last few decades the occupational character of caste has undergone some modifications. In place of their traditional occupations people have started accepting other vocations. The traditional system of caste interdependence under which artisan and occupational castes attach themselves to the families of agriculturists is still there. But the attached labourers of untouchable castes are showing signs of discontent and figures for the last ten years show twenty-one migrations of Madiga families to the city. Barbers, washermen and carpenters also openly express preference for a basis of cash payment as that enables them to negotiate and bargain and puts an end to the uncertainty and occasional high-handedness of the employer under the old system. The traditional arrangements involving the barter of occupational services between artisan castes too is now gradually breaking down and is giving place to a basis of cash payment.

In the ritual structure of the community no significant variations have been found. Under the Muslim régime, Hindus co-operated in the public ceremonies of the Muslims. With the spread of the revivalist and reformist ideas of the Arya Samaj greater interest was taken in the Hinduism of the holy books. Preachers invited from the city added to the folklore of the people some fragments of traditional Hindu mythology. However, the regional cults as well as the village cults still continue to retain their former position.

The Police Action undertaken by the Indian Union in 1948 changed the fortune and status of the State of Hyderabad. The most significant outcome was that political power changed hands —from an extremist communal party to the people of the State. It had a profound effect on the rural areas. However, sufficient time must elapse before we can evaluate its total influence on the life of the community. But it has set in motion certain trends which are not without interest to the student of social change in peasant communities.

The first definite change is that Muslims who occupied a privileged position during the former régime now no longer do so. On account of some of their un-neighbourly acts of terrorism during the last phase of extremist Muslim rule in the State some of them had become very unpopular. Fearing retaliation by the Hindus they ran away from the village temporarily. Now they have all returned. For some time they were jeered at and ridiculed, but at the time of our study cordiality had returned to the Hindu and Muslim sections of the population.

The second noticeable change is that under the administrative reforms initiated by the new administration forced labour and forced extraction of hospitality by government officials have been prohibited. In practice they still continue on a restricted scale. Government's decision to take determined steps against bribery and corruption has been announced; but firm action still remains to be taken in this direction.

Thirdly, the abolition of feudal estates has been a big step in the direction of land reform. With the end of the Jagirdari system Shamirpet has once again come under normal district administration. Further reforms ensuring a more equitable distribution of land, fixing a maximum limit on land holding and ending the evils of absentee landlordism are under contemplation. When these plans materialize substantial changes can be expected.

Fourthly, the government has intensified its welfare and nation-building activities. The village is to have a better school in the near future. The Public Health Department is already more active. The Agriculture and Veterinary departments are making a better planned and organized effort towards the introduction of more scientific methods in their respective fields. But the results of these efforts can be judged only after a few years.

Finally, there has been considerable activity in the rural areas by the political parties, culminating in the first general election of December 1951. This experience has been totally new to the villages in Hyderabad. As the Congress is the ruling party in the country, the loyalists have transferred their allegiance from the Nizam to the Congress. At any rate publicly they profess their loyalty to this organization. Because the headman of the village belongs to this group, the faction opposed to him in village matters allied itself to the Socialist party. The Communist party was illegal, but it had operated in the neighbouring area for a long time, and it was a candidate sponsored by it who ultimately won the election. Most people do not understand the intricacies of politics, and indeed frankly say so. Election propaganda has of course put several ideas into the minds of the people and raised new hopes. Those who have some educational or urban background are trying to come forward in this new field of activity. One observable consequence of this has been the revival of caste-ism. Although nearly every political party in its platform slogans paid lip service to the ideal of a casteless and classless society, in actual selection of the candidates due thought was given to the caste composition of the electoral districts. A candidate's pull over the members of his caste was an additional factor which was taken into account in such politically inexperienced territories as Hyderabad. In the countryside the election propaganda did take a sectarian turn and according to the occasion Hindu versus Muslim, or Reddi versus non-Reddi sentiments were freely exploited. Voting in several areas was largely done on caste considerations. The caste rivalries engendered by it lingered on even when the election was over.

Let us now briefly examine the motivation and mechanism of this process of social change. What are the major factors inspiring this change? And through what agencies does this change come about? In other words why is the community adopting new ways of life and thought, and under whose leadership are the traditional ways of the group being modified?

The reasons for change must be sought in a multiplicity of factors. In the words of Raymond Firth, 'Structural change is a product of social interaction, in which pressures are felt, advantages perceived, responsibilities recognized.'[1] Extending this approach to technical and organizational changes in peasant communities, we can attribute some changes in the life-ways of the people to State compulsion and legal prescription. In some spheres, particularly in material culture and technology, utility, convenience, availability and price determine to a great extent the adoption of new elements and traits. The prestige factor too is significant, for any externally induced or internally inspired change in the system of status evaluation brings in its wake significant modifications in the organization and life-ways of society. Innovation, variety and change for its own sake can also account for substantial variation from established norms in social behaviour at a given point of time. In a small rural community such as Shamirpet, which is situated near a big and modern city and is in everyday contact with it, the prevailing climate of opinion in social, economic and political matters in the city is bound to influence its general outlook and ways, for apart from their practical value city-ways are gradually coming to be regarded as more 'respectable' and 'progressive'.

So far State compulsion has been instrumental in bringing about little social and cultural change in the village community. Compulsory vaccination as well as inoculation at the time of an epidemic appear to be the only significant measures enforced by the State which have been accepted in the everyday life of the community. Although untouchability has been abolished by law, in actual practice it only gives to the hitherto untouchables an equal share in public utilities, for considerations of pollution bar all effective interaction between the high and the low castes especially in the social spheres of inter-dining and inter-marriage. Symbolic as it is, this gesture of the State has nevertheless brought about a considerable modification in the inter-group attitudes between the clean and untouchable castes.

The factors of utility, convenience and availability have played a more important role in bringing several new elements into the life of the community. Although indigenous herbs and magico-religious practices are still continued in the treatment of diseases, the efficacy and utility of allopathic drugs and injections have greatly changed the attitude of the people towards modern medicine. I have pointed out earlier that they eagerly seek these

[1] Raymond Firth, *Elements of Social Organization* (London, 1951), p. 85.

medicines and injections. The old beliefs and practices survive, partly because of the non-availability of quick and efficient modern treatment, and partly also because of its prohibitive cost. Besides the two systems do not conflict, and in order to be doubly sure, most people continue magico-religious practices along with modern medicinal treatment. Adoption of several new tools and instruments for occupational work, as well as of several other items of Western technology, such as buses, railways, razors, and electric torches, introduced in the comparatively recent times is due to their efficiency and utility. In the matter of dress and orna-ment other factors must also be taken into account. Mill-made cloth was not regarded only as cheap and more durable; it came to be looked upon as more respectable also. The coarse handloom cloth was regarded as rustic, the finer mill-cloth, on the other hand, was more refined and dignified. Further, mill-made cloth allowed a wider range of choice in the matter of colours, designs and patterns. The style of dress was influenced by a variety of factors. Under Muslim rule the style of dress of the rulers became fashionable. With Congress in power there was a sudden switch from the Muslim court-dress to Congress-patronized national dress. Modern Indian—as well as Western-style clothes—cigarettes, sun-glasses and tea are not only popular because of their utility, they possess a great prestige value as well.

Influence of the city has brought about adjustment and modi-fication in several spheres, but the need of balancing different extremes in the organization of the community has so far pre-vented any drastic structural change in village communities. Under the impact of the new socio-economic factors the family ties have weakened, the kin-group has lost some of its character-istic strength and in the system of status evaluation achieved-status is competing with traditionally ascribed status; but the society still continues to be caste-structured as caste plays a vital role in its social, economic and ritual organization. Democracy has brought in its wake party organization and elections which demand group formation and group allegiance: in several rural areas no new groups have emerged, the loyalties of the people have only been re-affirmed to the pre-existing caste groups. While no important social or economic projects and reforms have so far been put into operation, the first major political change—the introduction of democratic elections—has demonstrated the strength of the traditional system which has made a bid for absorbing 'political group formation' and 'democratic elections' in its all-embracing caste structure. Deeper and more far-reaching economic and technological changes, as well as externally induced social reform, touching the basic framework of rural societies, may present a different set of problems and test the strength of the caste structure. Under their new pressures and incentives the community may have to work out a new pattern of adjustment which may necessitate important structural changes.

Limited as this change has been, it is none the less not unimportant to ask who inspires and leads this movement towards modification of traditional ways and adoption of new elements of culture. To answer this question it is necessary to analyse the major cultural trends operating in India as a whole. Viewing the country broadly, we find three major trends: (i) the regional culture, founded on the traditions, customs and life-ways of the culture-area; (ii) the national culture, comprising some all-India traits inspired by the national renaissance, cemented by the struggle for self-government as well as by social and economic reform, and sustained by the will to find a rightful place in the comity of nations; the elements in this category being partly revivalistic and partly conscious innovations; and (iii) adoption of traits and elements from Western technology and culture. Besides these, in any given area the 'urban' and 'folk' or rural patterns are clearly distinguishable. While in the urban areas all the three trends delineated above are found to operate with more or less equal force, in the rural areas the folk variety of the regional culture is still predominant although it has been modified by national and Western elements. The inspiration and lead for modification in the traditional ways definitely come from the urban areas, brought into the village community by semi-urbanized people or inspired by the example of urban relatives. In the Indian setting while there is no polarity between 'folk' and 'urban' societies, for a proper perspective of social change this classificatory device can be used very effectively. On a limited scale the struggle for supremacy between 'old' and 'new' or between 'tradition' and 'progress' goes on in cities and smaller towns also, and every generation finds itself with a modified set of values. The rural communities clearly take the lead from the urban areas, although not without hesitation, misgivings, doubts and an initial resistance. The unfortunate class of people who are semi-rural and semi-urbanized find themselves rejected by both sides: they are held suspect by their fellow-villagers as demeaned by urban associations, and are looked down upon by their urban associates for their rustic ways. Petty government servants and town-returned village-folk are not expressly recognized as leaders of the community, but all the same they set the wheels of the community in motion in the direction of social change. It is through this class of people that urban items of regional culture, and several items of the national and Western cultures are brought into the community and hesitatingly absorbed into its life. Their selection or rejection naturally depends upon their need, utility, prestige-value and conformity with or opposition to the prevailing set of values in the community.

The village people have always idealized their traditional lifeways, and have shown unmistakable suspicion for those of the city, but have generally followed the lead of the élite, which formed the dominant social group, though sometimes with their own modifications and adaptations. The gradual adoption of Sanskritic ritual by the rural communities was the first major triumph of this group in the past. The process still continues, but now 'progressive' and 'modern' elements are gradually filtering in through the semi-urbanized village-folk.

To conclude, a few remarks may be made about the influence of these new trends on the ethos and world-view of the people.

The episodic, topical and complete life-histories recorded in the course of our investigations, supplemented by observation and records of conflicts and co-operative activities in Shamirpet, provide the material for these observations on the villagers' world-view. It is necessary to point out that so far no depth-psychology studies have been done in this area nor has there been any systematic attempt to study the cultural aspects of personality. In the absence of such studies, only an outline of the dominant attitudes and goals which are characteristic of the society can be attempted. In this context, following John Gillin, 'Ethos is taken to mean the constellation of acquired drives or motivations which are characteristic of a culture, plus the goals which are both explicit and implicit, towards which cultural activities are directed, or upon which high value is placed.'[1]

What is the universe according to the average way of thinking in this village community? Notwithstanding the historical traditions of the Andhra culture-area to which this village belongs, and the nearness of the settlement to the large cities of Hyderabad and Secundrabad the universe in people's thoughts remains extremely limited both in time and space. Some educated persons, especially the Brahmin and the Reddis, have vague ideas about the cultural traditions of Andhra and of the glorious past of India, but to the great bulk of the people caste-mythology is their only history. Traditional social institutions and life-ways are idealized: they originated long, long ago when men first appeared on the earth and the salvation of people lies in their faithful observance of these divinely ordained ways. It is customary to criticize the change of times in so far as the present is concerned; but the idealized past does not have much depth—at the most it goes to the great-grandfather's generation and above that to legendary heroes of caste-mythology. The Muslims have a fair acquaintance with the history of the origin of their religion, but not of their own connections with it. While people know about the existence of several different cultures, languages and religions in India, and also something about the lands beyond the seas, have been to places of pilgrimage and a few have even seen some of the larger cities of the land; their mental horizon is definitely regional. The village, their own caste, villages in the neighbourhood and some of the developments in the nearby capital city—generally only those affecting the rural areas—constitute their effective universe. The focus is local and regional, confined to family, kin, caste and some neighbouring villages. National consciousness is rather vague, and it was a surprise to us that in a village so near a large city there were many people who did not know the names of Mahatma Gandhi and Jawaharlal Nehru and had only the haziest of ideas regarding the struggles of the Indian National Congress against British rule. Recent political changes in Hyderabad and activities of the different political parties have sought to widen this universe, but so far the change has been extremely limited. Newspapers, increased political activity, and compulsory educa-

[1] Sol Tax, ed., *The Heritage of Conquest*, "Ethos and Cultural Aspects of Personality" by Gillin, p. 195.

tion will probably have modified this very considerably in a few decades.

The fundamental drive in the thought and activities of the group seems to be towards the goal of the adjustment of the individual to the universe. Several aspects of man's life are predetermined and he has to reconcile himself to his fate. But one need not therefore resign oneself to that fate, for actions in one's life-time can not only modify what has been predestined, but can also determine the course of life after death. Thus a life ordered according to the prescriptions of *dharma*, the traditionally approved 'correct way of life', mitigates some of the evils of the past and adds to one's merit which in its turn ensures happiness in this and future lives. The ideal pattern of adjustment with the universe is laid down by the *dharma* and comprises performance of sacramental rituals, observance of fasts and festivals, avoidance of acts and thoughts declared by religion as sinful, and rigid adherence to caste rules and taboos. Cheating in regard to some of the social and religious injunctions and prescriptions is practised, and is even regarded as permissible if it can be compensated with greater devotion in some other sphere. When such cheating becomes too open or hits the structural unity, stability and continuity of the community, it is punished; but as long as it remains personal and private one can hope to supplicate divine forces in other ways to win their forgiveness for some lapses and acts of omission and commission. All human acts are not attributed to individual volition; the unseen hand of destiny is found to motivate one's actions and decisions under many situations. Radical departures from traditional life-ways are often attributed to fate. On the whole rigid adherence to traditional life-ways is regarded as the ideal and most satisfactory method of adjustment with the universe and its unseen forces. Activities of political parties, particularly of the Communist Party, have tried to awaken people to a more positive attitude, not without total lack of success, but the new ideas are still greeted with frank dismay and scepticism and so far there has been very little change in their basic attitude towards life and the principal goal of the community, which still remains peaceful adjustment and adaptation to the laws that control the universe.

In inter-personal as well as inter- and intra-group relations, the people tend to view everything as hierarchically structured. All things, groups and people, must fit into higher, equal or lower levels. Castes are either superior, more or less equal, or inferior. This view extends to gods, animals and foods. This hierarchical setting does not denote status only, it denotes power as well. Thus people love to dominate; but they hate being dominated, and where they must accept domination of anyone higher, they in their turn seek to dominate all who occupy a lower position in the hierarchy. Man is superior to woman, therefore, she must obey him. But a mother is superior to children, to sons when they are not adults, and always to daughters and daughters-in-law, and she will therefore dominate them. A child must obey the elders, but he too can dominate a younger sibling. Superior castes can dominate inferior castes; the rich dominate the poor; those in authority dominate those who lack it. Age, kinship status, wealth and authority—together with caste—determine the superior and inferior statuses. When there are conflicts as a result of the desire to dominate in one, and hatred of domination in the other, either there is an open breach, or on 'respectable' levels there is a sort of vague compromise and adjustment under which the person with the superior status maintains the semblance of his authority by letting it become virtually ineffective and the person with the inferior status never challenges it seriously because in actual practice he does not feel its weight. Possessiveness and love of domination characterize most of the thoughts, ambitions and actions of the people, although under certain situations they are compelled to compromise with necessity and shed their power to maintain the fiction of their superiority. The new socio-political climate of the country has necessitated some adjustments and modifications in the nature of hierarchy and tone of domination; but basically the view of the people remains the same. As a concession to the changing times superior castes will not treat inferior castes harshly; but they still expect formal recognition of their superiority from the latter. A defiant low caste person would be subjected to several types of direct or indirect social presure; but one adhering to tradition and 'keeping his status in mind' would succeed in getting much better treatment.

The fundamental concepts of the rights and equality of men mean little to these people, whose visions are thus bounded by their own observation of the world. This is perhaps the most unexpected aspect of the village community for a Western mind to grasp, and it leads to its particular view of change. If people are asked to choose between tradition and progress, tradition would perhaps be their instinctive choice, although a second thought might induce them to take a few hesitating steps in the direction of change. Many still believe in a timeless present and take its continuity for granted notwithstanding its shortcomings and inequities; to many a deviation from tradition always signifies a deviation from the right way into a kind of blind alley. But the changing needs of time are also generally recognized, and while they will hold fast to the frame of their traditional structure, the people will not reject uncritically the benefits of new cultural elements. Indeed, from the readiness with which they have already adopted certain items of material culture, including Western medicines in so far as they are available, it is justifiable to predict that given suitable conditions the tempo of change would greatly increase.

Glossary

Allah. Islamic expression for God.

Arya Samaj. A modern reformist sect of the Hindus based mainly on the Vedas. Founded by Dayanand Saraswati, this sect discards idolatry and other later tendencies of Hinduism.

Ashramas. Four stages or periods in the life of a Hindu. The prescribed stages are: (1) Brahmacharya (the student life); (2) Grahastha (the householder's life); (3) Vanaprastha (the hermit's life); and (4) Sanyasa (the ascetic's life).

Atma. Soul or spirit.

Brahmacharya. Period of celibate education, the first stage in the life of a Hindu.

Chetla-kriya. Black magic.

Dharma. The approved way of life comprising righteousness, religious ordinances, rules of conduct, and duties of an individual peculiar to his stage and station in life. In English religion is often used to denote *dharma*, but this is misleading.

Dvija. The three 'twice-born' *varnas* who are eligible to perform certain special rites denoting spiritual rebirth.

Farman. A government order issued by a Muslim ruler.

Gotram. Clan, an exogamous division of caste.

Grahastya. A householder's life, the second stage in the life of a Hindu.

Jaggery. Crude brown sugar made from the juice of sugar-cane.

Jagir. A feudal estate or an assignment of land by a ruler to his feudal chief in return for military or other services.

Jagirdar. A feudal chief holding an assignment of land from a ruler in return for military or other service.

Jahannum. Muslim name for hell.

Jannat. Muslim name for heaven.

Jati. In Indian languages this word is used synonymously for caste as well as sub-caste. It denotes a small endogamous and occupational group forming the effective unit of caste system.

Karma. The law that binds everyone to enjoy or suffer the consequences of one's action in former life. This concept is based on the widely held Hindu theory of rebirth. In common talk it is used synonymously with fate or destiny.

Kharif. Crops sown in the rainy season.

Lingam (also *Linga*). Phallus, symbol of Shiva.

Lunar year. Counting of months by phases of the moon. Between two new moons the period is roughly twenty-nine and a half days; so every fourth lunar year an additional month is calculated to keep pace with the solar years.

Mantram (also *Mantra*). Incantation or spell. In Sanskrit, and in other languages derived from it, it also denotes hymn, sacred text, and mystical verse.

Moksha. Salvation; emancipation from the bondage of birth and death.

Muslim. Follower of Islam.

Narka. Hell.

Panchayat. Village council.

Pap. Sin.

Punya. Merit.

Rabi. Crops sown in winter.

Rupee. The unit of Indian currency. A rupee is equal to sixteen annas; an anna being subdivided into four pice or twelve pies. Rs.13/6 are equivalent to £1, and an American dollar is roughly equal to Rs. 5/-.

Sanyasa. The stage of renunciation during which a person abandons all worldly possessions and ties.

Shaiva. A Hindu sect worshipping Shiva as the greatest god, regarding him as the source and essence of the universe.

Swarga. Heaven.

Vaishnava. Hindu sect regarding Vishnu as the Supreme Being.

Vanaprastha. The third or hermit's stage in the life of a Hindu.

Vansham. Lineage.

Varna. Traditional scheme of classification of castes into four levels. The first three of these are regarded as twice-born, and the untouchables are kept outside the framework of caste system.

Yantram. Secret magical formulae and designs.

Bibliography

Bayley, F. G. 'An Oriya Hill Village.' *Economic Weekly*, Vol. V, No. 12, March 21, 1952.

Beals, A. R. 'Change in the Leadership of a Mysore Village.' *Economic Weekly*, Vol. V, No. 17, March 25, 1953.

Beals, Ralph L. *Cheran: A Sierra Tarascan Village*. Washington D.C., 1946.

Brand, Donald D. *Quiroga: A Mexican Village*. Washington D.C., 1946.

Brayne, F. L. *The Remaking of Village India*. London, 1929.

Carstairs, G. Morris. 'A Village in Rajasthan.' *Economic Weekly*, Vol. IV, Nos. 3 and 4, January 26, 1952.

—— 'Bhil Villages of Western Udaipur.' *Economic Weekly*, Vol. IV, No. 9, March 1, 1952.

Darling, M. L. *Wisdom and Waste in the Punjab Village*. London, 1934.

Davis, Allison, Burleigh B. Gardener and Mary R. Gardner. *Deep South*. Chicago, 1941.

Davis, Allison and John Dollard. *Children of Bondage*. Washington D.C., 1940.

Dollard, John. *Class and Caste in a Southern Town*. New Haven, 1937.

Dube, S. C. 'A Deccan Village.' *Economic Weekly*, Vol. VI, Nos. 19 and 20, May 8 and 15, 1954.

Embree, John F. *A Japanese Village : Suye Mura*. London and Chicago, 1946.

Emerson, Gertrude. *Voiceless India*, London, 1931.

Fei, Hsiao-Tung. *Peasant Life in China*. London, 1945.

Firth, Raymond. *Malay Fishermen : Their Peasant Economy*. London, 1946.

—— *Elements of Social Organization*. London, 1951.

Foster, George M. *Empire's Children : The People of Tzintzuntzan*. Washington D.C., 1948.

BIBLIOGRAPHY

Gillin, John. *Moche : A Peruvian Coastal Community.* Washington D.C., 1948.

—— *The Ways of Man.* New York, 1948.

—— 'Methodological Problems in the Study of Modern Cultures.' *American Anthropologist,* Vol. LI, No. 3, July–September 1949.

Gough, Kathleen. 'The Social Structure of a Tanjore Village.' *Economic Weekly,* Vol. IV, No. 21, May 24, 1952.

Hogbin, Ian. *Transformation Scene : The Changing Culture of a New Guinea Village.* London, 1951.

Homans, George, C. *The Human Group.* London and New York, 1951.

Hsu, F. L. K. *Under the Ancestor's Shadow.* London and New York, 1949.

Hutton, J. H. *Caste in India.* Cambridge, 1946.

Iyengar, S. Kesava. *Rural Economic Enquiries in the Hyderabad State 1949–51.* Hyderabad, 1951.

Kardiner, Abram and others. *The Psychological Frontiers of Society.* New York, 1945.

Lang, Olga. *Chinese Family and Society.* New Haven, 1946.

Lewis, Oscar. 'An Anthropological Approach to Family Studies.' *American Journal of Sociology,* Vol. LV. No. 5, March, 1950.

—— *Life in a Mexican Village : Tepoztlan Restudied.* Champaign 1951.

—— 'Group Dynamics in a North Indian Village.' *Economic Weekly,* Vol. VI, Nos. 15–18, April 10, 17, 24 and May 1, 1954.

Lynd, R. S. and H. M. Lynd. *Middletown.* New York, 1929.

Maine, H. S. *Village Communities in the East and West.* London, 1876.

Mandelbaum, David G. 'Technology, Credit, and Culture in an Indian Village.' *Economic Weekly,* Vol. IV, Nos. 32–33, August 8, 1954.

—— 'Social Organization and Planned Culture Change in India.' *Economic Weekly,* Vol. VI, No. 21, May 22, 1954.

Marriot McKim. 'Social Structure and Change in a U.P. Village.' *Economic Weekly,* Vol. IV, No. 34, August 23, 1952.

Mayer, Adrian C. *Land and Society in Malabar.* Bombay, 1952.

Miller, Eric J. 'Village Structure in North Kerala.' *Economic Weekly,* Vol. IV, No. 6, February 9, 1952.

BIBLIOGRAPHY

Miner, Horace. *St. Denis : A French Canadian Parish.* Chicago, 1939.

Mukherjee, Ramkrishna. 'Economic Structure of Rural Bengal : A Survey of Six Villages.' *American Sociological Review*, Vol. XIV, No. 3, 1949.

—— 'The Economic Structure and Social Life in Six Villages of Bengal.' *American Sociological Review*, Vol. XIV, No. 3, 1949.

Newell, W. H. 'A Himalayan Village.' *Economic Weekly*, Vol. IV, No. 8, February 23, 1952.

Opler, Morris E. and Rudra Datta Singh. 'The Division of Labour in an Indian Village.' *A Reader in General Anthropology* edited by Carleton S. Coon, New York, 1948.

—— 'Two Villages of Eastern Uttar Pradesh (U.P.) : An Analysis of Similarities and Differences.' *American Anthropologist*, Vol. LIV, No. 2, April–June, 1952.

—— 'Economic, Political and Social Change in a Village of North Central India.' *Human Organization*, Vol. II, No. 2, 1952.

Parsons, Elsie Clews. *Mitala : Town of the Souls.* Chicago, 1936.

Quain, Buell. *Fijian Village.* Chicago, 1948.

Redfield, Robert. *Tepoztlan : A Mexican Village.* Chicago, 1930.

—— *The Folk Culture of Yucatan.* Chicago, 1941.

—— *A Village That Chose Progress : Chan Kom Revisited.* Chicago, 1950.

—— and Villa R. Alfonso. *Chan Kom : A Maya Village.* Washington, 1934.

Rosser, Collin, 'A Hermit Village in Kulu.' *Economic Weekly*, Vol. IV, Nos. 19 and 20.

Rubin, Moston. *Plantation Country.* Chapel Hill, 1951.

Sarma, Jyotirmoyee. 'A Bengal Village.' *Economic Weekly*, Vol. V, Nos. 32–34, August 15, 1953.

Slater, G. *Some South Indian Villages.* University of Madras Economic Studies. London, 1918.

—— *Village Life in Madras Presidency.* Madras, 1918.

Smith, Marian W. 'Village Notes from Bengal.' *American Anthropologist*, XLVIII, No. 4, October–December 1946.

—— 'The Misal : A Structural Village Group of India and Pakistan.' *American Anthropologist*, Vol. LIV, No. 1, January–March 1952.

—— 'Social Structure in the Punjab Village.' *Economic Weekly*, Vol. V, No. 47, November 21, 1953.

BIBLIOGRAPHY

Srinivas, M. N. 'Social Structure of a Mysore Village.' *Economic Weekly*, Vol. III, Nos. 42–43, October 30, 1951.
—— 'A Joint Family Dispute in a Mysore Village.' *The Journal of the M.S. University of Baroda*, Vol. I, 1952.
—— *Religion and Society among the Coorgs of South India*. London, 1952.
Srinivasachari, C. S. 'Village Organization in the Madras Presidency at the Time of the Introduction of British Rule.' *Journal of the Annamalai University*, Vol. I, 1932.
Tax, Sol. 'Culture and Civilization in Guatemala Societies.' *Scientific Monthly*, XLVIII, May 1939.
—— 'World View and Social Relations in Guatemala.' *American Anthropologist*, Vol. XLIII, 1941.
—— and others. *Heritage of Conquest : The Ethnology of Middle America*. Glencoe, 1952.
Thomas, W. I. and Florian Znaniecki. *The Polish Peasant in Europe and America*. New York, 1927.
Tumin, Melvin M. *Caste in a Peasant Society*. Princeton, 1952.
Warner, W. L. and Paul S. Lunt. *The Social Life of a Modern Community*. New Haven, 1941.
—— and Leo Srole. *The Status System of a Modern Community*. New Haven, 1942.
West, James. *Plainville, U.S.A.* New York, 1945.
Wiser, Charlotte and William H. *Behind Mud Walls in India*. New York, 1930.
Yang, Martin C. *A Chinese Village*. London and Chicago, 1947.

Index

The names of authors appearing in the Bibliography are not given in the Index.

INDEX

Castes:
agricultural castes, 20, 35, 44, 116, 185
Ausula, 37, 53
Balja, 39, 40, 44
Balsantanam, 44
Brahmin, 20, 35–8, 40, 42, 54, 57, 62, 70, 79, 80, 82, 89, 95, 97–107, 111–14, 116–22, 124, 125, 128, 139, 162, 168, 172, 174, 176, 184, 188, 218, 232
Darzi, 67, 114
Dasari, 44
Erkala, 20, 25, 36, 37, 38, 44, 68, 82, 96, 101, 103, 106, 107, 124, 138, 173, 176
Gandla, 44
Gaondla, 20, 36, 37, 38, 41, 65, 87, 101, 114, 121, 172, 186, 224
Golla, 20, 25, 36, 37, 40, 41, 64, 97, 112, 114, 115, 121, 172, 185
Jangam, 39, 40, 103
Kamma, 44
Kammari, 37, 53, 66, 114
Kanchari, 37
Kapu, 20, 36, 37, 40, 57, 67, 116, 185
Kase, 37
Katike, 39, 40, 67
Komti, 20, 36, 37, 40, 44, 57, 62–3, 72, 82, 87, 89, 97–103, 105, 107, 112, 113, 114, 116–19, 122, 124, 130, 138, 139, 168, 172, 174, 176, 184, 185, 186, 218, 223
Kshatriya, 35, 38
Kummari, 20, 25, 36, 37, 40, 53, 57, 63–4, 107, 108, 111, 112, 114, 115, 121
Lambada, 44
Madiga, 20, 25, 26, 27, 37, 38, 41, 42, 46, 52, 53, 57, 59, 65, 67, 68–9, 72, 73, 78, 86, 87, 91, 96, 97, 101, 103, 104, 106, 107, 108, 111–15, 117, 119, 121, 122, 124, 129
Mala, 20, 25, 26, 27, 37, 38, 41, 46, 52, 68, 72, 101, 103, 106, 107, 111, 113, 124, 138, 162, 186

Castes—contd.
Mangali, 20, 36, 38, 39, 41, 53, 57, 66, 114, 115, 116, 124, 186
Muttarasi, 19, 36, 37, 40, 52
occupational castes, 4, 7, 18, 19, 35, 36, 60, 63, 64, 65, 85, 97, 99, 102, 122, 172, 174
Padmashali, 41
Panch Brahma, 20, 37, 38, 66, 98, 116, 118, 121, 172, 186
Pichha-Kuntla, 36, 37, 38, 41
Reddi, 19, 36, 37, 40, 44, 46, 52, 63, 72, 91, 97, 98, 100, 105, 106, 117, 129, 138, 168, 185, 188, 189, 212, 218, 227, 232
Sakali, 20, 25, 36, 38, 39, 41, 53, 57, 66, 111, 114, 115, 116, 124, 186
Sale, 20, 36, 37, 38, 41, 65, 101, 114, 121, 164, 185, 186
Sharda-galu, 44
untouchables, 20, 35, 68, 104, 113, 117, 162, 163, 164, 166, 168, 176, 187, 188, 206, 207, 224, 228
Vaddar, 20, 25, 36–9, 41, 59, 67–8, 85, 87, 96, 103, 106, 107, 138
Vaishya, 35, 38
Velma, 44
Wadla, 37, 53, 66, 114
Yenadi, 44
Cattle, 75, 82–4, 168; dead, 69; in Shamirpet, 82–4
Chandra Devi, Dr., xiii
Chants, 26, 129, 221
Chauti, see Festivals
Chetla-kriya, 129
Children: care of, 141, 144, 191–6; disciplining of, 149–50, 194; grandparents and grandchildren, 158–9; parent–child relationships, 148–53; relations between siblings, 156–8; sexual life of, 193–7
Clans, 43
Classical Hinduism, 88, 131
Communist party, 227, 233
Confinement, 118

243

INDEX

Conflict, conflicts, 138, 200–11; between villages, 55, 210–11; some cases of, 203–11
Corpse, 124, 126
Cremation, 108, 125
Cross-cousin marriage, *see* Marriage
Cults: local, 88; family, 88; village, 88; observed by castes, 88

Darzi, *see* Castes
Dasara, see Festivals
Dasari, *see* Castes
Day of Judgement, 90
Death, 51, 62, 63, 75, 93, 103, 124–6, 134; ceremonies associated with, among the Hindus, 124–6; ceremonies associated with, among the Muslims, 126; destiny of soul after, 125; impurity of, 125
Deepavali, see Festivals
Demons, 88
Deshmukh, 25, 45, 46, 50, 51, 52, 99, 103, 104, 112, 208, 213
Dharma, 92, 94, 127, 233
Diet, *see* Standard of living
Dispensary, 24, 25, 26, 221
Divination, 26, 221
Division of labour, 168–74; age and, 169, 173–4; men's work, 169–73; occupations, crafts and, 172–3; social status and, 169–70, 174; women's work, 169–72, 73
Division of property, 75, 140
Divorce, 55, 122, 124
Domestic animals, 82–4
Dowson, J., 39
Dress, 21, 22, 44, 168, 218–20
Durga, *see* Goddesses
Durgamma, *see* Goddesses
Dvija, 35

Ear boring, 119
Election, elections, 165, 215, 227, 230
Elementary family, *see* Family
Ellamma, *see* Goddesses
Embree, John F., 8
Endogamous, 36, 37, 38, 40, 41, 125
Endogamy, 54, 55

English, 165, 190, 217
Erkala, *see* Castes
Ethos, 4, 231
European, 219
Ex-communication, 39, 49
Exogamous, 42, 43
Exogamy, 55
Extended family, *see* Family

Family: allied families, 135, 136, 137; daughter-in-law, 153–6; elementary, 33, 34, 74, 134, 135, 137, 222; extended, 73, 134, 135; husband and wife, 141–7; interpersonal relations within, 141–60; joint, 34, 49, 74, 132, 133, 143, 145, 222; other relations within, 158–9; parents and children, 148–53; quarrels in, 138–41; relations outside, 159–60; separation from, 49, 55, 133, 134, 135; siblings, 156–8; structure of, 132–41
Fei, 8
Fertilizers, artificial, 80; chemical, 221
Festivals:
caste, 97; *Mallamma,* 97; *Maude Pochamma,* 97; *Saudamma,* 97
Hindu, 96–108, 116; *Ananta Chaturdashi,* 97, 102; *Chauti,* 97, 101; *Dasara,* 97, 103, 111, 115; *Deepavali,* 97, 104; *Holi,* 97, 107, 111; *Kartika Purnima,* 97, 102; *Kottalu,* 97; *Krishna Ashtami,* 97, 101; *Nagula Panchami,* 97, 100; *Narsimha Jayanti,* 97, 100; *Neela Gauri,* 97, 100; *New Eating,* 62, 97, 108; *Petramasa,* 97, 103; *Pitra Moksha Amavasya,* 39; *Rakhi Purnima,* 97, 101; *Rama Navami,* 97, 99; *Rath Saptami,* 97, 106; *Shivaratri,* 39, 97, 106; *Shravana Somwar,* 97, 101; *Til Sankranti,* 97, 105; *Toli Ekadashi,* 97, 100; *Ugadi,* 97, 98–99; *Vasant Panchami,* 97, 106
Muslim, 108–10; *Giarwin Sharif,* 108 109; *Id-uz-zuha,* 108, 110; *Meelad*

244

INDEX

Festivals—*contd.*
Muslim—*contd.*
   Sharif, 108, 109; *Moharram*, 108,
   109, 115; *Ramzan*, 108, 110; *Shabe*
   Barat, 108, 109; *Shabe Miraj*, 108,
   109
   village, 111–16; *Batkamma*, 97, 111,
   113; *Maisamma*, 97, 111, 114, 115;
   Pochamma, 97, 111, 112; *urs* (fair)
   of *Jalal Miyan*, 111, 115
Fetishes, 93
Firth, Professor Raymond, xiv, 227,
   228
Fishing, 84
Folk society, 3, 230
Fortes, Meyer, 43
Funeral, 126
Fürer-Haimendorf, Professor C., xiii,
   Mrs. Elizabeth, xiv

Gadi Maisamma, *see* Goddesses
Gandhi, 214, 232
Gandla, *see* Castes
Ganesha, 97, 101, 102
Ganges, 125
Gaondla, *see* Castes
Gauri, *see* Goddesses
Ghosts, 88, 93, 94, 127, 128, 129,
   130; categories of persons becom-
   ing, 129
Giarwin Sharif, *see* Festivals
Gillin, John, 8, 12, 231, 232
Godavari, 94, 96, 125
Goddesses: Balamma, 95; Durga, 104;
   Durgamma, 95, 96; Ellamma, 95;
   Gadi Maisamma, 96; Gauri, 97,
   100, 113; Katta Maisamma, 96;
   Lakshmi, 105; Mahakalamma,
   95, 96, 111; Maisamma, 95, 96,
   97, 111, 114; Mallamma, 97;
   Maude Pochamma, 97; Mutya-
   lamma, 95, 96, 111; Pinnamma,
   95, 96; Pochamma, 95, 96, 97,
   111, 112; Saudamma, 97; Sita, 95
Golla, *see* Castes
Gotram, 42, 43
Grave, graves, 109, 125
Graveyard, 124, 126

Hanuman, 95, 104
Heaven, 90, 91
Hell, 90, 91, 92
Hindu festivals, *see* Festivals
Hinduism, 35, 39, 94, 161
Hindu mythology, 225
Hindu scriptures, 95
Hindu trinity, 39, 94
Holi, *see* Festivals
Houses, types of, 28–31, 163
Hsu, F. L. K., 8
Hunting, 18, 84
Husband and wife, *see* Family

Id-uz-zuha, *see* Festivals
Impurity, 43, 92; of birth, 117, 118;
   of death, 125
Incest, 44
Indebtedness, 78
Indian National Congress, 214, 218,
   232
Inter-caste attitudes, *see* Inter-per-
   sonal relations
Inter-personal relations: educated vs.
   uneducated, 189, 190; within the
   family 141–60; inter-caste atti-
   tudes, 184–9; quality of, 181–4;
   urban vs. rural, 190–1
Islam, 93, 123, 132, 162
Islamic faith, 89

Jahannum, 90
Jangam, *see* Castes
Jannat, 90
Jati, 36, 54
Joint family, *see* Family

Kamadeva, 97, 107
Kamma, *see* Castes
Kammari, *see* Castes
Kanchari, *see* Castes
Kapu, *see* Castes
Karma, 90, 94
Kartika Purnima, *see* Festivals
Kase, *see* Castes
Kashi, *see* Benares
Katike, *see* Castes

245

Founded by KARL MANNHEIM
Late Professor of Education in the University of London

Edited by W. J. H. SPROTT
Professor of Philosophy in the University of Nottingham

The International Library

of

Sociology and Social

Reconstruction

ROUTLEDGE & KEGAN PAUL
BROADWAY HOUSE, CARTER LANE, LONDON, E.C.4

SOCIOLOGY OF EDUCATION

Mission of the University
JOSÉ ORTEGA Y GASSET. Translated and introduced by Howard Lee Nostrand   *Second Impression.* 12s. 6d.

Total Education
A Plea for Synthesis
M. L. JACKS, *Director of the Institute of Education, Oxford*   16s.

The Social Psychology of Education
An Introduction and Guide to its Study
C. M. FLEMING, *Reader in Education, Institute of Education, London*   11s.

Education and Society in Modern Germany
R. H. SAMUEL, *Professor of Germanic Languages, Melbourne*, and
R. HINTON THOMAS, *Lecturer in German, Birmingham*   16s.

The Museum
Its History and Its Tasks in Education
ALMA S. WITTLIN   *Illustrated.* 28s.

The Educational Thought and Influence of Matthew Arnold
W. F. CONNELL, *Senior Lecturer in Education, Sydney.* With an Introduction by Sir Fred Clarke   23s.

Comparative Education
A Study of Educational Factors and Traditions
NICHOLAS HANS, *Institute of Education, London*   23s.

New Trends in Education in the 18th Century
NICHOLAS HANS   21s.

From School to University
A Study, with special reference to University Entrance
R. R. DALE, *Lecturer in Education, University College, Swansea*   21s.

Adult Education
A Comparative Study
ROBERT PEERS   35s.

Education and Society
An Introduction to the Sociology of Education
A. K. C. OTTAWAY, *Lecturer in Education, Leeds.* With an Introduction by W. O. Lester Smith   *Third Impression.* 18s.

German Youth : Bond or Free
HOWARD BECKER   18*s*.

Parity and Prestige in English Secondary Education
OLIVE BANKS, *Lecturer in Sociology, Liverpool*   25*s*.

Helvetius
His Life and Place in the History of Educational Thought
IAN CUMMING, *Senior Lecturer in Education, Auckland*   25*s*.

Adolescence
Its Social Psychology: With an Introduction to recent findings from the
fields of Anthropology, Physiology, Medicine, Psychometrics and
Sociometry
C. M. FLEMING   *Fifth Impression.* 18*s*.

Studies in the Social Psychology of Adolescence
J. E. RICHARDSON, J. F. FORRESTER, J. K. SHUKLA and P. J.
HIGGINBOTHAM
Edited by C. M. FLEMING   23*s*.

From Generation to Generation
Age Groups and Social Structure
S. N. EISENSTADT, *Head of the Department of Sociology, Hebrew
University, Jerusalem*   42*s*.

The Social Purposes of Education
K. G. COLLIER   21*s*.

SOCIOLOGY OF RELIGION

The Economic Order and Religion
FRANK KNIGHT, *Professor of Social Science, Chicago,* and
THORNTON W. MERRIAM   18*s*.

Religious Behaviour
MICHAEL ARGYLE, *Lecturer in Social Psychology, Oxford*   25*s*.

SOCIOLOGY OF ART AND LITERATURE

Chekhov and His Russia: A Sociological Study
W. H. BRUFORD, *Schröder Professor of German, Cambridge*   18*s*.

The Sociology of Literary Taste
LEVIN L. SCHÜCKING   *Third Impression.* 9*s*. 6*d*.

3

*Men of Letters and the English Public in the 18th Century,
1660-1744, Dryden, Addison, Pope*
ALEXANDRE BELJAME, Edited with an Introduction and Notes by
Bonamy Dobrée. Translated by E. O. Lorimer   28*s.*

SOCIOLOGICAL APPROACH TO THE STUDY OF HISTORY

The Aftermath of the Napoleonic Wars
The Concert of Europe—An Experiment
H. G. SCHENK, *Lecturer in Political Economics, Fellow of Exeter College,
Oxford*   *Illustrated.* 18*s.*

Military Organization and Society
STANISLAW ANDRZEJEWSKI. Foreword by A. Radcliffe-Brown 21*s.*

Population Theories and the Economic Interpretation
SYDNEY COONTZ, *Assistant Professor in Forest Economics, State
University of New York, Syracuse*   25*s.*

Social Change in the Industrial Revolution
An Application of Theory to the Lancashire Cotton Industry, 1770–1840
NEIL J. SMELSER, *University of California, Berkeley*   40*s.*

SOCIOLOGY OF LAW

Sociology of Law
GEORGES GURVITCH, *Professor of Sociology, Sorbonne.* With an
Introduction by Roscoe Pound   *Second Impression.* 21*s.*

The Institutions of Private Law and their Social Functions
KARL RENNER. Edited with an Introduction and Notes by O. Kahn-
Freund   28*s.*

Legal Aid
ROBERT EGERTON. With an Introduction by A. L. Goodhart
                                        Second Impression. 12*s.* 6*d.*

CRIMINOLOGY

Juvenile Delinquency in an English Middletown
HERMANN MANNHEIM   14*s.*

Criminal Justice and Social Reconstruction
HERMANN MANNHEIM   *Second Impression.* 20s.

Group Problems in Crime and Punishment
HERMANN MANNHEIM   28s.

The Psycho-Analytical Approach to Juvenile Delinquency:
Theory, Case Studies, Treatment
KATE FRIEDLANDER   *Fourth Impression.* 25s.

The English Prison and Borstal Systems
LIONEL FOX, K.C.B., M.C., *Chairman of the Prison Commission for*
England and Wales   32s.

Crime and the Services
JOHN SPENCER, *Director of the Bristol Social Project*   28s.

The Criminal Area
A Study in Social Ecology
TERENCE MORRIS   25s.

THE SOCIAL SERVICES

Social Service and Mental Health
An Essay on Psychiatric Social Workers
M. ASHDOWN and S. C. BROWN   18s.

The Social Services of Modern England
M. PENELOPE HALL, *Lecturer in Social Science, Liverpool*
                            Fourth Edition (Revised). 28s.

Lunacy, Law and Conscience, 1744-1845
The Social History of the Care of the Insane
KATHLEEN JONES   21s.

British Social Work in the 19th Century
A. F. YOUNG and E. T. ASHTON, *Department of Social Studies,*
Southampton University   25s.

5

Social Policies for Old Age
B. E. SHENFIELD, *Lecturer in Social Studies, University of Birmingham* 25*s*.

Voluntary Societies and Social Policy
MADELINE ROOFF, *Lecturer in Social Policy and Social Administration at Bedford College, London* 35*s*.

Children in Care
The Development of the Service for the Deprived Child
JEAN S. HEYWOOD 25*s*.

In Place of Parents
A Study of Foster Care
GORDON TRASLER, *Lecturer in Social Psychology, University of Southampton* 25*s*.

SOCIOLOGY AND POLITICS

Social-Economic Movements
An Historical and Comparative Survey of Socialism, Communism, Co-operation, Utopianism; and Other Systems of Reform and Reconstruction
H. W. LAIDLER *Second Impression. Illustrated.* 37*s*. 6*d*.

Dictatorship and Political Police
The Technique of Control by Fear
E. K. BRAMSTEDT 20*s*.

Nationality in History and Politics
A Psychology and Sociology of National Sentiment and Nationalism
FRIEDRICH HERTZ *Fourth Impression.* 32*s*.

The Logic of Liberty: Reflections and Rejoinders
MICHAEL POLANYI, F.R.S., 18*s*.

The Analysis of Political Systems
DOUGLAS V. VERNEY, *Lecturer in Government, University of Liverpool* 28*s*.

The Political Element in the Development of Economic Theory
GUNNAR MYRDAL. Translated by Paul Streeten   25*s*.

Higher Civil Servants in Britain
From 1870 to the Present Day
R. K. KELSALL, *Head of the School of Social Studies, Sheffield*   25*s*.

Democracy and Dictatorship: Their Psychology and Patterns of Life
Z. BARBU, *Lecturer in Social Psychology, Glasgow*   28*s*.

How People Vote: A Study of Electoral Behaviour in Greenwich
MARK BENNEY, A. P. GRAY, and R. H. PEAR   25*s*.

Economy and Society
A Study in the Integration of Economic and Social Theory
TALCOTT PARSONS, *Chairman of the Department of Social Relations, Harvard*, and NEIL J. SMELSER   *Second Impression.* 35*s*.

The Functions of Social Conflict
LEWIS COSER, *Associate Professor of Sociology, California*   18*s*.

The American Science of Politics
BERNARD CRICK   28*s*.

FOREIGN AFFAIRS, THEIR SOCIAL, POLITICAL & ECONOMIC FOUNDATIONS

Patterns of Peacemaking
DAVID THOMSON, *Research Fellow, Sidney Sussex College, Cambridge*, E. MEYER and ASA BRIGGS, *Professor of History, Leeds*   25*s*.

French Canada in Transition
EVERETT C. HUGHES, *Professor of Sociology, Chicago*   16*s*.

State and Economics in the Middle East
A Society in Transition
A. BONNÉ, *Professor of Economics. Director, Economic Research Institute, Hebrew University, Jerusalem*   *Second Edition (Revised).* 40*s*.

The Economic Development of the Middle East
An Outline of Planned Reconstruction
A. BONNÉ   *Third Impression.* 16*s*.

Studies in Economic Development
With special reference to conditions in the Underdeveloped Areas in Western Asia and India
ALFRED BONNÉ
32s.

Peasant Renaissance in Yugoslavia, 1900-1950
A Study of the Development of Yugoslav Peasant Society as Affected by Education
RUTH TROUTON
28s.

Transitional Economic Systems
The Polish-Czech Example
DOROTHY W. DOUGLAS
25s.

Political Thought in France from the Revolution to the Fourth Republic
J. P. MAYER
14s.

Central European Democracy and its Background
Economic and Political Group Organization
RUDOLF SCHLESINGER
30s.

ECONOMIC PLANNING
Private Corporations and their Control
A. B. LEVY
Two Volumes. 70s. the set

The Shops of Britain
A Study of Retail Distribution
HERMANN LEVY
Second Impression. 21s.

SOCIOLOGY OF THE FAMILY AND ALLIED TOPICS
The Family and Democratic Society
J. K. FOLSOM, *Professor of Economics, Vassar College*
35s.

Nation and Family
The Swedish Experiment in Democratic Family and Population Policy
ALVA MYRDAL, *Swedish Ambassador to India*
28s.

The Deprived and the Privileged
Personality Development in English Society
B. M. SPINLEY, *Educational Psychologist, Sheffield Child Guidance Clinic* 20s.

8

Prosperity and Parenthood
J. A. BANKS, *Lecturer in Sociology, Liverpool*   21*s*.

Family, Socialization and Interaction Process
TALCOTT PARSONS and ROBERT F. BALES   30*s*

The Home and Social Status
DENNIS CHAPMAN, *Senior Lecturer in Social Science, Liverpool*
                                                119 *tables, diagrams and plates,* 35*s*.

Women's Two Roles: Home and Work
ALVA MYRDAL and VIOLA KLEIN   25*s*.

The People of Ship Street
MADELEINE KERR   23*s*.

TOWN AND COUNTRY PLANNING
HUMAN ECOLOGY

The Social Background of a Plan: A Study of Middlesbrough
Edited by RUTH GLASS. With Maps and Plans   42*s*.

City, Region and Regionalism
A Geographical Contribution to Human Ecology
ROBERT E. DICKINSON. With Maps and Plans   25*s*.

The West European City: A Study in Urban Geography
ROBERT E. DICKINSON. With Maps and Plans   42*s*.

Revolution of Environment
E. A. GUTKIND   *Illustrated.* 32*s*.

The Journey to Work
Its Significance for Industrial and Community Life
K. LIEPMANN, *Research Fellow in Economics, Bristol.* With a Foreword
by Sir Alexander Carr-Saunders   *Second Impression* 16*s*.

Stevenage: A Sociological Study of a New Town
HAROLD ORLANS   30*s*.

The Genesis of Modern British Town Planning
A Study in Economic and Social History of the Nineteenth and Twentieth
Centuries
W. ASHWORTH, *Professor of History, London School of Economics*   21*s*.

9

The Urban Community
A World Perspective
NELS ANDERSON, *Research Director, Unesco Institute of Social Sciences, Cologne*   35*s.*

SOCIOLOGICAL STUDIES OF MODERN COMMUNITIES

Negroes in Britain
A Study of Racial Relations in English Society
K. L. LITTLE, *Reader in Anthropology, Edinburgh*   25*s.*

Co-operative Living in Palestine
HENRIK F. INFIELD   *Illustrated.*   12*s.* 6*d.*

Co-operative Communities at Work
HENRIK F. INFIELD   18*s.*

Colour Prejudice in Britain
A Study of West Indian Workers in Liverpool, 1941-1951
ANTHONY H. RICHMOND, *Lecturer in Social Theory, Edinburgh*   18*s.*

The Absorption of Immigrants
S. N. EISENSTADT   25*s.*

Studies in Class Structure
G. D. H. COLE   21*s.*

The Study of Groups
JOSEPHINE KLEIN, *Lecturer in Social Studies, Birmingham*   21*s.*

City Life in Japan
A Study of a Tokyo Ward
R. P. DORE   45*s.*

The Changing Social Structure of England and Wales 1871—1951
DAVID C. MARSH   28*s.*

The Sociology of an English Village : Gosforth
W. M. WILLIAMS, *Lecturer in Geography, Univ. Coll. of North Staffs.* 25*s.*

Rural Depopulation in England and Wales
JOHN SAVILLE, *Lecturer in Economic History, University of Hull*   28*s.*
(Dartington Hall Studies in Rural Sociology)

The History of a Soviet Collective Farm
FEDOR BELOV   21*s.*

Class in American Society
LEONARD REISSMAN, *Tulane University*

English Rural Life
Village Activities, Organizations and Institutions
H. E. BRACEY, *Department of Economics, University of Bristol*   30s.

SOCIOLOGY OF INDUSTRY

Mobility in the Labour Market
MARGOT JEFFERYS   15s.

Patterns of Industrial Bureaucracy
ALVIN W. GOULDNER, *Professor of Sociology, Illinois*   21s.

Wildcat Strike
A Study of an Unofficial Strike
ALVIN W. GOULDNER   16s.

Recruitment to Skilled Trades
GERTRUDE WILLIAMS, *Professor of Social Economics, Bedford College,*
London   23s.

The Country Craftsman
A Study of some Rural Crafts and the Rural Industries Organisation
in England. (Dartington Hall Studies in Rural Sociology).
W. M. WILLIAMS   25s.

Apprenticeship
An Enquiry into its Adequacy under Modern Conditions
KATE LIEPMANN   23s.

ANTHROPOLOGY

The Sociology of Colonies: An Introduction to the Study of
Race Contact
RENÉ MAUNIER   *Two volumes.* 63s. *the set*

A Chinese Village: Taitou, Shantung Province
MARTIN C. YANG   23s.

*A Japanese Village: Suye Mura**
JOHN F. EMBREE, *Associate Professor of Anthropology, California*

The Golden Wing: A Sociological Study of Chinese Familism
YUEH-HWA-LIN, *Professor of Social Anthropology, Yenching*   18s.

* **This book is temporarily out of print.**

12

SOCIOLOGY AND PSYCHOLOGY OF THE PRESENT CRISIS

Diagnosis of Our Time
Wartime Essays of a Sociologist
KARL MANNHEIM   *Sixth Impression.* 18*s.*

Farewell to European History or the Conquest of Nihilism
ALFRED WEBER   18*s.*

The Fear of Freedom
ERICH FROMM   *Seventh Impression.* 21*s.*

The Sane Society
ERICH FROMM   28*s.*

Freedom, Power, and Democratic Planning
KARL MANNHEIM. Edited by Hans Gerth and E. K. Bramstedt 28*s.*

Essays on Sociology and Social Psychology
KARL MANNHEIM. Edited by Paul Kecskemeti   30*s.*

Essays on the Sociology of Culture
KARL MANNHEIM. Edited by Ernest Manheim and Paul
Kecskemeti   28*s.*

SOCIAL PSYCHOLOGY AND PSYCHO-ANALYSIS

Psychology and the Social Pattern
JULIAN BLACKBURN, *Associate Professor of Psychology, McGill University, Canada*   *Fifth Impression.* 14*s.*

The Framework of Human Behaviour
JULIAN BLACKBURN   *Second Impression.* 15*s.*

A Handbook of Social Psychology
KIMBALL YOUNG, *Professor of Sociology, North-western University*
                                             Revised edition. 35*s.*

Solitude and Privacy
A Study of Social Isolation, Its Causes and Therapy
PAUL HALMOS, *Lecturer in Psychology, University College of N. Staffs.* 21*s.*

The Human Group
GEORGE C. HOMANS, *Associate Professor of Sociology, Harvard*   28*s.*

Sigmund Freud: An Introduction
A Presentation of his Theories and a Discussion of the Relationship between Psycho-analysis and Sociology
WALTER HOLLITSCHER   *Second Impression.* 12s.

The Social Problems of an Industrial Civilization
ELTON MAYO   *Second Impression.* 15s.

Oppression
A Study in Social and Criminal Psychology
TADEUSZ GRYGIER. Foreword by Hermann Mannheim   28s.

Mental Health and Mental Disorder
A Sociological Approach
Edited by ARNOLD M. ROSE, *University of Minnesota*   40s.

Disaster
A Psychological Essay
MARTHA WOLFENSTEIN   23s.

APPROACHES TO THE PROBLEM OF PERSONALITY

The Cultural Background of Personality
RALPH LINTON, *Prof. of Anthropology, Yale.* *Fourth Impression.* 14s.

The Feminine Character: History of an Ideology
VIOLA KLEIN. With an Introduction by Karl Mannheim   16s.

A History of Autobiography in Antiquity
GEORG MISCH, *Professor of Philosophy, Göttingen,* Translated by E. W. Dickes.   *Two volumes.* 45s. *the set*

Personality and Problems of Adjustment
KIMBALL YOUNG   *Second Edition (Revised).* 40s.

Towards a Measure of Man
The Frontiers of Normal Adjustment
PAUL HALMOS   28s.

PHILOSOPHICAL AND SOCIAL FOUNDATIONS OF THOUGHT

Homo Ludens: A Study of the Play Element in Culture
J. HUIZINGA   18s.

The Ideal Foundations of Economic Thought
Three Essays on the Philosophy of Economics
WERNER STARK, *Reader in Economics, Manchester*
                               Third Impression. 16*s.*

The History of Economics in its Relation to Social Development
WERNER STARK   *Fourth Impression.* 12*s.*

America: Ideal and Reality
The United States of 1776 in Contemporary European Philosophy
WERNER STARK   12*s.*

Society and Nature: A Sociological Inquiry
HANS KELSEN, *Department of Political Science, California*   25*s.*

Marx: His Time and Ours
R. SCHLESINGER   *Second Impression.* 32*s.*

The Philosophy of Wilhelm Dilthey
H. A. HODGES, *Professor of Philosophy, Reading*   30*s.*

Essays on the Sociology of Knowledge
KARL MANNHEIM   35*s.*

The Sociology of Knowledge
WERNER STARK   36*s.*

GENERAL SOCIOLOGY

A Handbook of Sociology
W. F. OGBURN, *Professor of Sociology, Chicago,* and
M. F. NIMKOFF, *Professor of Sociology, Bucknell*
                            Third Edition (Revised). 30*s.*

Social Organization
ROBERT H. LOWIE, *late Professor of Anthropology, Chicago*   35*s.*

Professional Ethics and Civic Morals
EMILE DURKHEIM. Translated by Cornelia Brookfield   30*s.*

Systematic Sociology
KARL MANNHEIM
Edited by W. A. C. STEWART and J. S. EROS   24*s.*

Value in Social Theory
GUNNAR MYRDAL
32*s*.

The Logic of Social Enquiry
QUENTIN GIBSON, *Senior Lecturer in Philosophy, Canberra University College*
24*s*.

FOREIGN CLASSICS OF SOCIOLOGY

Wilhelm Dilthey: An Introduction
A comprehensive account of his sociological and philosophical work, with translations of selected passages.
H. A. HODGES
Second Impression. 14*s*.

From Max Weber: Essays in Sociology
Translated, Edited and with an Introduction by H. H. GERTH and C. W. MILLS
Third Impression. 28*s*.

Suicide: A Study in Sociology
EMILE DURKHEIM. Translated by J. A. Spaulding and George Simpson
28*s*.

Community and Association
FERDINAND TONNIES. Edited and supplemented by Charles P. Loomis
21*s*.

Socialism and Saint-Simon
EMILE DURKHEIM, *Preface by Marcel Mauss*
28*s*.

DOCUMENTARY

Changing Attitudes in Soviet Russia
Documents and Readings. Edited with an Introduction by
RUDOLF SCHLESINGER
Volume 1: *The Family in the U.S.S.R.*
30*s*.
Volume 2: *The Nationalities Problem and Soviet Administration*
30*s*.

Psychology in the Soviet Union
BRIAN SIMON, *Lecturer in Education, University College, Leicester*
32*s*

Soviet Youth: Some Achievements and Problems
Excerpts from the Soviet Press
Edited and translated by DOROTHEA L. MEEK
28*s*.

All prices are net and subject to alteration without notice